DAVE TODD

Y0-BGT-607

JAPANESE SUBMARINE RAIDERS 1942

A Maritime Mystery

JAPANESE SUBMARINE RAIDERS 1942

A Maritime Mystery

Steven L. Carruthers

Casper Publications

Published by Casper Publications Pty Ltd
A.C.N. 67 064 029 303
PO Box 225, Narrabeen, NSW 2101 Australia
Ph: +61 (0)2 9905-9933 Fax: +61 (0)2 9905-9030
Website: http://www.casperpublications.com

First published 1982
Revised edition 2006

© Steven L. Carruthers 2006

National Library of Australia
Cataloguing-in-publication data

Carruthers, Steven L., 1951-
　　Japanese submarine raiders, 1942 : A maritime mystery

　　Rev. ed.
　　Bibliography.
　　Includes index.
　　ISBN 0 9775063 0 4

　　1. Japan. Kaigun - Submarine forces. 2. World War,
　　1939-1945 - Naval operations, Japanese. 3. World War,
　　1939-1945 - Naval operations - Submarine. 4. Midget
　　submarines. 5. Sydney (N.S.W.) - History - Bombardment,
　　1942. II. Title. Carruthers, Steven L., 1951- Australia under
　　siege : Japanese submarine raiders, 1942. II. Title.

　　940.545952

Cover design: Imogen Mellifont, Studio Canvas.
Sub-editor: Ray Trowbridge, Outsource Proofreading and Editorial Services.
Printed in China by Everbest Printing Co. Ltd.

All rights reserved. Apart from any fair dealing for the purposes of private study, research, criticism or review, as permitted under the *Copyright Act 1968*, no part may be reproduced, stored in or introduced into a retrieval system, or transmitted, in any form or by any means (electronic, mechanical, photocopying, recording or otherwise). Inquiries should be addressed to the publisher.

DEDICATED TO
JEAN ANDREW
In her centenary year

CONTENTS

Acknowledgements 11
Dates, Times and Measurements 13
Preface 15
Introduction 21
01 No Cause for Alarm 27
02 Sunday Evening, Sydney Harbour 33
03 Japan Comes Nearer 43
04 Australia Looks to America 61
05 The Secret War 71
06 Warnings Ignored 81
07 From Hyde Park to Hollywood 95
08 Defences Unprepared 101
09 The Attack Commences 113
10 Sydney's Wildest Night 127
11 Kuttabul Sinks 141
12 Chaos and Indecision 153
13 Censorship and the People 165
14 Attack Post-Mortem 171
15 Campaign of Destruction 185
Author's Note 203
Epilogue 209
Appendices 231
Appendix A: Official Report, 16 July 1942 233
Appendix B: Preliminary Report, 22 June 1942 243
Appendix C: Chart recovered from midget submarine, 10 June 1942 246
Appendix D: Chart recovered from midget submarine, 10 June 1942 247
Appendix E: Reconstruction of midget submarine, 10 June 1942 248
Bibliography 249
Index 257

ACKNOWLEDGEMENTS

I am very grateful to the many people who have helped me in the preparation and writing of this book. The task of researching and compiling this story has been a difficult one. I owe a special thanks to Reginald Andrew who provided me with a vivid account of the Japanese midget submarine attack on Sydney Harbour, and to his wife Jean for her patience and hospitality.

A debt of gratitude is also owed to Harold Anderson, James Nelson, James Cargill, Charlie Brown, George Chipley, Tulla Brown and John Hector who have also been most helpful in the sorting out of events and contributing important information.

I wish to thank Kensuki Zusuki, Bureau Chief of Kyodo News Service while in Australia for his assistance in obtaining the official Japanese War History detailing the planning and execution of the Japanese attack on Sydney Harbour. A special debt of gratitude is also owed to members of the Japan Midget Submarine Association who provided an accurate account of Japan's midget submarine operations during World War II.

No book of this kind can be compiled without the help of others and to all of these people I express my most sincere gratitude:

Itsuo Ashibe, Koichi Ban, Peter Blazey, Wendy Borches, P. Bradfield, Jack Breyon, John Burden, John Burdett, Ian Burgess, John Burton, Alex J. Burwasser, Margaret Chambers, John DeBoer, Tim Donnellan, Peter Dunn, Bill Fitzegerald, William O. Floyd (Rear-Admiral, USN), Walter C. Ford (Rear-Admiral, USN), Laurie Glenman, June and Ray Henman, E. Jim Higgins, Laurie. E. C. Hinchliffe (Lieutenant-Commander, RAN), Geoffrey Hitchcock, Jikyo Ishino (Admiral, Japanese Navy), Jim James, Shigeko Kimura, George Kittredge (Captain, USN), Junie and Noel Kohler, Marie Kuliffay, Lance LeCornu, John MacKenzie, Kazuko Matuo, M. J. McCann, Hermon J. Mecklenberg (Captain, USN), Imogen Mellifont, "Boy" Messenger, Mark Morgan, John Moyle, Harvey Newcombe (Captain, RAN), Roland J. Obey (Captain, USN), Stella O'Brien, Damien Parer, Vern Pascal, Rick Poole, Lynn Quale, Neil Roberts, W. O. C. Roberts, Neil Robson, Vicki Rowlands, Rachel Rovay, Frank Rudd, Hirokazu Sano, Quentin Saunders, Gavin Souter, William A. South (Commander, USN), Peter Taylor, Pippa Thompson, Roy Turner, Tony Turner, Kazuo Uyeda, John Verren, Tony Ward, Kevin Warwick, Tony Wheeler, Jeff Whenan, Jim Whitbread, Jim Whitfield, Teddy Willis, Teiji Yamaki, Yoichi Yokoborii. ●

DATES, TIMES AND MEASUREMENTS

The dates and times in this book vary in a number of instances from those recorded in official Australian documents. For example, the reconnaissance flight over Sydney Harbour by a Japanese seaplane occurred in the early morning hours of 29 May, not 30 May 1942 as recorded in the official Australian history. Other inaccuracies in the historical record include the time when the dockyard floodlights were extinguished on Garden Island at 12:25 am on 1 June; not an hour earlier at 11:25 pm on 31 May 1942 as recorded in the official naval history.

All times are expressed according to local geographical time zones. During World War II, Japanese naval activities operated on Japanese time (GMT +9). Times taken from Japanese historical records have been converted to local geographical times.

The Japanese Imperial Navy also used the metric system of measurement, while the Allied Navies used the Imperial system. All measurements in this narrative are expressed according to their source to better reflect the period.

Many historical accounts of the attack on Sydney Harbour adopt the names of the midget submarines recorded in the official history. In fact, the official report lists four midget submarines, whereas only three took part in the Sydney Harbour raid. For simplicity, I have named the midget submarines to correspond with that of their carrier submarine. ●

Preface

PREFACE

In deciding to write this book my primary aim was to canvass and describe the events that took place on the night of 31 May 1942 when the Japanese launched a surprise midget submarine raid on Sydney Harbour. But, as I began to delve into the incidents surrounding the attack, it became increasingly clear that I had set myself a mammoth task. It was necessary to research a multitude of incidents which preceded the attack in order to fully understand what happened that befogged night; and when I tried to track down official documents, there were very few to be found. Only one 13-page official report relating to the whole affair had been written and submitted to the Australian Naval Board.

Since the surprise attack on Sydney Harbour, the whereabouts of the midget submarine from I-24 has become one of Australia's greatest maritime mysteries, second only to the location of the light cruiser, *HMAS Sydney*, sunk off the Western Australian coast by the disguised German raider, *Kormoran*, in November 1941. Japanese historical records confirm the craft did not return to its carrier submarine after the Sydney Harbour attack, and through the intervening years there have been many theories about its whereabouts, intensifying the mystery of what happened to the midget submarine and its crew, Lieutenant Katsuhisa Ban and Petty Officer Mamoru Ashibe. Several unconfirmed reports of its discovery over the years were met with strong editorials espousing that the wreck should be left alone and treated as a war grave for the two crew trapped inside, as would be the wishes of the Japanese people. Contrary to these assertions, the relatives of the two sailors are anxious for the craft to be found and they have expressed their wishes in separate letters to the Australian Government:

LETTER OF APPEAL

Dear Sirs,
According to the latest news from your country, we have been informed that what is believed to be the midget submarine of the Japanese Navy has been discovered near Sydney Harbour.

If the identity of that object can be ascertained, I have no doubt that it would be the sunken midget submarine on which my elder brother was on board under the command of Lieutenant Ban.

During the war, we were taught that a sailor's life was to perish as a part of the ocean. However, after the long waiting time for this news, my heart burns with aches for my brother.

I should be most grateful if you would be kind enough to ascertain the identity of this object and allow the remains of the crew to be salvaged. I am aware that my wish is such that causes your Government troubles. I apologise for the damage my brother caused your country during the war.

As all my four brothers were killed in World War II, and none of their ashes have been returned to Japan, I hope you would understand my feelings, being the only surviving member of the family, to wish that just one of my brothers' ashes could come back.

I thank you most sincerely for your kind attention on this matter.

Signed by ITSUO ASHIBE on 12 April 1978.

LETTER OF APPEAL

Dear Sirs,
I wish to express respectfully my appreciation for the careful attention paid by your Government to the matters concerning my brother Katsuhisa Ban, who was one of the crew of the midget submarine.

Please accept my sincere apologies on behalf of Katsuhisa for the detriment he had caused to your esteemed country. Katsuhisa, having been a member of the Imperial Navy, had to perform his military duties which necessitated his actions. I am sure that his personal feelings were not resentful of your country. I hope that you would give your thoughtful consideration in this regard and forgive my brother.

I have been deeply impressed with the warm and gallant treatment that your Royal Australian Navy had given to the crew of the two other midget submarines, Lieutenant Matsuo and Lieutenant. Chuma.

I am most grateful for the effort your Government has taken to search for the third submarine of which my brother was a member of the crew.

As his elder brother, it is my life-long wish that Katsuhisa's ashes would be returned to his homeland and sleep restfully with his deceased parents.

Beyond the sentiments of the past hostilities now being forgiven, I seek your kind consideration on this matter.

Signed by KOICHI BAN on 13 April 1978.

My involvement in this story began in late 1977 when, while carrying out an abalone tagging programme for the NSW Fisheries Department, I came across a wreck in Sydney Harbour, thought to be part of the missing submarine. It was not. Until that time I had hardly been aware, like so many of my generation, that there had been a Japanese raid on Sydney Harbour. As a result of the publicity that followed, I received an interesting letter from a naval veteran who had commanded one of the patrol boats on the harbour the night of the attack. Curiosity aroused, I visited him and he told me his story, which varied from the official account. So, I set out to discover what really happened that night.

The Sydney Harbour raid was as daring as the midget submarine attack on Pearl Harbor in December 1941, and had there been greater loss of life the conduct of the defences of Sydney would have been revealed. After the Darwin air attack in February

1942, the government had no alternative but to order a Royal Commission, the results of which, had they been publicly released at the time, would have caused an outcry. Even today, the true number of fatalities from the Darwin air attack remain unknown. With the Sydney Harbour attack following so closely, the government could not afford another official investigation.

Today, only a few of our war veterans of that era remain, which has made it difficult, in the absence of documentation, to cover every aspect of the Sydney Harbour attack. It is now evident that military secrecy and government censorship was a major factor why few details emerged until many years after the Sydney raid. Had there been an official investigation, it would have revealed serious flaws in the harbour defences, as well as the failure of some personnel; it also would have revealed the gallantry of many Australian defenders.

In this revised edition, I hope I have filled in the gaps in those areas where I felt the first edition was deficient. It wasn't until after *Australia Under Siege* was first published in 1982 that many survivors and participants on the harbour that night, and members of the public, came forward with their stories. Additions include further accounts from *HMAS Kuttabul* survivors, from former crew members of *USS Chicago* and *USS Perkins*, the role of censorship in war-time Australia, the role of suicide attacks as a weapon of war, and the theories surrounding the location of the missing Japanese midget submarine. ●

Steven L. Carruthers, 2006

INTRODUCTION

INTRODUCTION

Just over three months after the surprise air raid over Darwin, Australians were once again shaken when the Japanese launched a surprise midget submarine attack on Sydney Harbour, Australia's premier city. The attack was among the most audacious actions carried out in Japanese naval history. It occurred at a time when Japan's Imperial Army was advancing on Port Moresby, and three weeks after the Japanese had seemingly won a tactical victory against the United States Pacific Fleet in the Battle of the Coral Sea.

The Japanese greatly valued surprise. It had devastated Pearl Harbor and they expected similar unpreparedness when they launched their submarines into crowded Sydney Harbour, which then contained over 40 ships of war from all the Allied Navies fighting in the Pacific. Present were a number of American warships, including the heavy cruiser *USS Chicago*, plus British, Indian, Dutch and Australian vessels.

The Sydney Harbour attack was preceded by a similar attack at Diego Suarez Bay, Madagascar, during which the midget raiders sank the tanker *British Loyalty* and damaged the battleship *HMS Ramilles*. Had the Diego Suarez Bay attack been known to Sydney, then it is possible the Australian defence authorities might have strengthened the harbour's defences, particularly in view of previous warnings over preceding days indicating the presence of Japanese submarines operating close to Sydney. However, these warnings were ignored and the British Admiralty did not warn Australia of the Diego Suarez Bay attack. Consequently, the harbour's defences were not strengthened.

Shortly before moonrise on 31 May 1942, three large Japanese submarines launched their midget submarines off Sydney Heads. Each craft was manned by two highly trained men; an officer and a non-commissioned officer. At 8:01 pm the first submarine entered the harbour undetected; but at 8:15 pm became hopelessly entangled in the anti-submarine boom net strung across the inner harbour entrance. At 8:30 pm it was discovered and reported; however, an incredible two hours passed before the alarm was raised. Although the Naval Officer-in-Charge of Sydney Harbour had received earlier reports of a suspicious object entangled in the boom net, it was not until 10:35 pm, when the midget submarine self-destructed that he finally realised an enemy submarine was in the harbour.

Two hours later the second submarine to enter the harbour dispatched two torpedoes towards the *USS Chicago*, one of which passed narrowly ahead of the heavy cruiser, and under the Dutch submarine *K-9* and the Australian barracks vessel, *HMAS Kuttabul*, permanently moored at Garden Island. The torpedo struck the sea wall beneath the

Kuttabul, killing 21 sleeping naval ratings and injuring another 10. The second torpedo passed astern of the heavy cruiser before running harmlessly aground on Garden Island.

After firing its torpedoes, the midget submarine seemingly escaped from the harbour, but failed to rendezvous with the Japanese submarine attack force waiting off the coast south of Sydney. The whereabouts of this midget submarine has become one of Australia's greatest maritime mysteries.

The third midget submarine successfully penetrated deep into the harbour but, because of damage sustained to the craft earlier in the night, was unable to fire its two torpedoes. The submarine was sighted on the surface and sunk by depth charges.

In the dark there was panic and indecision. Although Sydneysiders thought an air raid was in progress, the naval authorities clearly knew otherwise.

The attack may be regarded as ending a long period of apathy and half heartedness about the war. After 31 May 1942 it was impossible to ignore the closeness of Japanese forces. In fact, that last weekend of May in Sydney might be regarded as the last weekend of peace – or, perhaps, the end of the "phoney war", that quiescent period of half-war and half-peace which ended abruptly for England when the Germans invaded France.

It was certainly the high point in a period of rapid change in social and sexual mores that had never before occurred in Australia, the lasting results of which earned Sydney its reputation of "Sin City". This appellation was richly rewarded when the American High Command decided to make Sydney an R&R base during the Vietnam War.

In retrospect, the explosions and gunfire on the harbour that night put a sudden end to an astonishing period of Australia's social history. After that Sydney raid things were never again quite the same. The war was finally regarded as being in earnest, the politicians became more pious, and the multitude of Americans in Australia began to experience a slow decline in public favour.

In the weeks that followed the Sydney Harbour raid, the Japanese launched a large scale campaign to terrorise and destroy commercial shipping off the east coast of Australia. A week after the Sydney raid, two submarines surfaced off Sydney and Newcastle and commenced shelling the suburbs, which resulted in alarmed residents putting their homes up for sale and fleeing to safer inland areas. Between June 1942 and December 1944, a total of 27 merchant ships were sunk in Australian waters, resulting in 577 fatalities. Nearly 300 of these were in one attack when the Australian hospital ship, *Centaur*, was sunk off the Queensland coast in May 1943.

Official documents about the Sydney Harbour attack are rare and many of them have been lost or destroyed. Unlike Pearl Harbor and the Darwin attack, no official investigation was held to examine the conduct of defences. This should have been a matter of routine. In the words of Lieutenant Athol. G. Townley, one of the defenders on Sydney Harbour:

> This was war in one's backyard, so to speak, and yet there was little publicity about it. One wonders if a similar attack… on New York or San Francisco… would have been permitted to pass as did this one – almost without official comment.

24. JAPANESE SUBMARINE RAIDERS 1942 *A Maritime Mystery*

Military authorities in Australia were well aware that the country was a likely target for the Japanese. General Douglas MacArthur, in Australia at the time, had known in advance of the impending sea invasion of Port Moresby. From intelligence obtained through a highly secret source known as "Ultra", he was able to inform the Australian government of the strength of the Japanese forces and the time that the invasion would occur. Even with this prior knowledge, the Allies did not muster sufficient air and naval forces to inflict a decisive defeat on the advancing Japanese forces.

On the Australian mainland necessary precautions against attack were either inadequate or non-existent. A few instances, particularly of the preparations and handling of the Sydney Harbour attack, demonstrate the general complacency that prevailed at such a critical time in Australia's history.

After the Darwin air attack the government introduced legislation forbidding all reports of the war being released to the public, except those approved by Prime Minister Curtin. In this manner the government was able to withhold the true details of the actual attack, the casualties suffered, and of the looting, the panic and mass exodus of civilian and military personnel. Radio and press censorship had the effect of inflaming the already exaggerated rumours running through the nation. Censorship summaries report there was a feeling of general panic amongst Australians during this period, with the expectation of defeat by the Japanese. For that reason, the Government watered down any Australian disaster in regards to attacks on Australian soil, to prevent the population from "getting scared". Censorship also allowed the government to cover up mismanagement of the war effort, peculiarities in defence conduct, and even Australian casualties.

When news of the midget submarine attack on Sydney Harbour became known in Japan, thousands of Japanese youths volunteered their lives to the *kaiten* (human torpedo) units, hoping to emulate the courage and self-scarifice of their heroes. Although not technically a suicide mission, the midget submarine crews knew they would not return.

As Japan became more desperate towards the end of the war, suicide attacks became formalised and ritualised. While the early *kaiten* were equipped with escape hatches, their crews had no intention of using them. Later *kaitens* had no means of escape. After aiming a two-person *kaiten* at their target, the two crew members traditionally embraced and shot each other in the head. Similarly, in the blue skies above the Pacific, *kamikaze* pilots flew to their deaths in the thousands.

Social support for such choices was strong, due in part to Japanese cultural history, in which *seppuku*, honourable suicide, was part of *samurai* duty. In the modern age, suicide attacks have become the defining act of political violence. ●

CHAPTER ONE
No CAUSE FOR ALARM

CHAPTER ONE

NO CAUSE FOR ALARM

Ito's seaplane was seen and heard, but still no one suspected the presence of a Japanese force so close to Australia's largest city.

Ports of N.S.W. June 1978,
Volume 2, No.1.

On Friday 29 May 1942, in the early hours of the morning before dawn, Able-Seaman Leslie Bland was on sentry duty alongside *HMAS Kuttabul*. The *Kuttabul*, a passenger ferry before the war, had been requisitioned by the navy and converted to a barracks ship to accommodate naval ratings in transit. She was now permanently moored on the south-eastern side of Garden Island Naval Base.

Bland was looking out over the harbour, trying to keep warm from the winter chill when he heard and saw an aircraft flying down the harbour at low altitude. He knew this was an unusual occurrence at that time of the morning but as no one else on the harbour seemed alarmed he regarded the aircraft as a welcome relief to an otherwise tedious watch. The thought that it could be a Japanese aircraft on a reconnaissance mission never occurred to him. A short time later it reappeared over Man-of-War Anchorage. Suddenly, searchlights pencilled the sky looking for the aircraft which had now disappeared into the dense cloud lingering over the harbour.

The unidentified aircraft was piloted by 27-year-old Flying Warrant Officer Susumu Ito who had been specially chosen to fly the reconnaissance aircraft from an I-class submarine, the largest type of submarine in the Japanese navy. This quietly spoken man was one of Japan's crack night flyers. He and a team of mechanics had succeeded in putting the float plane with collapsible wings into the water just before moonrise. After servicing it, Ito and his observer taxied across the choppy sea and took off at 3:47 am from a point 30 miles east of North Head. Because his plane had no identification marks or guns, Ito was hoping to fly low enough and long enough with his navigation lights on and still escape any ground guns or enemy aircraft.

The thick cloud level was at about 600 metres and Ito flew low over North Head at about 400 metres; he descended to 300 metres then 200 metres to allow his observer to sketch the position of the anti-submarine net at the harbour entrance and to locate its opening. He then flew down the harbour but with the moonlight obscured by clouds he couldn't see clearly. The plane passed over the Harbour Bridge and Cockatoo Island dockyard beyond where he saw flashes from welding plants on the ground. Ito was using an Admiralty map to navigate his aircraft but was unable to understand some of the markings and became lost. He tried to find Mascot aerodrome so he could get his bearings and was soon rewarded when the aerodrome switched on its landing lights. He later recounted on a visit to Sydney in 1957 that he "did not know whether they expected a friendly plane or mistook me for one but it was helpful".

Ito headed back towards the harbour and circled Garden Island and Man-of-War Anchorage where he saw a cluster of large warships. He later recounted that he circled Man-of-War Anchorage twice, descending to 30 metres, below the height of ship mastheads, to allow his observer to sketch the position of the warships. When the searchlights came on, he climbed into the clouds and headed back towards North Head and out to sea to rendezvous with his submarine; but it wasn't there. Ito searched the area for a few minutes before returning to North Head to start another approach. As he turned again he flashed on his lights while he counted to five. The submarine waiting on the surface responded by switching on its searchlight for a few seconds to show Ito where to land. However, while he was reconnoitring Sydney Harbour, the wind had strengthened and the sea had become rough. As the aircraft touched the sea it overturned. Ito and his observer managed to scramble clear unharmed and swam through the cold sea to the submarine. A short time later the plane's floats were punctured so it would sink.

The first sighting of the aircraft was made by the army artillery battery at George's Heights, near Middle Head, the majestic cliff that guards the harbour entrance. The battery commander reported the plane to the duty intelligence officer at Garden Island, Lieutenant P. F. Wilson, informing him that there was no cause for alarm as it was an American Curtiss Falcon float plane (a remarkable deduction considering it was dark and the plane had no distinguishing markings).

Wilson later told Australian historian, G. Hermon Gill, that he "was quite aware that *Chicago*'s planes were on its deck and that no other American cruiser was anywhere in the vicinity". Wilson sought permission from the security officer, Lieutenant Commander C. F. Mills, who had also heard and seen the aircraft from Garden Island, to proceed to the *USS Chicago* to inquire if they knew anything about it.

The officer-of-the-deck on *Chicago*, Ensign E. Jarman, an aviator, was the only person on the heavy cruiser to see the aircraft and he identified it as an enemy plane. Immediately after returning to Garden Island, Wilson telephoned fighter sector headquarters at Asta Flats in the city to report that an unidentified aircraft had been sighted at low altitude over the naval anchorage area. At 5:07 am fighter headquarters issued an official alert and dispatched Wirraway fighters from Richmond airbase to investigate. By this time the aircraft had escaped to sea. Based on the army battery report, Ito's plane was officially identified as friendly and the fighter aircraft returned to their airfield.

Although it was prohibited for aircraft to fly over Sydney Harbour, the sighting failed to inspire any apprehension in the Naval Officer-in-Charge (NOIC) of Sydney Harbour's defences, Rear-Admiral Gerald Charles Muirhead-Gould, who had been posted to the Australian Station from the Royal Navy. He did not raise the alarm or initiate any precautionary defence measures. He conceded in his report some days later that: "The attack was probably preceded by aerial reconnaissance, which may have been carried out on 29, 30 and 31 May."

Over the previous two weeks the Australian authorities received several more warnings of Japanese units operating close to Sydney; but they failed to draw any conclusion from these as possibly presaging an attack on the harbour.

On 16 May the Russian ship *Wellen* was attacked by a submarine 40 miles east of Newcastle. The Japanese submarine surfaced almost alongside *Wellen* and commenced firing with her deck gun. After firing off seven rounds the submarine submerged, the sound of hissing air clearly audible on *Wellen's* bridge. *Wellen's* captain sent off a distress call to the naval authorities in Sydney and Newcastle announcing he was being attacked. Rear-Admiral Muirhead-Gould closed Sydney and Newcastle ports to outward-bound merchant shipping, but re-opened them 24 hours later following a fruitless search of the area by the Dutch cruiser *Tromp*, the Australian corvette *Arunta*, and the American destroyer *Perkins*.

Other warnings of Japanese submarines close to Sydney were ignored when on 26 May, and again on 29 May, the New Zealand naval authorities intercepted Japanese radio transmissions east of Sydney. The New Zealand Naval Board notified the authorities in Australia of an enemy unit, probably a submarine, operating approximately 700 miles, then 40 miles, east of Sydney Harbour. However, these warnings were also ignored.

Yet another warning came when Japanese radio chatter was heard aboard *USS Chicago* over several nights preceding the Sydney raid. The ship's communications officer, Lieutenant-Commander H. J. Mecklenburg, reported the chatter to the Garden Island Operations Room, but his report went no further.

After the Japanese surprise attack on Pearl Harbor, both civilian and military personnel in Australia developed a profound complacency, a feeling that "it can't happen here" – even as they followed accounts of the rapid southward advance of the Japanese forces. They avoided the unpleasant issues and faced reality only when confronted with it. That the Japanese might actually attack Sydney was unthinkable.

In general, Australians objected to the disruption of their lives and blamed the government for the beer shortage and food rationing. Black marketing and racketeering became common practice amongst military personnel as well as the civilian population. Further, people were irritated by frequent air raid drills being imposed on them. According to newspapers of the day, the National Emergency Service (NES), a "dad's army" style organisation, held an air raid test on 30 May involving 20,000 NES personnel in 10 suburban municipalities. Simulated bomb casualties were treated for shocking injuries and fire brigades fought imaginary fires. The test lasted for two hours after which the NES announced that a similar test would be held in the Eastern Suburbs the following week.

The next morning the *Daily Telegraph* headlines announced "British Counter in Libya". Many Sydney residents had formed the habit of scanning the newspapers daily, anxious for news of the battle areas overseas where their loved ones and friends might be. After this ritual had been completed, the reader studied the rest of the news. On that morning, it was revealed actor John Barrymore had died from pneumonia at the age of 60 years and Reinhard Heydrich, the Nazi butcher of Czechoslovakia, was hanging between life and death after an assassination attempt. The main news item that caught readers attention, however, was the announcement that the beer ration for June would be increased by 15%; but it was thought doubtful whether the increase would greatly relieve the Sydney beer shortage.

Meanwhile, 30 miles off Sydney Heads, Captain Hankyu Sasaki, commanding the Third Submarine Company, was encouraged by Ito's reconnaissance report and prepared his attack order to launch a midget submarine attack into the harbour.

The Third Submarine Squadron consisted of five I-class submarines which had been assembling off Sydney Harbour since 24 May in preparation for the attack. The 3,000-tonne I-class submarines were then the world's largest. Three of these submarines carried midget submarines clamped to their decks, piggy-back style, and two carried reconnaissance aircraft.

The midget submarine crews included Lieutenant Keiu Matsuo who was a key strategist in the planning of the unsuccessful midget submarine attack on Pearl Harbor on 7 December 1941. When none of the craft from that operation were recovered, he returned to Japan and went to work learning how to improve the midget submarines' performance.

The commander of the Japanese Combined Fleet, Admiral Isoroku Yamamoto, was deeply affected by the loss of the 10 crew members from the midget submarine operation at Pearl Harbor, but he was convinced by those associated with them, and the crews themselves, that a second midget submarine operation would be successful if the craft were modified and the raid carried out on a harbour which was weakly defended. Subsequently, plans were drawn up for simultaneous surprise attacks in the Indian and South Pacific Oceans.

In February 1942, Yamamoto ordered I-25 to proceed to Australian waters to carry out aerial reconnaissance over Sydney, Melbourne and Hobart, to pinpoint harbour defences and to locate the heaviest concentration of Allied naval shipping. The Japanese also studied aerial photographs of major ports in the South Pacific including Sydney Harbour, taken from Australian periodicals published in 1938. The Japanese naval authorities had also acquired Admiralty charts of the Australian coastline and its ports and harbours prior to the War in the Pacific.

At the beginning of April 1942, a force of six submarines, under the command of Captain Hankyu Sasaki, was ordered to proceed to Australian waters to search for major naval vessels. One submarine was sunk en route, reducing Sasaki's force to five. Only after determining the location of the greatest concentration of naval shipping was the attack to take place, sometime at the end of May when the moon would be bright.

Following an aerial reconnaissance over Sydney on 23 May that reported battleships and cruisers in the harbour, Captain Sasaki ordered his submarine force to assemble off the harbour entrance. Arriving off Sydney on 28 May, he launched a second reconnaissance flight to re-affirm the presence of large warships in the harbour. Sasaki ordered the attack to commence shortly after sunset on 31 May. He shrewdly calculated that on that day Australian defences would be less alert than usual. Indeed, Australian apathy and the action of wharfies in holding up the unloading of warships had prompted a Sydney joke to the effect that Japan was fighting a total war while Australia was only engaging in a five-day-a-week war. ●

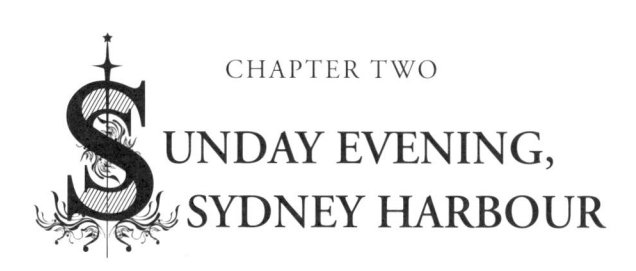

CHAPTER TWO
SUNDAY EVENING, SYDNEY HARBOUR

CHAPTER TWO

SUNDAY EVENING, SYDNEY HARBOUR

We got into Port Jackson early in the afternoon and had the satisfaction of finding the finest harbour in the world in which 1000 sail of line may ride in perfect security.

Arthur Phillip, 23 January 1788

In the pre-twilight hours of Sunday 31 May 1942, a crisp and wet southwesterly wind moistened Sydney Harbour. Sunset came at 4:53 pm and a full moon was due to rise at 7:15 pm. The ragged coastline from Dee Why to Bondi was majestically silhouetted against the waning light, with Middle and South Heads visible against the foreshore lights of the harbour suburbs. It was the end of another Sunday and Sydney residents were settling into their lounge chairs to listen to the war news on their wireless sets.

Inside the harbour the calm waters were dark and occasionally lit by moonlight which penetrated the overcast sky. The serenity was disturbed only by fishing boats sprinkled about the harbour, their crews busy setting nets for the night. The Manly ferry plied the harbour as she transported her passengers to Circular Quay and the cinema.

For the past two months Sydney had been crowded with American servicemen, and the Australian way of life had become decidedly lighthearted. At the State theatre Abbot and Costello in *Keep 'Em Flying* was into its second week. (Ironically, the same feature film had been playing in Honolulu the night before Pearl Harbor was attacked.) A reduced admittance fee of one shilling for men and women in uniform had caused a long queue to form along the footpath. The theatre soon sold out and about 300 people were turned away.

A new group of American sailors, recently returned from the Coral Sea, flocked to the David Jones restaurant on Elizabeth Street where a party was held in their honour. Australian girls crowded the entrance to catch the eye of an American GI, or a wandering sailor.

On the harbour, Hornby Light at Inner South Head and Macquarie Light at Outer South Head came on as usual. The floodlights at Garden Island were switched on where work was being done on the construction of a new dry-dock. The obtuseness of defence authorities in allowing these lights to be used gave the Japanese a floodlit scene before they were eventually extinguished.

The harbour was filled to capacity with naval and commercial shipping. Wharves and buoys were fully occupied with many more vessels at anchor. There were no large transport

The Northampton-class American heavy cruiser, *USS Chicago*.

The Mahan-class American destroyer, *USS Perkins*.

vessels in the harbour; the *Queen Mary I* and her sister ship, *Queen Elizabeth I*, had sailed some weeks earlier, their decks crowded with thousands of troops en route to battle areas overseas. The Flagship of the Australian Squadron, the heavy cruiser *HMAS Australia*, had gone to sea only a few days earlier.

Over preceding days, the Dutch/Australian hospital ship, *Oranje*, had been discharging wounded troops from the Middle East, among them the distinguished Roden Cutler who had earned the Victoria Cross for heroic action in Syria. At 4.10 pm, *Oranje* slipped her moorings and proceeded out of the harbour with her decks aglow; but the Third Submarine Company merely watched and allowed her to pass unmolested.

Commercial shipping movements were heavier than usual that evening. Between 5:17 am and 6:55 pm the merchant ships *Cobargo*, *Erinna* and *Mortlake Bank* entered the harbour and made their way down to Walsh Bay to unload their cargoes. In addition to commercial shipping, there were over 40 Allied naval vessels congesting the harbour on that Sunday evening. This unusually large contingent was present because a number of vessels had recently returned from northern waters to repair, rearm and refuel following the historic Battle of the Coral Sea. The heavy cruiser, *USS Chicago*, had taken up her mooring at Man-of-War Anchorage after completing a minor refit at Cockatoo Island dockyard where her 1.1-inch machine guns were replaced with automatic, rapid fire "Bofers". Similarly, her destroyer escort, *USS Perkins*, had just completed an overhaul after six months of steady steaming at sea, often at high speed. The most valuable targets from the Japanese point of view were the five American, British and Australian cruisers, three of which were carrying aircraft and highly explosive aviation fuel.

As darkness descended on Sunday 31 May, a mood of tranquillity came over the harbour and defence personnel relaxed for the evening. At Farm Cove, seven off-duty channel patrol boats (CPBs) had stood down for the night. The crew of *HMAS Leilani* had gone ashore for the night, leaving only a quartermaster on board. The leader of the Channel Patrol Boat Flotilla, Lieutenant-Commander E. Breydon, moved his boat, *HMAS Silver Cloud*, to Rushcutters Bay to be near his residence. The commander of *HMAS Steady Hour*, Lieutenant A. G. Townley, relinquished command of his patrol boat early in the evening, but decided to remain onboard to allow the new skipper, who had family in Sydney, to go ashore for the evening.

Lieutenant R. T. Andrew assumed command of *HMAS Sea Mist* at 4:00 pm. Since he was not rostered for patrol duty until the following morning, he decided to retire early. Also in Farm Cove was *HMAS Marlean* and *HMAS Toomaree*, which were manned, fuelled, and on standby to proceed on patrol.

HMAS Yarroma, commanded by Sub-Lieutenant H. C. Eyres, was rostered for duty and slipped her moorings at Farm Cove at 6:00 pm to proceed to the harbour entrance and the West Gate boom net opening, which was still under construction. On arriving there he decided to drop anchor. *HMAS Lolita*, commanded by Warrant Officer H. S. Anderson, slipped her moorings in Farm Cove at the same time to patrol the East Gate channel opening.

At Rushcutters Bay, Naval Auxiliary Patrol Boat (NAP) flotilla leader, L. H. Winkworth, slipped the moorings of *HMAS Lauriana*, also at 6:00 pm, and proceeded to the harbour

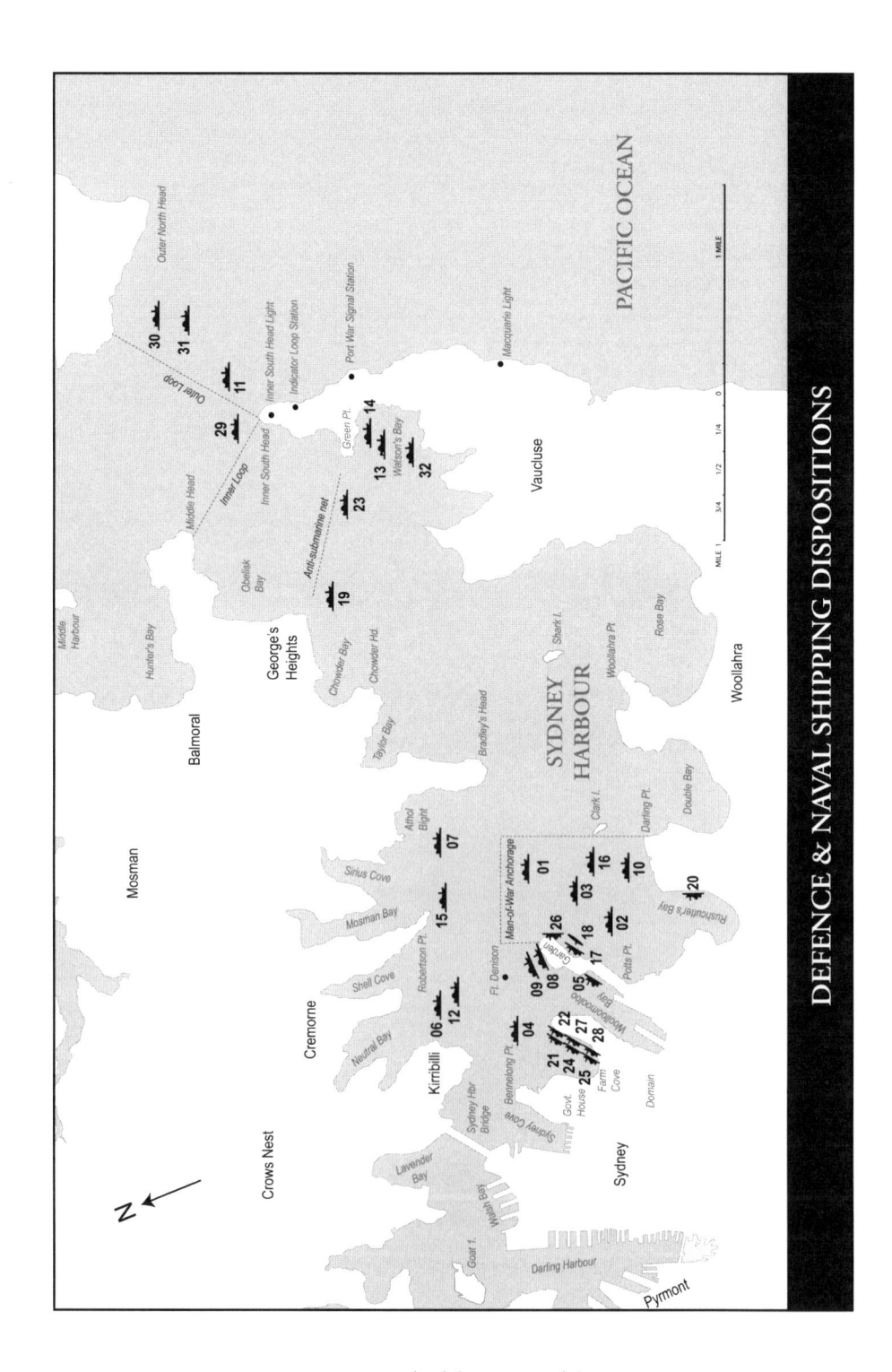

38. JAPANESE SUBMARINE RAIDERS 1942 *A Maritime Mystery*

NAVAL SHIPPING IN SYDNEY HARBOUR 31 MAY - 1 JUNE 1942

01. *USS Chicago* - heavy cruiser
02. *USS Dobbin* - destroyer tender
03. *USS Perkins* - destroyer
04. *HMAS Canberra* - heavy cruiser
05. *HMAS Adelaide* - light cruiser
06. *HMS Kanimbla* - armed merchant cruiser
07. *HMAS Westralia* - armed merchant cruiser
08. *HMAS Geelong* - corvette
09. *HMAS Whyalla* - corvette
10. *HMIS Bombay* - corvette
11. *HMAS Yandra* - anti-submarine vessel
12. *HMAS Bingera* - anti-submarine vessel
13. *HMAS Goonambee* - minesweeper
14. *HMAS Samuel Benbow* - minesweeper
15. *HMAS Doomba* - minesweeper
16 *HMAS Bungaree* - minelayer
17. *HMAS Kuttabul* - barricks vessel
18. *RNS K-9* - submarine
19. *HMAS Yarroma* - channel patrol boat
20. *HMAS Silver Cloud* - channel patrol boat
21. *HMAS Steady Hour* - channel patrol boat
22. *HMAS Sea Mist* - channel patrol boat
23. *HMAS Lolita* - channel patrol boat
24. *HMAS Toomaree* - channel patrol boat
25. *HMAS Marlean* - channel patrol boat
26. *HMAS Miramar* - channel patrol boat
27. *HMAS Leilani* - channel patrol boat
29. *HMAS Esmerelda* - channel patrol boat
28. *HMAS Lauriana* - auxiliary patrol boat
30. *HMAS Allura* - auxiliary patrol boat
31. *HMAS Yarrawonga* - auxiliary patrol boat
32. *HMAS Adele* - examination vessel

The Australian heavy cruiser, *HMAS Canberra*. *(From the personal effects of Captain F. E. Getting)*

Inspecting troops on the deck of the *Queen Mary I*. (L to R): Commander R. B. Irving, captain of the troop transport ship, the Governor-General, Lord Gowrie, Commodore G. C. Muirhead-Gould, and Brigadier J. J. Murray in charge of the troops aboard the *Queen Mary I* (Photograph taken 15 September 1940).

entrance. Winkworth contacted flotilla vessels *HMAS Yarrawonga* and *HMAS Allura* shortly afterwards, giving them instructions to patrol between North and South Heads with the anti-submarine vessel, *HMAS Yandra*.

At 6:15 pm Winkworth contacted *Yarroma* at the West Gate and received information on the local fishing boats which were permitted to fish in certain restricted areas. Winkworth recorded in his vessel's running log that it was then dark and *Lauriana* proceeded on patrol between the heads with all her lights out. The moon was up but a patchy sky clouded it at frequent intervals. There was a steady roll coming through the heads, and no ships were sighted entering the harbour.

At Garden Island, some of the ship's company of *HMAS Kuttabul* had gone ashore for the night, while others were rostered for duty or remained behind to catch up on their letter writing. Also billeted on *Kuttabul* was Leading Seaman Diver W. L. Bullard. The previous afternoon he had secured the 42-foot diving pinnace between *Kuttabul* and the sea wall, taking the woollen gear, helmets, suits and telephone to the diving shed, but leaving all the heavy gear in the boat including pumps, air hoses, breast lines, boots and weights. He then proceeded ashore to his home in the inner Sydney suburb of Gladesville.

Also at Garden Island, the duty staff officer, Lieutenant Commander C. F. Mills, handed the watch over to his assistant, Lieutenant P. F. Wilson, who maintained his watch from Rear-Admiral Muirhead-Gould's staff offices on the eastern side of Garden Island. The Operations Room looked out over Man-of-War Anchorage and the harbour. Wilson had a direct telephone link with both Combined Defence Headquarters located in the city, and "Tresco" at nearby Elizabeth Bay, the official residence of the Naval Officer-in-Charge of Sydney Harbour. Muirhead-Gould was fond of entertaining and on this particular evening he had invited *Chicago's* commanding officer, Captain H. D. Bode, and other ship's officers to dine with him at Tresco.

On the other side of the harbour, at Admiralty House, the Governor-General, the Earl of Gowrie VC, who played an important behind-the-scenes role in Australian politics, had just arrived in Sydney from Canberra. The Governor-General's official Sydney residence, situated on Kirribilli Point, had a dress circle view of the harbour.

Shortly before sunset, the Third Submarine Company took up position 7 to 10 miles east of the harbour and prepared to launch three midget submarines. Those who turned in early in preparation for the coming week, were destined to be savagely awakened by a pandemonium of gunfire and explosions as the Australian forces reacted to a surprise raid by Japanese midget submarines. ●

CHAPTER THREE
JAPAN COMES NEARER

CHAPTER THREE

JAPAN COMES NEARER

Getting lunches and soft drinks, it's like going on a hike.

Sub-Lieutenant Akira Hiroo
On boarding his midget submarine for Pearl Harbor

When Japan entered the war, the Supreme Commander of the Combined Squadron, Admiral Isoroku Yamamoto, was not keen at first to support the use of midget submarines in the attack on Pearl Harbor. However, he was swayed by the enthusiasm of the personnel directly associated with them and he adopted a plan to use them in the coming operation.

The men selected to crew the midget submarines were small in stature, their average height about 1.52 metres. Most were bachelors, with some exceptions, who showed an aptitude for submarine warfare. Keiu Matsuo was such a man. The son of an elementary school teacher, he graduated from the 66th Term at Kure Naval College in September 1938, after which he was ordered to serve a training period on a destroyer attached to the Combined Fleet. He was promoted to Second-Lieutenant in June 1939, and Lieutenant in November 1940. While attached to the Combined Fleet, he applied for service in the Flying Corps but failed to qualify and was ordered to undergo training for midget submarines. He graduated from the midget submarine school at Kure Naval Dockyard in April 1941 and became one of the first to pilot these experimental submarines.

Matsuo's intelligence was highly regarded by his peers and superior officers who earmarked him for greater responsibility. Along with Lieutenants Naoji Iwasa and Saburo Akieda, he became one of the first to propose the use of these craft in a sneak attack, convincing Yamamoto that the crews could be safely recovered after a successful attack.

In addition to these three men, further eight officers, three warrant officers and 12 petty officers were selected to commence training in midget submarines. Each craft was designed to carry two men – an officer responsible for navigation, speed, communications and target calculations, and a non-commissioned officer responsible for steering, engineering, air purifying and firing of torpedoes.

The first two experimental midget submarines were cigar-shaped with a conning tower to house the periscope. The success of these two craft resulted in another 41 vessels being built and powered by 600hp electric motors. However, they had no generators and so the batteries had to be removed for recharging, either by their carrier

Midget Submarine graduates of the 2nd Term at Kure Naval Dockyard.
Back row (L to R): Akira Hiroo (Pearl Harbor), Teiji Yamaki (assigned to Sydney Harbour), Kazuo Sakamaki (Pearl Harbor), Katsuhisa Ban (Sydney Harbour), Kuromi, Matsumoto.
Front row (L to R): Kenshi Chuma (Sydney Harbour), Keiu Matsuo (Sydney Harbour), Masaharu Yokoyama (Pearl Harbor), Shigemi Furuno (Pearl Harbor), Kanda, Otosaka.

PEARL HARBOR MIDGET SUBMARINE OPERATION

Submarine	Captain	Midget Crews
I-16	Commander Kaoru Yamanda	Sub-Lieutenant Masaharu Yokoyama Petty Officer Sadashi Uyeda
I-18	Commander Kiyonori Ohtani	Sub-Lieutenant Shigeru Furuno Petty Officer Kunhan Yokoyama
I-20	Commander Takashi Yamanda	Sub-Lieutenant Akira Hiroo Petty Officer Yoshio Katayama
I-22	Commander Kiyoi Ageta	Lieutenant Naoji Iwasa Petty Officer Naokichi Sasaki
I-24	Commander Hiroshi Hanafusa	Sub-Lieutenant Kazuo Sakamaki Petty Officer Kiyoshi Inagaki

46. JAPANESE SUBMARINE RAIDERS 1942 *A Maritime Mystery*

vessels or in a dockyard. The midget submarines used at Pearl Harbor were 23.7 metres in length, 1.8 metres in diameter and weighed 46 tonnes. Each had a crew of two. Although experimental in design, they were advanced for their time. For short periods, they could run at 24 knots on the surface and 19 knots submerged, but their endurance was greatly reduced to only 55 minutes. At a submerged speed of 4 knots, however, the midgets had an effective range of 100 miles or an endurance of 25 hours. Each carried two 18-inch torpedoes mounted one above the other, and a scuttling charge to avoid capture. The size of each torpedo warhead approximated 1,000 pounds of explosive. These craft were completed only months before the Pearl Harbor attack, allowing little time for crew training.

First sea trials commenced in the Seto Inland Sea. During the ensuing months extensive workups and exercises were carried out to bring the midget submarines and their crews to a high level of efficiency. The seaplane carriers *Chiyoda* and *Nisshin* were speedily converted to carry 12 midget submarines each. These two vessels transported the midget submarines to their operational exercise areas and their callsigns were altered to disguise their real purpose.

It was soon realised that these vessels would have to transport the midget submarines to within about 30 miles of a target area. This, of course, was undesirable, as the seaplane carriers would be detected by enemy patrols, even under the cover of darkness. Considerable thought was directed towards employing the craft in fleet-against-fleet operations instead, but this idea was also abandoned when it was decided that they still lacked a suitable vehicle to carry them. Naval experts then considered transporting the craft mounted on the rear deck of a larger submarine. Carrying the midget submarines in this fashion was a brilliant concept as it would allow a carrier submarine to transport its ward to the mouth of a harbour while submerged. Then, when night fell, it could surface to release the craft, almost within sight of the target. Subsequently, the "I-16 class" submarines were selected to undergo modifications to allow the craft to be clamped to their decks.

On one occasion during training exercises, while learning how to dive under anti-submarine nets, one of the midget submarines failed to return. Piloted by Lieutenant Matsuo with Lieutenant Teiji Yamaki as co-pilot, the craft suddenly stopped when the forward part became trapped in mud. Matsuo gave the order to blow the torpedo tubes, but it was unsuccessful in freeing the craft. Yamaki recounted many years after the war that he suggested the pressure should not be wasted but released slowly, and Matsuo immediately accepted the idea.

> So we stopped the blowing and decided to await the rescue ship. Although this was my idea to wait, the acceptance of this advice showed Matsuo's calm and he never over-reacted to this situation.

Both Matsuo and Yamaki conserved their energy and, over four hours later, bubbles were sighted by *Chiyoda* and the midget submarine was recovered.

Yamaki described Matsuo as a very enthusiastic officer and when there was no training, he spent his time practising kendo and judo with Lieutenants Naoji Iwasa and Kenshi Chuma, whom he had befriended during training.

Japanese submarine I-16, one of the carrier submarines which took part in both the Pearl Harbor and Diego Suarez Bay attacks.

Commander Kiyoi Ageta, commander of the carrier submarine I-22, who took part in the midget submarine attacks on both Pearl Harbor and Sydney Harbour.

Matsuo had a sense of humour and from time to time we visited a small island in the middle of the Seto Inland Sea when there was no training. We collected a group of boys and girls on this island to sing traditional songs and pray together. These three men were just ordinary navy officers … If there was an exceptional factor, it was Matsuo's mother who was a school teacher and a poetess who composed many poems about her son.

To maintain the secrecy over the midget submarine operations, the codename "Ko-Mark" was adopted when describing the craft. They were also referred to as "SSBs", "hanger-sheaths", or simply "sheaths". The deception was so successful in concealing their true identity and purpose that Captain Shojiro Iura, who served as the Naval Staff Officer of the Submarine Fleet for the coming Pearl Harbor operation, was unaware what was going on. The masquerade continued until September 1941 when plans for the Pearl Harbor attack were revealed to Chief Staff Officers and Commanders at the Tokyo Naval College.

In mid-October, Matsuo's training exercises were interrupted when he was assigned to special espionage duty in Hawaii. This interruption prevented him taking part as a crewman in the coming operation. Matsuo arrived in Honolulu on 5 November aboard the ocean liner, *Taiyo Maru*, listed on the ship's passenger list as a doctor. While in Hawaii, he met with Takeo Yoshikawa, the local spymaster, who drew maps of Pearl Harbor and provided information about the navigation markers leading into the harbour, the position of the anti-submarine net, and the location of ships. Matsuo returned to Japan on 15 November where he submitted his report to the General Staff.

Meanwhile, on 23 October 1941, the captain of I-22, Commander Kiyoi Ageta, received orders to proceed to Kure Naval Base to undergo modifications to his boat. Similar orders were received by four other I-16-class submarines. Ageta secured the submarine alongside the naval arsenal where it was swamped with a team of workmen who began to demolish the rear deck. The following night, under a shroud of mystery, a midget submarine was loaded on to the rear deck, followed some days later by Lieutenant Naoji Iwasa and Petty Officer Naokichi Sasaki who were to operate the craft.

Captain Hankyu Sasaki, the Commander of the First Submarine Squadron, was chosen to lead the midget submarine attack on Pearl Harbor. The squadron consisted of – I-16, I-18, I-20, I-22 and I-24. Sasaki flew his flag in I-22. Soon after Matsuo's return from Hawaii, he summoned his commanders to Kure where he revealed their part in the Pearl Harbor operation. In the early evening of 18 November, the First Submarine Squadron left Kure Naval Base with midget submarines strapped to their decks. Matsuo joined his friend Iwase in I-22, disappointed he would take part in the coming attack. After exiting the narrows of the Inland Sea, the squadron fanned out at 20 mile intervals, travelling over the surface until they reached the American-controlled Wake Islands. They then submerged during the day and travelled over the surface at night. The squadron maintained radio silence throughout the voyage.

Soon after departing Kure, Commander Ageta informed his crew of their destination and the purpose of their mission, which was met with great excitement. During the voyage, the midget submarine crews checked and re-checked their equipment and studied detailed charts of Pearl Harbor and the surrounding waters to develop their attack plans.

Admiral Isoroku Yamamoto, Commander-in-Chief of the Japanese Combined Fleet.

Courtesy Kyodo News Service

Captain Hankyu Sasaki, operational commander for both the Pearl Harbor and Sydney Harbour attacks.

Courtesy Japan Midget Submarine Association

On 26 November, Captain Sasaki received a radio transmission from the Naval Staff Officer of the Submarine Fleet for the Pearl Harbor operation announcing that negotiations with the United States were now hopeless. On 2 December, he received another communication confirming that the attack was scheduled for 7 December, Hawaiian time. Sasaki received a final report some days later giving the disposition of American naval vessels at Pearl Harbor, which included eight battleships, but no aircraft carriers.

As the First Submarine Squadron advanced on Hawaii, weather and sea conditions deteriorated, making maintenance and last minute work on the midget submarines difficult. Charging batteries, "topping-up with air", and "lining-up" the torpedoes had to be carried out in difficult conditions because the submarine decks were usually awash. The squadron finally arrived 5 to 10 miles off Pearl Harbor on the night of 6 December. In addition to the five midget submarine carriers, another 22 Japanese submarines took up position in the waters around Oahu. All five midget craft were launched before the planned aerial attack so they would be in position to commence the attack in conjunction with the air strike.

Although Lieutenant Iwasa was the senior officer, each craft operated independently. The original orders were specific. The midget submarines were to lay on the habour floor during the air strike, then attack the surviving capital ships on the night of 7 December and escape. However, Iwasa asked permission to launch his attack immediately after the air strike instead of waiting for night, and Admiral Yamamoto agreed to his request.

In preparation for the attack, Iwasa and his crewman Petty Officer Naokicki Sasaki, cleaned their bodies with alcohol and sprayed perfume on their underclothes before changing into new uniforms. Matsuo wished his friend good luck and, realising Iwasa had no ceremonial sword, presented him with his own. Iwasa entered the craft first followed by Petty Officer Sasaki who closed and secured the small conning-tower hatch behind him. A few minutes later Iwasa reported everything was in readiness and Commander Ageta gave the order to cut the phone cable and to release the straps holding the midget to the carrier submarine's deck. I-22 then submerged to send the midget submarine on its way.

Similar procedures were carried out on the other carrier submarines. The first midget submarine was launched from I-16 at midnight, manned by Sub-lieutenant Masaharu Yokoyama and Petty Officer Sadashi Uyeda. A 1:16 am, I-22 released her craft crewed by Iwasa and Petty Officer Sasaki, followed by the midget from I-18 at 2:15 am and manned by Sub-Lieutenant Shigemi Furuno and Petty Officer Kunhan Yokoyama. At 2:57 pm, the fourth midget submarine was launched from I-20, crewed by Sub-Lieutenant Akira Hiroo and Petty Officer Yoshio Katayama. As Hiroo boarded his special purpose submarine he was reported to say with a smile, "Getting lunches and soft drinks, it's like going on a hike". Last to leave their carrier submarine was the midget from I-24 at 3:33 pm. Crewed by Sub-Lieutenant Kazuo Sakamaki and Petty Officer Kiyoshi Inagaki, the craft's departure had been delayed by a faulty gyro compass. The torpedo officer aboard I-24, Lieutenant-Commander Mochitsura Hashimoto, records this incident in his book, *Sunk*:

Pearl Harbor, Honolulu, Hawaiian Islands. This Japanese midget submarine attempted to enter Pearl Harbor before the air attack, but later ran aground on the beach at Bellow's Field where Sub-lieutenant Kazou Sasamaki was captured.

52. JAPANESE SUBMARINE RAIDERS 1942 *A Maritime Mystery*

It was decided to go ahead without the gyro at 1:00 am [5:30 am Hawaiian time]. The officer commanding the midget went calmly up to the bridge to make his final report and then took his place in the midget. The parent submarine dived, the securing clamps were cast off, and the midget was off to the Pearl Harbor entrance.

Sakamaki's midget submarine immediately turned somersault after leaving I-24. Many years after the war, he recounted how he could only control the steering by increasing speed and relying on the moonlight to advance towards the harbour entrance. When he put the helm up, the submarine floated rapidly to the surface, and when the helm was put down the craft continued to descend, even after the helm was returned to a neutral position. To maintain any sort of trim, Inagaki, a former engine driver, had to struggle with shifting ballast deposited on the bottom of the submarine from front to the rear, and vice versa, and both crewmen suffered severe pain in their eyes and throats caused by gas generated from spilled sulphuric acid contained in the secondary battery compartment.

One of the fears of the attack planners was that the presence of the submarines would give away the Japanese intent. The fear was justified; however, US forces did not understand the significance of sighting a submarine within the Pearl Harbor defensive zone until too late. The first submarine was sighted at 3:42 am by the minesweeper *USS Condor* 1-3/4 miles south of the Pearl Harbor entrance buoys. The minesweeper sighted a periscope and notified the night patrol destroyer *USS Ward* by blinker light, whose commander, Captain William Outerbridge, searched without success until 4:45 am. The next sighting came an hour later when *USS Antares*, towing a target into the harbour, spotted a submarine following them in. The submarine's conning tower was fully exposed. A Navy Catalina flying boat dropped "smoke pots" in the vicinity at 6:33 am, giving the night patrol destroyer an approximate location. Four minutes later *Ward* spotted the midget behind the *Antares* making a run for the harbour. Captain Outerbridge made a decision in just three minutes to attack. Sounding general quarters at 6:40 am, the aging destroyer's engines surged full ahead as the gun crews loaded the deck guns. No. 1 gun opened fire at 6:45 am and missed; immediately No. 3 gun fired, hitting the submarine at the base of the conning tower. The submarine heeled to starboard and slowed. The destroyer depth-charged the midget submarine still on the surface before it disappeared for the last time. At 6:54 am, Captain Outerbridge sent a coded message to the naval authorities in Pearl Harbor reporting the destroyer had sunk a submarine off the harbour entrance, but because of delays in decoding the duty officer did not receive the message until almost 20 minutes later. The decoded report didn't reach the Commander-in-Chief of the Pacific Fleet, Admiral H. E. Kimmel, until shortly before the air attack had begun at 7:58 am.

At 8:17 am, a second midget submarine was spotted by the destroyer, *USS Helm*, hung up on the starboard side of the channel entrance. The submarine submerged but immediately popped up again. The *Helm* fired on the submarine before it submerged again and slipped away.

This craft was crewed by Sub-Lieutenant Sakamaki and Petty Officer Inagaki who were still experiencing gyro compass problems. After many vicissitudes, Sakamaki and

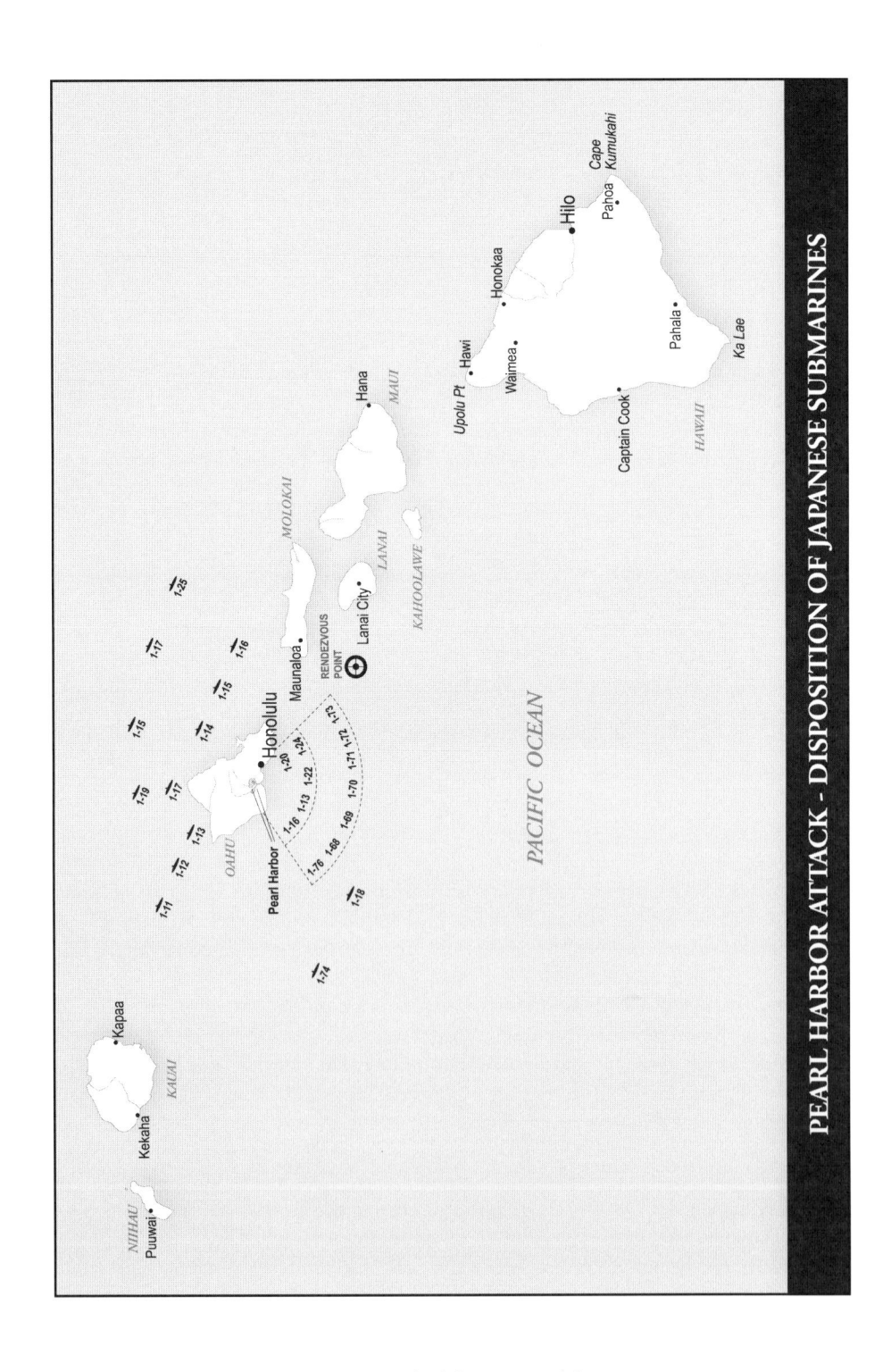

54. JAPANESE SUBMARINE RAIDERS 1942 *A Maritime Mystery*

Inagaki made a further attempt to enter the harbour, but the gyro compass continued to play tricks and the craft ran aground twice, eventually stranding on a coral reef 200 yards from the beach. Unable to complete his mission, and overcome by foul gas, Sakamaki lit the demolition charge before jumping into the sea. However, the fuse sputtered out and he survived to reach the beach. The body of Inagaki washed ashore some days later, his remains showing evidence that he had died from a gunshot wound to the head.

At 8:30 am, a third midget submarine, commanded by Lieutenant Iwase and Petty Officer Sasaki, was sighted four miles inside Pearl Harbor by the seaplane tender *USS Curtiss*. The *Curtiss* fired at the submarine and scored a hit on the conning tower before it submerged and fired a torpedo at the seaplane tender that missed. The destroyer, *USS Monaghan*, also spotted the submarine and ran at full speed toward it in an attempt to ram, striking a glancing blow as a second torpedo passed harmlessly beneath the destroyer and exploded on the bank at Ford Island. *Monaghan* dropped two depth charges which finished off the submarine.

The fate of a fourth midget didn't become known until 1960 when it was discovered in 75 feet of water off the harbour entrance, her torpedoes still intact but her crew missing.

The whereabouts of the fifth craft still remains a mystery although recent studies of Pearl Harbor attack photographs have led some historians to believe that it was in place off "Battleship Row" as the Japanese torpedo planes came in, and may have fired its torpedoes at *USS Oklahoma* or *USS West Virginia*.

In 1993, Commander John Rodgaard, US Naval Reserve (Retired), a senior image analyst at Autometric, Inc., met Dan Martinez, an historian at the National Park Service's *USS Arizona* Memorial, and Burl Burlingame, a noted Pearl Harbor historian and local journalist. Martinez showed a copy of what many consider to be one of the twentieth century's most dramatic photographs. It was taken from a Japanese Nakajima B5N2 "Kate" torpedo bomber during the first attack wave. Martinez saw something intriguing in the photograph and asked Rodgaard if he could determine whether a tiny object in the photograph was one of the Japanese midget submarines. An enlargement of the area in question revealed the presence of a black, rectangular object sitting atop a dark linear structure, followed by "rooster tail" plumes. The analysis determined the image to be a midget submarine, its conning tower and contra-rotating propellers exposed by the concussion of a torpedo hit on the battleship *West Virginia*.

The photographic evidence indicates the fifth midget submarine had successfully penetrated Pearl Harbor and positioned herself in the south-east loch where she waited to launch her torpedoes at the capital ships on Battleship Row. These ships were identified as the *Oklahoma* and *West Virginia*. At 8:03 am, soon after the aerial strike began, the midget fired her first torpedo at the *West Virginia*, then turned to port and fired her second torpedo. With her second torpedo heading toward the *Oklahoma*, the midget increased speed and began her run toward the harbour entrance to escape.

While making her escape, the midget was struck by a series of concussion waves. Rodgaard concluded that because of a loss of trim owing to the release of her torpedoes, the effects of her speed, and the oncoming concussions from aerial torpedoes that had struck their targets, that the midget broached the surface when she was buffeted by the cavitation

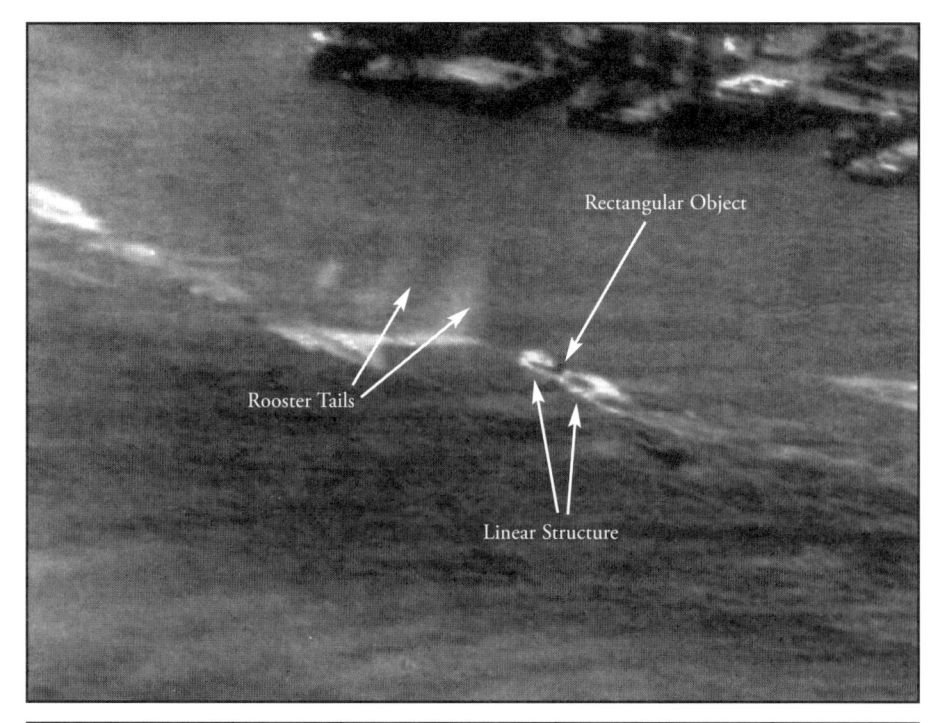

56. JAPANESE SUBMARINE RAIDERS 1942 *A Maritime Mystery*

effects generated by the underwater explosions, exposing the midget's rudder and contra-rotating propellers and causing "rooster tail" sprays to form. This craft was the midget launched from I-16 crewed by Sub-lieutenant Yokoyama and Petty Officer Uyeda.

After the attack, Captain Sasaki assembled his submarine squadron within sight of each other, seven miles off Lanai Island, about 70 miles south-east of Pearl Harbor, and continued to wait for the midget submarines throughout the night. At 22:41 pm, I-16 received a radio message from Sub-lieutenant Yokoyama reporting: "We succeeded in the surprise." Following this there was a lull until 1:11 am on 8 December when I-16 heard from Yokoyama once again, the midget's batteries now completely exhausted: "We cannot sail anymore." After this there was silence. At dawn, Captain Sasaki ordered his squadron to submerge for the day, out of sight until the following night when they would assemble again at the recovery point. After several nights, he gave the order to abandon the wait and for his force to make their way independently to Kwajalein in the Marshall Islands.

The combined air and underwater attack on Pearl Harbor lasted for less than two hours after which it was realised that the American Navy and Army had suffered 3,435 casualties and the loss of five battleships (including the *Oklahoma* and *West Virginia*), three destroyers, three light cruisers and a number of smaller vessels. One hundred and eighty-eight aircraft were lost or severely damaged. The carefully planned attack resulted in the loss for Japan of 29 aircraft from a force of 353 launched, and all five midget submarines. By a stroke of luck, not one of the Western Pacific Fleet's three aircraft carriers was in Pearl Harbor that day. They, and the undamaged American submarine force, soon launched offensive operations into the Western Pacific.

According to American historian Gordon W. Prange, the Japanese Navy concluded that at least three midget submarines had penetrated Pearl Harbor and, after the air raid, had inflicted severe damage, including the destruction of a capital ship. The word quickly spread that the midget submarines had sunk the US battleship *Arizona*. The Japanese Navy released this to the press in the spring of 1942 and the midget submariners were venerated as veritable gods, to the resentment of the flyers, who knew exactly when and under what circumstances the *Arizona* had exploded.

When I-22 arrived at Kwajalein following the Pearl Harbor attack, Lieutenant Matsuo transferred to I-16 for the return voyage to Japan where he went to work gathering information from other submarine commanders and looking for ways to improve the performance of the midget submarines. Although none of the crews returned, those associated

Pearl Harbor attack, 7 December 1941 - The first wave of torpedo planes attack "Battleship Row", seen from a Japanese aircraft. Ships are, from lower left to right: *Nevada* with flag raised at stern; *Arizona* with *Vestal* outboard; *Tennessee* with *West Virginia* outboard; *Maryland* with *Oklahoma* outboard; *Neosho* and *California*. *West Virginia*, *Oklahoma* and *California* have been torpedoed, as marked by ripples and spreading oil, and the first two are listing to port. Torpedo drop splashes and running tracks are visible at left and centre. White smoke in the distance is from Hickam Field. Grey smoke in the centre middle distance is from the torpedoed *USS Helena*, at the Navy Yard's 1010 dock. Japanese writing in lower right states that the image was reproduced by authorisation of the Navy Ministry.

with the midget submarines, and the crews themselves, insisted that after certain modifications, intensive crew training, and at a location where enemy defences were slacker than Pearl Harbor, that it would be possible to conduct a successful attack and recover the crews. This view was finally adopted by Command Headquarters of the Combined Squadron on 16 December 1941 and preparations for a second midget submarine operation began.

Admiral Yamamoto recognised that a great deal of study and many preparatory exercises would be required if a second attack were to be successful. Even then, he articulated doubts as to whether the crews could be recovered safely. Still, he agreed to proceed with the modifications and crew training.

The approval to go ahead with a second midget submarine operation was met with considerable enthusiasm by those associated with the craft and modifications began. The inability to communicate between the parent submarine and the midget after submerging was recognised as a major problem. Another was that the carrier submarine had to surface and the crew had to walk to the rear deck before transferring to the craft. Not only was this method undesirable at locations where rigid enemy defences were employed, but was also impractical for conducting routine maintenance and service. Subsequently, modifications to allow the crew to transfer while submerged were made by adding a "traffic sheath" (hatchway) that connected the midget to its parent submarine. The lugs securing the craft to the carrier submarine were made detachable from inside the midget submarine. Work was also done to improve the gyro compass, and an eye glass on each side of the conning tower assisted the pilot when leaving or rejoining the carrier submarine. However, the craft could not be controlled from the conning tower, as the steering gear was located in the control room below.

An addition to the midget submarines was a nose guard. The net cutting apparatus used in the Pearl Harbor midgets were replaced with vertical fin cutters with a tensioning wire to the conning tower, which was faired over with steel guards. The tensioning wire then continued to the tail fin. The new modifications were designed to allow the craft to nose under boom net defences. Additional skew strengthening rods were welded to the cage-like structure around the propellers to give additional protection against fouling nets when the contra-revolving propellers were going astern.

The modified midget submarines included a single ballast tank of 52 cubic feet capacity situated in the bow. The ballast tank served to stabilise the craft once the torpedoes were fired to prevent the midget submarine bobbing to the surface. However, the fundamental problem of being unable to recharge the midgets' batteries still remained. Due to wartime scarcity, the Navy Department would not fit a generator into the craft. Thus, their operational radius remained the same – 100 miles at 4 knots.

The most advanced of the refitted craft was 24 metres, slighting longer than its Pearl Harbor counterpart, fabricated in three sections and bolted together. The modified craft were fitted with two self-demolition charges, one located forward and the other in the control compartment amidship. They were able to operate at a maximum depth of 300 feet, but capable of lying on the ocean bottom at much greater depths. They could remain submerged for at least 12 hours and were able to operate in any harbour for up to seven days, provided they could lie hidden somewhere on the surface during the night in order to ventilate. However, they were still difficult to steer in a horizontal direction, and they lacked a suitable hydrophone to enable the crew to detect approaching vessels.

During the modification period, Admiral Yamamoto made an inspection of the training base at Kure where he gave the crews encouraging words. Plans were now drawn up to use them in Japan's intended southward advance.

As a preliminary to the planned operation in Australian waters, I-25 was ordered to sail from the Marshall Islands and carry out reconnaissance flights in eastern Australian waters. She was equipped with a small one-man seaplane with a three-hour operating duration. The seaplane carried out a daring reconnaissance flight over Sydney on 17 February 1942, taking photographs of Cockatoo Island and Garden Island dockyards. Undetected by Sydney defences, the pilot successfully rejoined his carrier submarine waiting off the coast. The submarine then proceeded south and conducted flights over Melbourne on 26 February and Hobart on 1 March before crossing the Tasman to New Zealand to reconnoitre Wellington on 8 March and Auckland on 13 March.

The fact that these flights went undetected gives some idea of the preparedness of Australian defences at the time. Continuing her astonishing progress, I-25's seaplane flew reconnaissance flights over Suva and later Pago Pago in American Samoa before turning north to make her report. This same seaplane later flew reconnaissance flights over the Midway Islands prior to that historic naval battle.

By mid-March 1942 there were two main factors influencing the strategy for a southward advance. The Japanese had obtained information that considerable forces had been positioned in the Indian Ocean. Although the war in waters north of Australia had calmed down, sea traffic in the Indian Ocean was still active and formed a supply line from Britain to the Middle East via the African east coast. The other important factor was the effectiveness of the United States Navy. While initially damaged at Pearl Harbor, it was starting to function effectively out of Hawaiian and South Pacific bases.

The Japanese Planning Staff favoured an advance to Samoa and Fiji to cut Pacific communications and isolate Australia. Since the beginning of February a number of attacks had been carried out on Japanese bases, and it was presumed that the United States was trying to support the Australian forces via Fiji, New Caledonia and New Zealand.

While the Chief of the Operations Division of the Combined Fleet, Captain Kameto Kuroshima, favoured an offensive against Ceylon and the Indian Ocean and a linkup with their German and Italian allies, Yamamoto and his Chief-of-Staff wanted to thrust eastward towards Midway and Hawaii for a final reckoning with the United States' Pacific Fleet. It was Kuroshima's suggestion that led the Japanese General Staff to draw up plans for simultaneous midget submarine attacks in the Indian Ocean and South Pacific.

On 10 April, Yamamoto ordered the Eighth Submarine Squadron, under the command of Rear-Admiral Noburu Ishizaki, to collect their midget submarines at Penang, on the west coast of Malaya (now Malaysia), and then proceed to the Indian ocean to locate the largest concentration of naval vessels. The midgets were transported to Penang on the disguised seaplane carrier *Nisshin*.

The Third Submarine Company, under the command of Captain Hankyu Sasaki, were to first co-operate with the Port Moresby invasion and then collect their midget submarines from the converted carrier *Chiyoda* at Queen Carola Harbour in the Solomon Islands. They would then proceed to Australia and New Zealand where reconnaissance flights would be made over enemy ports and harbours to locate the heaviest concentration of Allied naval shipping.

Sasaki's force originally consisted of four submarines with facilities to carry midget submarines (I-22, I-24, I-27 and I-28), and two boats fitted with seaplanes (I-21 and I-29). Sasaki flew his flag in I-21. Following the Port Moresby invasion, I-21 and I-29 were to reconnoitre Sydney, Noumea and Auckland while the others collected their midget submarines. After ascertaining the position of the enemy's main vessels, the submarine force would then assemble near that area for a scheduled attack at the end of May, when the moon would be full. The midget submarines would be launched within one hour after sunset, or soon after moonrise, and the crews were to be recovered the following morning. If the crews did not return within the planned time, then the recovery phase would continue for another two nights. Immediately after the attack, an aircraft reconnaissance was to be made to determine the results of the attack.

In mid-April, the Eighth Submarine Squadron and Third Submarine Company left their home bases in Japan and proceeded to the Indian and South Pacific Oceans, respectively. After many months of intensive preparations, the attack was finally underway and confidence and morale was running high. Regardless of the outcome, Australians were about to be shaken into a realisation that war was at their doorstep. ●

CHAPTER FOUR
Australia Looks to America

CHAPTER FOUR
AUSTRALIA LOOKS TO AMERICA

> The first thing any government does when faced with a war crisis is to manipulate the truth by taking control of the news.
>
> *Darwin 1942*,
> Timothy Hall.

With paralysing rapidity the Japanese Imperial Forces moved southward and occupied Rabaul, New Britain, in the middle of January 1942. A wave of disbelief swept through the nation as men were quickly mobilised from Australia's already thin ranks and sent north to combat the "yellow peril".

Australians were caught between a strange mixture of apathy and panic, the former being most apparent to Australian waterside workers who organised a series of recurring strikes to hinder American shipping. A general apathy perhaps stemmed from a sense of fatalism that if the Japanese were going to invade Australia, there was little that could be done to stop them.

At the same time, however, a wave of muted alarm rippled through the civilian population as they followed the Japanese advance towards Australia. There were, of course, many reasons for panic. Months earlier on the night of 8 December 1941 the Australian Labor Prime Minister, John Curtin, in a radio broadcast to a woefully undefended nation, told the people that Australia was at war with Japan.

It is interesting to retrace the Australian declaration of war which occurred the day after the Japanese attack on Pearl Harbor on 7 December, and the constitutional difficulties which delayed the formal proclamation of war by the Australian Parliament until 17 December. Curtin told the Australian people on radio:

> We are at war with Japan. That has happened because, in the first instance, Japanese naval and air forces launched an unprovoked attack on British and United States territory; because our vital interests are imperilled and because of the rights of free people in the whole Pacific are assailed. As a result, the Australian Government took the necessary steps which will mean that a state of war exists between Australia and Japan. Tomorrow, in common with the United Kingdom, the United States and the Netherlands East Indies Governments, the Australian Government will formally and solemnly declare the state of war it has striven so strenuously to avoid.

In the early hours of that morning, first news of a surprise attack on Pearl Harbor had reached Australia from a shortwave radio transmitter monitored around the clock by the Department of Information in Melbourne. At 5:45 am on 9 December, a flash was intercepted from Washington announcing that Pearl Harbor and military installations at Manila in the Philippines were under attack by Japanese aircraft.

Curtin and most of the War Cabinet were in Melbourne. After retiring to his room at the Victoria Palace Hotel at 1:00 am, he was awakened by his press secretary and informed of the attacks. The information was immediately passed on to members of the War Cabinet and Australian military leaders. The War Cabinet was summoned and, by breakfast time, it was clear that Japan had entered the war.

The War Cabinet met again later in the day with the Chief of the General Staff, Air Staff and Naval Staff in attendance to discuss what action Australia should take. Curtin reported at that meeting that the Japanese were shelling and attempting to land on the east coast of Malaya. He also revealed that an Australian warship had intercepted a cable from the British Admiralty ordering the British Navy in the Far East to "commence hostilities against Japan at once". In the absence of any direct British communiqué, the War Cabinet immediately agreed that this cable provided sufficient weight for the Australian Government to declare war on Japan, which happened on 9 December.

But, Curtin could only announce that the Australian people, as opposed to the Australian Government, were at war: he instructed the Australian Charge d'Affairs in Tokyo to inform the Japanese Government about his announcement.

Although this decision was made by Curtin in consultation with the War Cabinet, it raised a constitutional dilemma. There was no provision in the Australian Constitution regarding the procedure to follow in making a declaration of war. In addition, the King of England had not delegated any authority to the Australian Governor-General to declare war on his behalf.

The answer to this problem was either to enact legislation to clarify the constitutional position or for the King to give express authority to his representative to make such a declaration. Curtin telegrammed the Australia High Commissioner in London to seek a "draft instrument" for the King's signature, authorising the Governor-General, Lord Gowrie, to declare a state of war between Australia and Japan.

It took one week for the Australian Government to receive the "draft instrument" signed by the King. Consequently, it was not until 16 December that the Governor-General's proclamation of war was tabled in Parliament by Curtin who declared that "Japan had struck like an assassin in the night" and that the attacks against the United States and British territories constituted a direct attack upon Australia also.

On 17 December the "Declaration of War" was endorsed by Parliament. At the same time Curtin created a precedent in Australian parliamentary history by moving a resolution to approve his earlier actions of declaring war on Japan. The resolution was passed.

Although it was not realised until after the war, Australia had already begun hostilities against Japan before the Pearl Harbor attack. On 8 December, at 2:40 am eastern Australia time, the Japanese had commenced shelling Malaya, and had landed at 3:05 am. Australian Hudson aircraft, attempting to repel the landing, had succeeded in sinking one

Japanese transport and in damaging another two. One hour later the Japanese landed on Thailand, and at 4:25 am, attacked Pearl Harbor.

The Director of Naval Intelligence in Melbourne, the respected Commander R. B. M. Long, was present at the Australian War Cabinet meetings held in December. He foresaw the possibility of Japan penetrating the northern islands off Australia, including the New Hebrides (now Vanuatu), New Caledonia, Fiji and Samoa. He also predicted that a direct attack against Australia and New Zealand was unlikely and that "it is likely, in view of Japan's present attack against Hawaii that raids will be made by heavier units, other than submarines, against coastal areas such as Newcastle. These attacks may take the form of shelling by a squadron of naval units or air attacks from aircraft carriers".

Australian military leaders further advised the government: "A probable initial Japanese course of action would be an attempt to occupy New Guinea… An attack on Rabaul is a likely first step."

The military's appreciation of the situation was realised in January 1942 when the Japanese invaded Rabaul, to the north-west of New Guinea.

The first indications of Japanese submarines close to the Australian mainland came on 17 January when the American cruiser *USS Houston* sighted two submarines close to Darwin. The submarines had been attempting to lay mines at the harbour entrance. *Houston* immediately informed the naval authorities at Darwin and the Australian corvettes *Deloraine*, *Katoomba* and *Lithgow* were dispatched to search and destroy the enemy.

Three days later, while searching the reported position of the submarines, *Deloraine* was attacked by a torpedo from I-124, which she evaded. The corvette succeeded in locating the submarine on underwater detection equipment (ASDIC) and carried out a series of depth charge attacks lasting over an hour, after which air bubbles and an oil slick appeared on the surface. With her depth charges expended, the *Deloraine* returned to Darwin to replenish her armaments and left *Katoomba* and *Lithgow* to continue the attack; but I-124 was already in her death-throes. This was the first submarine to be sunk by the Australian Navy; but Australia's elation about this success was to be short lived.

On 19 February Vice-Admiral Chuichi Nagumo who, less than three months earlier had launched his aircraft on Pearl Harbor, moved his carrier force within striking distance of the Australian mainland. Nagumo launched his bombers and fighter aircraft towards an unsuspecting Darwin. For the first time in history, Australia was attacked on its own soil. The final death toll of 243 was certainly lower than the true figure.

The Curtin Government withheld the true details of the actual attack, the casualties suffered, and of the looting, the panic and the mass exodus of civilian and military personnel that followed. The War Cabinet immediately ordered a news black-out, and the propaganda they released has since become part of our verbal history. From his sick bed in Sydney's Saint Vincent Hospital, where he was recovering from a gastritis attack, Curtin announced to the people that: "The Government has told you the truth. Face it like Australians."

Over two months before the attack, Australian military authorities had advised Curtin and the War Cabinet that Darwin was a likely target for the Japanese: "…an attack by bombardment squadron or carrier-borne aircraft is a strong possibility". Darwin was the

Courtesy Sydney Morning Herald

Prime Minister Curtin moving a resolution approving the Declaration of War against Japan in the House of Representatives, 17 December 1941. The motion was seconded by Opposition leader Fadden (not pictured) and was carried unanimously. Seated on front bench, (L. to R): Mr Beasley (Supply and Development), Dr Evatt (Attorney General and External Affairs), Mr Makin (Navy and Munitions), Mr Frost (Repatriation and War Service Homes) and Mr Lawson (Transport).

only main base for Allied naval forces operating in the eastern end of the Malay Barrier and stored some 100,000 tonnes of naval fuel. It was also an air force base and therefore provided an attractive target.

In spite of this warning, Darwin was a source of embarrassment to Curtin, even before the attack occurred. Dishonesty amongst wharf and railway workers had been rife; continual industrial strife had caused delays in essential shipping of up to three weeks; there was no co-ordination between government departments; and facilities in the harbour had been appalling. By the end of January 1942, management of the port had become severely defective, causing American Brigadier-General Barnes to protest in the strongest terms to the Australian War Cabinet. He had asked for military labour to assist on the wharves, but Curtin refused. As a result, on 19 February, the harbour was dangerously congested and weakly defended.

The day after the Darwin attack, on 20 February, Curtin summoned the members of Parliament and moved a resolution that all further sittings and discussions of Parliament would be held in secret, including reports of the war. All "strangers" were ordered to withdraw until after the secret and confidential reports of the war had been discussed, after which they were re-admitted. It was agreed that senators be allowed to remain. Curtin's resolution was accepted and gazetted into a regulation under the *National Security Act*. No information from these sittings could be divulged or published except those statements officially emanating from the Prime Minister.

In this manner, Curtin was able to suppress vital war news and reports on the conduct of Australian military and civil defence personnel to the Australian public. This censorship had the effect of inflaming the already exaggerated rumours running through the nation.

Faith of the people in Curtin and the Australian Government began to wane. The government's chief censor reported a general feeling of panic amongst Australians during this period, with the expectation of defeat by the Japanese. For that reason the government watered down any Australian disaster in regard to attacks on Australian soil – to prevent Australians from "getting scared". In addition, this watering down provided the government with an excellent excuse to cover up information regarding mismanagement of the war effort, peculiarities in defence conduct, and even Australian casualties.

The censor's report, quoted in Sir Paul Hasluck's *The Government and the People*, also revealed extremely bitter criticism of Churchill and the British Government which, it was felt, had let Australia down: "… it is very evident that there is developing a grave loss of confidence in Great Britain". The censor added that the Australian public were not being told the facts about the progress of the war and accused both Australian and British leaders of being merely self-seekers who turned circumstances in which they found themselves to their own advantage.

From the beginning of 1942 relations between Curtin and Churchill reached an all time low. Curtin carried on a long and acrimonious feud with the British Prime Minister, making no attempt to conceal his disdain. He seized every opportunity to provoke the British leader and exchanges of cables between the two were acid; but Curtin was no match for Churchill's wit.

Curtin, the Australian Government and the general public now thoroughly distrusted Britain following her neglect of the desperate situation in the Far East. Curtin's dislike for

Churchill was cemented 19 days after Pearl Harbor when 4,600 American troops arrived in Australia and he made his historic declaration: "Without any inhibitions of any kind I make it quite clear that Australia looks to America, free of any pangs as to our traditional links or kinship with the United Kingdom."

Although Curtin attacked Churchill at every opportunity, he saw this as a means of appeasing the Australian people's resentment of the Empire's leaders – which also took the focus off the more important issues closer to home. In spite of Curtin's veiled threats of severing ties with the British Government, he had no intention of doing so.

Nevertheless, when Singapore fell on 15 February, the colonial dream that Australia would be defended by the mother country was shattered for all time and Curtin insisted that Australian troops destined for Burma be redirected to Australia; much to Churchill's chagrin. It was finally realised that Australia's only hope for strong support lay with America.

On 17 March 1942, General Douglas MacArthur landed at Batchelor Field, south of Darwin, after escaping from the Philippines. He was greeted with tremendous adulation by the Australian people who lined the streets to cheer and pay homage to the Great General – Australia's new saviour. They followed his regal progress from Darwin to Alice Springs, then by rail to Melbourne where he arrived on 21 March and was given a hero's welcome at Spencer Street station. He was met there by a military guard of honour and Australian Service Chiefs, after which he immediately set about establishing his headquarters. In his book, *Reminiscences*, MacArthur recalled with candour the day his train puffed into Melbourne. Tumultuous as the welcome was he could not help noticing that a "sense of dangerous defeatism had seized upon a large segment of the Australian people".

No sooner had MacArthur shaken the dust off his hat when he was rushed to Canberra for a dinner given in his honour by the Prime Minister. Weary and red-eyed from the long drive overland during the night, he learnt that he had been awarded the Congressional Medal of Honor by the President of the United States.

In his book, MacArthur described Curtin as the sort of man Australians called "fair dinkum". He wrote of this occasion that as he rose to leave, he put his arm around Curtin's strong shoulder and said: "Mr Prime Minister, we two, you and I, will see this through together. We can do it and we will do it. You take care of the rear and I'll handle the front."

The day after MacArthur's arrival in Australia, on 18 March, President Roosevelt cabled the British Prime Minister:

> There is no use giving a single thought to Singapore or the East Indies. They are gone. Australia must be held and we are willing to undertake that.

At the same time, Roosevelt had sent a message to Curtin suggesting that it would be quite acceptable to him if the Australian Government would nominate MacArthur as the Supreme Commander of the Allied Forces in the South-West Pacific. Curtin readily agreed and immediately announced the appointment.

On 26 March MacArthur was invited to attend a meeting of the War Cabinet, where he outlined his views regarding the war situation in the Pacific. His opinions echoed strongly of those of Commander Long's appreciation three months earlier.

MacArthur believed that Japan would not invade Australia as he thought "the spoils were not sufficient to warrant the risk". This assessment may have been accurate but hardly flattering. He said that the main dangers were from air raids and that the Japanese may try to secure air bases in the north of Australia. He emphasised that it was essential to provide adequate anti-aircraft defences for the main cities and air bases.

MacArthur frequently expressed the point of view that the relative importance of the Pacific War would depend on the outcome of the European theatre as a whole. This view had already been formulated by Roosevelt and Churchill in a "Grand Strategy" document which outlined a "beat Hitler first" policy.

The existence of the "Grand Strategy" document was unknown to the Australian Government at the time of MacArthur's appointment. Churchill and Roosevelt's desire to withhold the document from the Australian government was, in addition to other factors, because it was formulated before the Japanese attacked Pearl Harbor and America was still a neutral country. Had the contents of the document been revealed to the American Congress or to the public, the President of the Unites States would have undoubtedly been accused of treasonable activities.

When MacArthur was appointed the Supreme Commander of Allied Forces in the South-West Pacific, his directives were based on this "Grand Strategy" document. MacArthur's orders were to hold key regions of Australia as bases for future offensive operations against Japan as soon as Hitler was defeated in Europe. He was also ordered to check, as far as possible, the enemy advance across Australia if it occurred and to keep all the essential lines of communication open.

It was not until May 1942 that Dr Evatt, Australia's Minister for External Affairs, discovered the existence of the "Grand Strategy" document while on a visit to London. He sent the following cable to Curtin:

> The strategy contemplates Germany's defeat before that of Japan. In a phrase, "beat Hitler first". The existence of this written agreement came as a great surprise to myself and, no doubt to you. We were not consulted about the matter… Owing apparently to the United States Government's desire for secrecy, it took some little insistence to get the document here.

Evatt remarked later, in spite of the "beat Hitler first" policy, and the fact that the Australian Government was unaware of its existence, there were clauses in the document which insisted that the security of Australia must be maintained. He also remarked: "I think that we can now appreciate the background in which General MacArthur's directive was drafted."

Although MacArthur's strategies were defensive in nature, he also undertook limited offensive operations against the Japanese when the opportunity arose. In the months ahead, he was able to make surprisingly accurate "predictions" of enemy movements in the South-West Pacific – too accurate to be mere guesswork. ●

CHAPTER FIVE
THE SECRET WAR

CHAPTER FIVE

THE SECRET WAR

Battles were won because we had advance knowledge of enemy plans, could influence those plans, and could anticipate enemy actions by methods heretofore concealed.

A Man Called Intrepid,
Sir William Stephenson.

The Australian Government was unaware that MacArthur's predictions of enemy movements were derived from a source that he was unable to confide to the government or even to Curtin.

Prior to the war in Europe, the British Secret Service had obtained a German cipher machine which they later developed to enable Churchill and the key Chiefs of Staff to monitor both German and Japanese naval, army and air movements. The stolen machine was originally known as an "Enigma" machine – a name taken from the Greek, meaning "puzzle" – and was probably the most jealously guarded secret in military history.

It is now evident that deciphering the enemy's codes played a major role during World War II. For 35 years after the war, military historians tended to believe in such concepts as "great men", like Churchill and Roosevelt, or gifted military leaders, such as Montgomery and MacArthur. The defeat of the Axis powers was brought about by these leaders and the men they led, coupled with the eventual superiority of western firepower. But an incalculable advantage was in knowing beforehand what the Axis powers intended to do. The Allies possessed the Enigma machine as early as 1939; but it wasn't until 1974 that historians learnt of its existence and necessitated a revision of the history of World War II. We now know that the Allies had privileged access to most of the secret enciphered and coded messages that emanated from both German and Japanese High Commands.

This single advantage, which neither the Germans nor Japanese seriously suspected, was the decisive factor in winning both the European and Pacific wars. The British called the information gained from it "Ultra", and the Americans "Magic". If there were some shadowy areas where Ultra's effectiveness was diminished by the need to keep it secret, they were outnumbered by the decisive battles which were won as a result of its information.

In the Pacific theatre, the Battle of Midway Island in June 1942 was the turning point in the Pacific War. Ultra information played a crucial role in this when precise dates were intercepted from Japanese Imperial Headquarters of an impending attack by Japanese forces on Midway Island. This information was vital to the successful deployment of the American Pacific Fleet.

Again, almost a year later, Ultra information played a key role with the assassination of Admiral Isoroku Yamamoto. A Japanese signal was intercepted and decoded which gave the precise date, time and itinerary of Yamamoto's planned inspection of the Bougainville and Truk area. The message was rushed to Washington where, after a midnight meeting with the Secretary of the Navy, President Roosevelt made the decision to ambush Yamamoto's aircraft over Bougainville. The death of this revered hero shattered the morale of Japanese forces.

The part played by Ultra in the Pacific is still only vaguely known. Ultra's existence was first authoritatively revealed in 1974, when F. W. Winterbotham published *The Ultra Secret*. Soon after there appeared the international bestseller – *A Man Called Intrepid* by William Stevenson. This book detailed the part played by Sir William Stephenson (not the author) in the secret war and who, on Churchill's orders, established in New York and Bletchley Park in London, a high level, secretly liaisoned organisation called British Security Co-ordination (BSC). This organisation dealt with Ultra information and passed on the deciphered interceptions to the appropriate authorities.

A primitive version of the Enigma machine had been obtained by the British Secret Service as early as 1938. Its function was explained by a Polish engineer who had been working in a German factory which was building the secret cipher machine. The German machine was theoretically incapable of having its cipher broken because of its incredibly complex operation. However, the Pole took careful note of the various components and, with the help of other Polish workers in the factory, was able to piece together its function. The Pole was then smuggled to Paris where he reconstructed the machine from memory for the British Secret Service. Although it had common parts, he was unable to provide cipher experts with any of the specifics they required and a decision was made to steal a production model. After learning that one such machine was to be delivered to a German frontier unit, the truck carrying the machine was ambushed and the cipher machine stolen. The truck was then set on fire and fake coils, springs and rotors planted in the charred remains to fool the German investigators.

The Japanese had purchased an early uncomplicated version of the Enigma machine from the Germans in 1930, and adapted it for their own use for diplomatic traffic. Its use was also shared with the Japanese military. Although diplomatic and military traffic was concealed by complicated codes, it became increasingly apparent that Japan was also moving towards naked aggression. The US Army's Signal Intelligence Service duplicated the Japanese machine and called it "Purple". By September 1940, Japanese codes were being intercepted and gradually deciphered. From this point on the Americans gave it the code name "Magic".

After September 1939 there was always the possibility that Britain would be conquered by the Nazis. Churchill appointed the Canadian industrialist William Stephenson as the Chief of British Secret Intelligence to set up a combined American and British secret intelligence organisation in neutral United States. Stephenson established BSC in New York with the covert approval of President Roosevelt who realised that America's own intelligence organisation had many shortfalls and was incomparable to that of Britain. In these troubled times, he saw the need to collaborate with Churchill.

American William "Wild Bill" Donovan was appointed by Roosevelt to be groomed as Stephenson's successor and to set up BSC's American equivalent, the Office of Strategic Service (OSS). Until Donovan was ready to take over, Stephenson co-ordinated both American and British intelligence.

Through Stephenson, Britain ran the most intricate, integrated intelligence organisation in history. His mandate assumed that Britain might be conquered, so New York was chosen as the junction box through which all Allied secrets could be pooled as it was the commercial and communications centre of the world. If Britain fell, as seemed possible, the secret war could still be directed from BSC.

It was from this shadowy world that the "beat Hitler first" policy was formulated and the task of keeping that knowledge secret rested with Stephenson. Had this clandestine alliance between the United States and Britain become known to the American press or Congress, there could have been a call for the President's impeachment through violation of American neutrality.

When the stolen Enigma machine arrived in London, Stephenson established his main secret intelligence organisation at Bletchley Park, 60 miles from London. It was here that the German ciphers were broken and the information used by Churchill, without compromising his source, for Britain's profit. As a result of Stephenson's diplomatic persuasion, the US Army Signal Intelligence Service handed over a model of its Japanese version to the British, which was also installed at Bletchley Park. Churchill now had access to both German and Japanese traffic.

By 1942, Stephenson's secret intelligence network had grown throughout the world with intercepted Japanese wireless traffic coming from Australia, India, Ceylon, New Guinea and Singapore direct to Bletchley with copies to New York. Over 30,000 experts were now linked to the British Secret Service but only a handful of people knew or had access to its information.

Churchill was reluctant to impart Ultra's existence to Curtin. He distrusted the Australian Government which he felt was complacent. Since the invasion of Australia seemed possible, Churchill considered that the Australian Government would compromise Ultra by using the information in its own defence against Japan. Indeed, Churchill only told Roosevelt as much as he felt he needed to know.

Through Ultra it was learned that there was an impending bombing raid on Coventry in Britain. Churchill decided not to evacuate the city or to warn the population, in the event of risking Britain's pre-knowledge of the bombing to the Germans. Many people were killed in that raid. Although the decision was considered right, Churchill later wrote that Coventry was the most painful decision he had to make during the war.

To reduce the risk of an Ultra leak, Churchill confided its existence to the fewest British leaders possible. He felt it was necessary to confide in Roosevelt to demonstrate that Britain could repel an invasion from across the English Channel. Churchill urgently needed the American destroyers and other defence hardware which the American President had promised, but first he had to prove that this hardware would not be captured by the Germans and eventually used against the United States. Churchill stated: "We must make an exception with Mr Roosevelt. To him, and to him alone, the truth should be confided…"

Meanwhile, at Bletchley Park, Special Liaison Units (SLU) were being trained to decipher and rephrase Ultra information, so that if it was intercepted by the enemy during redirection, it would not resemble the original signal. These units were then sent to various locations throughout the world. Such a unit, SLU9, was sent to Brisbane, Australia, at the beginning of 1942 under the control of Australian Colonel Alastair W. Sandford. Sandford had received his training at Bletchley and was the only man empowered to convey Ultra information to American, British, and Dutch or Australian military Chiefs of Staff.

It is interesting to note that the only Australian war records uncovered of Sandford's activities appeared in the Army list under Special Wireless Section, Australian Intelligence Corps. His army career was recorded up until the beginning of 1941, after which he seems to have vanished. He re-emerged in the latter half of 1943 where the Army List records him as being attached to the Central Bureau, Intelligence Corps – the same organisation set up by General MacArthur which evaluated Ultra information.

Colonel Sandford also channelled all intercepted Japanese wireless traffic to Arlington House, Nebraska Avenue, Washington, where it was analysed by Stephenson's second in command. This man was Commander Laurence F. Safford – code-name "Crusader" – who headed the intelligence unit at Washington Naval Headquarters (NEGAT). According to Safford, every wireless transmission emanating from the Japanese in the Pacific, including Japanese submarine traffic off the coast of Australia, had been intercepted since the beginning of 1942.

With the installation of the Australian SLU, information containing Japanese naval, army and air movements was now being received in London, Washington and Brisbane.

Situated on the sixth floor of the Australian Mutual Provident (AMP) building in Queen Street, information gained from Ultra suffered from severe restrictions imposed by General MacArthur regarding who should have what information and, although rigid security was imposed, only some of the information obtained was siphoned to Australian military leaders in Melbourne without compromising its source.

The person in charge of setting up SLUs around the world, Fred Winterbotham, a senior Air Staff representative in the British Secret Intelligence Service for 10 years, records the distribution of information in his book, *The Ultra Secret*. On a visit to Brisbane in early 1942, he wrote:

> I wanted to make my number with the Australian Chief of Air Staff, Air Commodore Jones. I found him unhappy about the amount of information that was being passed to him from Brisbane. He certainly wasn't getting all that he should have, so I decided to look into the Brisbane distribution as soon as possible ... I found the Ultra set-up in Brisbane was most efficient, but it suffered a little from restrictions imposed by General MacArthur, on "who should have what". Nevertheless, I was able, with the co-operation of Colonel Sandford, the young Australian officer in charge who I had known in London when we were teaching him the job, to sort out some of the distribution problems ...

Winterbotham recounts that no history of naval warfare in World War II can now be regarded as complete without mention of the information which was available to the Allied admirals. It was this information which created the sea air battles in the Pacific. The Japanese plan aimed to outflank New Guinea by going far to the east to the Coral Sea before closing on Port Moresby. The plan was received on 17 April 1942 and passed to Admiral Nimitz. It gave him time to move his ships to meet the threat and, in fact, fight the Battle of the Coral Sea in early May. The Battle of the Coral Sea was not the decisive victory but it did stop the Japanese moving southwards, and the threat to Port Moresby was averted.

After the outbreak of war the overall Australian intelligence organisation had come under the control of General Sir Thomas Blamey. Its operations were limited but after the fall of Singapore, the Special Operations Executive (SOE), quartered in New York and a secret cell of BSC, sent British businessman G. S. Mott to whip it into the most effective intelligence organisation in the Pacific. Mott had received his formal training in intelligence at Singapore prior to the war and was given the wartime rank of Colonel.

Mott developed a reputation as a cold and calculating man who had wide business interests in both Australia and the Far East. After the fall of Singapore he harboured a deep resentment against the Japanese who had caused the collapse of his Asia-wide business of Maclaine, Watson & Co Ltd. The American Allison W. Ind, attached to MacArthur's Allied Intelligence Bureau (AIB) in Australia, in his book *Spy Ring Pacific*, describes Mott as a moody, dark, saturnine man with a short temper, who had the ability to act quickly and get things done. It is now known that Mott was guided by Stephenson and reported directly to London.

Surrounded by a small staff of specialist British, Dutch and Australian officers, Mott established a security tight base behind the walls of a fashionable Toorak house called "Airlie". It was also known as the "department of dirty tricks".

After meeting with some opposition from the Australian Government, Mott formed the Inter-Allied Services Department (IASD), which was merely an innocent cover name for his activities. His organisation intercepted highly revealing cryptograms from the Japanese, which Mott channelled directly to 10 Downing Street and BSC in New York. He also kept Churchill informed of Curtin's attitudes and wartime policies. Even General MacArthur, when he established his own Allied Intelligence Bureau, was unaware of the full extent of Mott's activities.

With the entry of America into the war MacArthur became one of the few Americans to have access to Ultra information. He established his own intelligence organisation in Melbourne under the fiery leadership of Colonel C. Willoughby. Washington offered the services of clandestine agents attached to the American department of BSC, titled Office of Strategic Services (OSS, the forerunner of the CIA) and led by William Donovan. But MacArthur refused, saying that he disliked having personnel under his command whom he could not control. Willoughby also resented anyone interfering in his intelligence domain. Nevertheless, "Wild Bill" Donovan channelled the appropriate Japanese intercepted traffic to MacArthur, which became the governing factor of his strategies.

MacArthur was extremely grateful for Donovan's information and later described him as the most determined, resourceful and gallant soldier that he had ever known. Donovan replied that he knew too much about war to glory in it. He added that wars were made by politicians who neglected to prepare for it.

By June 1942 MacArthur had amalgamated Mott's secret intelligence organisation into his own AIB, labelling it the Central Bureau. This section was controlled entirely by Willoughby and Mott who distributed information only on a need-to-know basis, which included the Supreme Commander of the South-West Pacific.

Allison W. Ind, in his book, *A History of Modern Espionage*, described the Central Bureau as having accomplished the incredibly difficult task of establishing wireless reporting stations in the East Indies. Within the Central Bureau, MacArthur also formed an Allied Translator and Interpreter Section (ATIS), which translated Japanese radio interceptions and captured documents. This section was led by American Colonel Sydney F. Mashbir, a master intelligence agent with a long and distinguished career as a translator, who had a fine insight into the Japanese mind. Prior to Mashbir's arrival in Australia, the ATIS was headed by Queensland-born Oxford University graduate George Caiger who had spent 10 years as an English lecturer in Tokyo before the war.

By mid-April, intercepted Japanese communications, together with northern coast watcher reports, revealed to Mott and Caiger's organisations details of Admiral Yamamoto's plans for the imminent sea invasion of Port Moresby, New Guinea. From there the Japanese intended to carry out further attacks on Australia.

On 17 April Colonel Willoughby in Melbourne passed the plans to MacArthur and Admiral Chester Nimitz, Commander in Chief of the United States Pacific Fleet based in Hawaii. Despite this ample forewarning, MacArthur and Nimitz were still unable to muster the forces necessary to inflict a decisive defeat on the Japanese naval forces in what was to become known as the "Battle of the Coral Sea".

Yamamoto's plans announced the forces to be used would be three aircraft carriers, five heavy cruisers, four light cruisers, 12 destroyers, and Captain Hankyu Sasaki's submarine force. Willoughby also advised Nimitz that the invasion would occur during the first week of May. MacArthur informed Curtin and the Australian Government of the impending invasion and added that this information was derived from coast watcher reports.

Admiral Yamamoto's objective was to launch a seaborne invasion of Tulagi in the Solomon Islands and then Port Moresby, thus securing Japanese lines of communications to the north of Australia. Once this objective was achieved, the Japanese would then be able to launch air attacks against an isolated Australia, and also against Nauru and the Ocean Islands, culminating in the capture of their phosphate deposits.

Once Yamamoto had issued his invasion plans, however, he found it difficult to determine the strength of the opposing forces. His limited intelligence organisation revealed the presence of only a small Allied naval force in the Coral Sea. Due to this uncertainty, Yamamoto added another two submarines to Captain Sasaki's Third Submarine Company, with orders to locate and "destroy the enemy fleet".

Unknown to Yamamoto, Rear-Admiral Fletcher and his *USS Yorktown* force were already near the Coral Sea area by 25 April. Nimitz ordered the *USS Lexington* force, which was already a week out of Pearl Harbor, to proceed to rendezvous in the Solomon Sea on 1 May with the heavy cruiser *Chicago* and the destroyer *Perkins*, which were escorting the fleet oiler *Tippecanoe* from Noumea. In addition, the Australian Squadron, under the command of Rear-Admiral Crace of the Royal Navy, was ordered to reinforce the *Yorktown* and *Lexington* groups, and sailed from Sydney accordingly.

The main action of the naval battle did not occur until 8 May when planes from the American aircraft carriers sank the Japanese carrier, the *Shoho*, and seriously damaged another, the *Shokaku*. The Americans lost the *Lexington* and two others ships. The *Yorktown* was also badly damaged. Although the Americans suffered greatly, it was considered a victory because the Japanese fleet turned back to Rabaul due to a lack of adequate air defences. After learning of their withdrawal, Yamamoto ordered them south again to "annihilate remaining enemy forces", but because of the distances between the opposing forces, no further contact was made.

The Battle of the Coral Sea was the first in naval history of enemy surface vessels being beyond sight of one another, and the battle being decided by their opposing aircraft. The result checked the Japanese in their southward drive and their objective to invade Port Moresby was denied them and the capture of Nauru and Ocean Islands was postponed. Also, because of the outcome of the forthcoming Battle of Midway, a massive 300-aircraft attack on Townsville and the planned invasions of New Caledonia, Fiji and Samoa had to be postponed and eventually abandoned in July.

The War Cabinet met on 13 May 1942 and, largely based on MacArthur's appreciation of the previous day, severely criticised the conduct of the Coral Sea operation. MacArthur had observed that the backbone of the striking power was the aircraft carriers which did not belong to his command. The results of this meeting expressed the government's views to be:

> ... rather disappointing, the more so as we had ample warning of the enemy's intention, the prospective date of the attack and the strength of his forces. With the advantage of this information we should have been able to concentrate the superior strength necessary to have ensured a complete victory. As it was, an opportunity to inflict losses on the enemy was lost.

Curtin cabled both Churchill and Roosevelt of the War Cabinet's viewpoints. He also emphasised in the cable that in view of the Coral Sea engagement, it was vital to build up and maintain Australia's strength sufficiently to repel any further Japanese attacks.

This communication to Churchill and Roosevelt was not sent through secret channels. The cable was an open one, in which Curtin stated that "We knew the strength of the enemy concentration, we knew his intentions, and we knew the prospective date of his attack..." This knowledge he would not have divulged so freely had he been aware of Ultra and the security surrounding the information obtained in it.

From the outset Churchill had insisted on the utmost secrecy for Ultra, evidenced by the example of his inaction over the German bombing of Coventry. To inform Curtin of its existence was an added and unnecessary risk, as Churchill doubted that Curtin had sufficient strength to sacrifice Australians under similar circumstances.

Indeed, the closing sentence of Curtin's cable, "Fortune will not continue to favour us with these opportunities if we do not grasp them", suggests that he would have used these opportunities, as Churchill feared, to protect Australia against attack – a step he could not have taken without arousing enemy suspicion of Ultra's existence when it would be realised by the Japanese that their codes had been deciphered.

The Coral Sea engagement, though not a military success did, however, grant Australians a reprieve from the imminent threat of invasion. A tide of relief swept through the nation. Although the Japanese failed to capture Port Moresby, parts of Sasaki's Third Submarine Company were already in Australian waters, watching and waiting to strike a blow at the heart of urban Australia, thousands of miles from the New Guinea war front. ●

CHAPTER SIX
WARNINGS IGNORED

CHAPTER SIX

WARNINGS IGNORED

> Not one of the midgets has returned. In spite of that, the young officers are keen to carry out the next plan. But only once more. If the midgets do not return next time I say there will be no more midget submarine operations.
>
> *Vice-Admiral Shigeru Fukutome,*
> Japanese Imperial Navy.

In spite of setbacks to plans for the invasion of Port Moresby, the Japanese were not seriously concerned since they felt, with the capture of Tulagi near Guadalcanal, that Port Moresby could be captured at will. In the meantime, they still intended to proceed with attacks on enemy bases in the South Pacific and the Indian Ocean. Their target was naval game, the intention being to disrupt naval communications rather than to molest merchant supply lines. Accordingly, preparations for midget submarine attacks in the South Pacific and Indian Ocean were made when the "MO Operation" (Port Moresby invasion) was postponed.

The Commander of the Sixth Submarine Fleet, Vice-Admiral Daigo, was relegated to Operational Commander of the Third Submarine Company. In late April, Japanese reconnaissance aircraft from Rabaul reported the presence of two American aircraft carriers south of the Jomard Passage, at the eastern tip of the New Guinea mainland. This was part of the Australian Squadron under Rear-Admiral Crace's command retiring to the Great Barrier Reef and included *USS Chicago* and *USS Perkins*. Daigo believed they were making their way south to refuel and replenish supplies somewhere in the South Pacific and ordered I-21 to proceed to Fiji and I-29 to New Caledonia to look for them. He also ordered those submarines with facilities to carry midget submarines - I-22, I-24, I-27 and I-28 - to proceed to Queen Carola Harbour in the Solomon Islands to embark their midgets from the converted seaplane carrier, *Chiyoda*. Prior to this, I-22, I-24 and I-28 were marauding in the Coral and Solomon Seas looking for targets of opportunity, and I-27 was operating off the coast of Brisbane, watching for Allied naval vessels.

On reaching New Caledonia, I-29 launched her sea plane to reconnoitre Noumea. Unable to locate any naval warships, the pilot returned to the carrier submarine waiting on the surface. Unknown to the submarine's commander, the *USS Yorktown* force, which included *Chicago*, *Perkins* and *Tippecanoe*, had sailed from Noumea a few days earlier to rendezvous with the *USS Lexington* force in the Solomon Sea and he failed to make contact with them.

Lieutenant Keiu Matsuo, commander of midget submarine I-22.

Courtesy Japan Midget Submarine Association

Portrait of Petty Officer Masao Tsuzuki, Lieutenant Matsuo's crew member on midget I-22.

AWM 128896

On 5 May, I-29 attacked the American ship *John Adams* off New Caledonia. Only one torpedo struck the ship – over-sensitive adjustments caused the others to explode before reaching their target. The *John Adams* caught fire and eventually sank the following day. While still in the waters between Noumea and Brisbane, I-29 also pursued and sank the Greek ship *Chloe* on 7 May.

Captain Sasaki in I-21 arrived off Fiji and launched his reconnaissance aircraft over Suva Harbour. Again, unable to locate any carrier or other naval vessels, he proceeded to New Zealand where, on 24 May, the seaplane reconnoitred Auckland Harbour; but due to dense fog, the pilot was unable to find any carrier or naval vessels in that harbour.

Returning to events in the Coral Sea, Japanese naval movements had been hindered by the increased Allied aircraft and submarine reconnaissance activity. At 4:00 pm on 11 May, Vice-Admiral Daigo switched the midget submarine transfer location from Queen Carola Harbour to Truk Lagoon in the Caroline Islands. However, misfortune overtook I-28 at daybreak on 17 May when she was sighted by an American submarine south-south-east of Truk. *USS Tautog* was 23 days out of Pearl Harbor on passage to Fremantle and sighted I-28 on the surface with numerals and men clearly visible on the bridge. *Tautog* fired one torpedo and scored a direct hit. The Japanese submarine replied with gunfire but *Tautog* fired a second torpedo which struck I-28 below the conning tower and effectively sealed her fate. The submarine disappeared in an eruption of smoke and debris, sliding quickly below the surface with the entire crew. The demise of I-28 reduced the attack capacity of the Third Submarine Company by a quarter and was the first of several mishaps to occur during the coming submarine operation.

In order to avoid a similar incident occurring, the remaining three submarines – I-22 (Commander Kiyoi Ageta), I-24 (Commander Hiroshi Hanafusa) and I-27 (Commander Iwao Yoshimura) – travelled over the surface at night and submerged during the day. They eventually all arrived at Truk Lagoon at daybreak on 18 May.

By evening, I-24 had taken delivery of her midget submarine, commanded by 24-year-old Lieutenant Teiji Yamaki. However, on the second night out of Truk an explosion occurred during routine maintenance of the midget submarine. Yamaki had entered the submarine when one of the maintenance crew switched on the light, which ignited some gas that had escaped from the batteries and caused a small explosion. The co-pilot, Petty Officer Shizuka Masumoto, who was entering the hatch, was caught in the blast and thrown into the sea. The submarine searched for six hours, but Masumoto was not seen again. The explosion also caused severe burns to Yamaki's leg. Without a co-pilot and with a damaged midget submarine, I-24 returned to Truk where the damaged craft was removed and replaced by one crewed by Lieutenant Katsuhisa Ban and Petty Officer Mamoru Ashibe. The carrier submarine slipped her moorings in the early hours of 20 May and proceeded southward to Australian waters without further incident.

From documents recovered from the midget submarine after the attack, it is evident Lieutenant Matsuo, in I-22, studied the Admiralty charts and photographs obtained by I-25 three months earlier during her reconnaissance of eastern Australia and New Zealand bases. He would have noted the channels leading into the various enemy harbours, including Sydney Harbour whose underwater corridors were narrow and complicated.

Photograph of midget submarine trainees in Kure, Japan. Identified left is Lt Keiu Matsuo; and rear left is Lt Kenshi Chuma, both commanders of midget submarines launched from carrier submarines I-22 and I-27, respectively, in the attack on Sydney Harbour on 31 May 1942. Both officers were among the four bodies subsequently recovered.

Masas Tsuzuku, who had been selected to accompany Matsuo, supervised the maintenance of the craft. Tsuzuku was the son of a poor farmer. As a boy he was unable to obtain formal schooling because of the long distance of school from his home in the mountains. He decided to become a naval cadet at the age of 18 years but, because of his poor education, he failed the examination. Determined, Tsuzuku embarked on a study program using borrowed books. He sat for the examination again the following year and, this time, was successful. After he graduated from the Torpedo and Submarine School at Kure, he joined the specially selected midget submarine force.

Meanwhile, I-29 had arrived off the Australian coast on 13 May. The first of several warnings indicating the presence of enemy submarines off the eastern Australian coast came in the evening of 16 May when I-29 sighted the Russian ship *Wellen* on passage to Newcastle. The submarine surfaced 30 miles off Newcastle and fired seven rounds at 100 yards range. The *Wellen* replied with machine-gun fire before the submarine submerged. The *Wellen's* captain, one officer and another rating were injured.

Wellen's captain sent out a distress call which was intercepted by Australian naval authorities in Sydney. The officer-in-charge of Sydney and Newcastle harbours', Rear-Admiral G. C. Muirhead-Gould, ordered the Dutch cruiser *Tromp*, USS *Perkins* and the Australian corvette *HMAS Arunta* to search for the submarine. As a precautionary measure, he closed Sydney and Newcastle ports to outward bound merchant shipping. However, the surface and air search for the submarine was unsuccessful and *Wellen* arrived in Newcastle without further incident.

The implications of the *Wellen* incident went unnoticed by Muirhead-Gould who concluded the submarine was alone and had already departed the area. Twenty-four hours later he re-opened Sydney and Newcastle ports to merchant shipping and ordered *Tromp*, *Perkins* and *Arunta* back to Sydney.

After the *Wellen* incident, I-29 continued to watch Sydney and Newcastle. At 3:00 am the following morning, while lurking close inshore, the submarine observed what its commander thought was a "Warspite" battleship and destroyer-escort. The I-29 pursued these ships for over four hours, but was unable to get into an attacking position and abandoned the chase when they entered Sydney Harbour.

There was a lull of activity until 23 May when I-29 launched her reconnaissance seaplane and carried out a dawn flight over Sydney Harbour. The pilot observed three large cruisers or battleships dotted about the harbour with numerous smaller naval vessels tied up at the wharves. Some vessels were aglow with bright lights and the pilot assumed that they were under repair. He also observed four destroyers and several patrol boats, plus many merchant ships beyond the Harbour Bridge. The reconnaissance seaplane went undetected, however, it is thought the aircraft was damaged on landing and sunk.

The Japanese document, "Submarine Operations During the Second Phase of Operations (April 1942 to August 1942)", prepared in 1947, records that, "… as the aircraft on both I-21 and I-29 were damaged, no reconnaissance could be made". This is a reference to the attack plan that aircraft reconnaissance takes place immediately before and after the attack. Since no aerial reconnaissance was made after the attack, it is presumed that the Third Submarine Company no longer had any reconnaissance aircraft left.

During the reconnaissance flight over Sydney Harbour on 23 May, Captain Sasaki was still lurking off Auckland Harbour. Although he was disappointed no aircraft carriers had been included in the Sydney Harbour report, he was encouraged by the news of battleships and cruisers. Shortly after midnight on 24 May, Sasaki made the decision to attack that harbour and ordered the Third Submarine Company to rendezvous off the coast of Sydney.

Australian authorities were unaware of I-29's reconnaissance flight over Sydney Harbour until after the war. Japanese authorities were uncertain of the exact date of the flight, because all reports from I-29 were lost in July 1944 when that submarine was sunk off the Philippines. However, naval historian G. Hermon Gill records British "sources" were able to confirm that the reconnaissance flight occurred on 23 May. This lays claim to the fact that British intelligence within Australia had, through Ultra, intercepted Sasaki's telegraphic orders to the Third Submarine Company.

On the evening of 26 May there was another warning of the close proximity of Japanese submarines off Sydney. This occurred when Japanese radio traffic was intercepted by New Zealand naval authorities.

While en route from Auckland to Sydney, Captain Sasaki telegraphed all submarines in the Third Submarine Company outlining the alterations to his initial attack order. This transmission was intercepted by the New Zealand Naval Board who notified the authorities in Australian, presumably the Australian Naval Board, of an enemy unit, probably a submarine, operating 700 nautical miles east of Sydney.

At 6:00 pm on 26 May, Sasaki sent the following telegraphic order to his submarine force now converging on Sydney Harbour:

TELEGRAPHIC ORDER NO. 3

The following alterations are made re: Sydney Attack –

1. Date of the attack will be by a special order (scheduled 31 May).
2. Order of dispatching the "hanger sheaths" will be I-27, I-22 then I-24. The time and order for the "sheaths" passing through the heads will be I-27, 20 minutes after moonrise, then I-22 and I-24 following at 20 minute intervals.
3. Targets for the attack will be up to the discretion of the "sheath" commanders but try as much as possible to attack the following targets:
a. If there is a battleship or large cruiser beyond the Harbour Bridge, then I-22 is to attack the battleship and I-24 the cruiser. If there are two cruisers, then I-22 and I-24 will attack them and I-27 will attack the battleship.
b. If there is a battleship or aircraft carrier outside the Harbour Bridge, then attack it.
c. If there are no suitable targets outside of the Harbour Bridge, then try as much as possible to attack the battleship and large cruiser beyond the bridge.
4. After the completion of the attack, the following recovery rendezvous is to be taken.
    Day 1… No 4 recovery rendezvous (off Broken Bay)
    Day 2… No 2 recovery rendezvous (off Port Hacking).

Sasaki arrived off Sydney Heads during the evening of 28 May, having travelled over the surface from Auckland through rough weather. On 29 May, he decided to carry out a second reconnaisance flight over Sydney Harbour to confirm the concentration and location of capital warships in the harbour, and to ascertain the position of the anti-submarine boom net at the harbour entrance and the location of its opening. This reconnaissance report formed the basis for Sasaki's final attack order. At 6:00 pm on 29 May, he sent the following transmission to the Third Submarine Company:

TELEGRAPH ORDER NO. 4

1. Day of attack…. 31 May.
2. The enemy situation in Sydney Harbour is as follows:
a. One US battleship 400 metres east of Garden Island. One large US transport ship at 900 metres north of Garden Island. Several destroyers wharved on the west side of Garden Island. (Those have wharfing lights on.) Cockatoo Island has no enemy vessels around it. However, there are two light cruisers and a destroyer inside the dockyard.
b. No detection made on the defences of the enemy, but seeing the frequent passage of enemy vessels (in night-time, too) it is presumed that there must be an opening for sea passage. No recognition of enemy patrol boats.
c. There are no control lights inside the harbour, the lights at Barrenjoey lighthouse are on.
d. There are frequent movements of merchant ships in and out of the harbour and those ships have their lights on. However, there may be false (decoy) wharving lights on.
3. The following alterations are made to Telegraphic order No. 3.
a. Day one… No. 2 Recovery rendezvous (off Port Hacking, south of Sydney). Setting the starting point at 180 degrees 4 km off Port Hacking, position at 100 degrees the following vessels: I-29, I-27, I-22 and I-24 (in that order). Distance 4 km, 190 degrees 6 km from the centre position of the retrieval for I-21.
b. For daytime standby (and night-time withdrawal), set the metre reading for submergence at 190 degrees and 10 degrees.
c. Depending upon the situation, some submarines may be ordered to search the foreshores after the second day.
4. Note: The reconnaissance aircraft overturned on landing but no casualties reported.

Sasaki's telegraphic order was again intercepted by the New Zealand naval authorities. At 7:10 pm on 29 May, the New Zealand Naval Board notified the authorities in Australia of the presence of an enemy unit, "probably a submarine", approximately 40 miles east of Sydney Harbour. Inexplicably, this warning of Japanese submarines operating close to Sydney was not acted on by the Australian authorities.

Japanese radio chatter was also heard on *USS Chicago* over several nights preceding the attack. Although the ship's communications officer, Lieutenant-Commander H. J. Mecklenburg, reported the chatter to the Garden Island Operations Room, the information went no further. *Chicago's* radio direction finding (RDF) equipment placed the transmissions coming from the Blue Mountains.

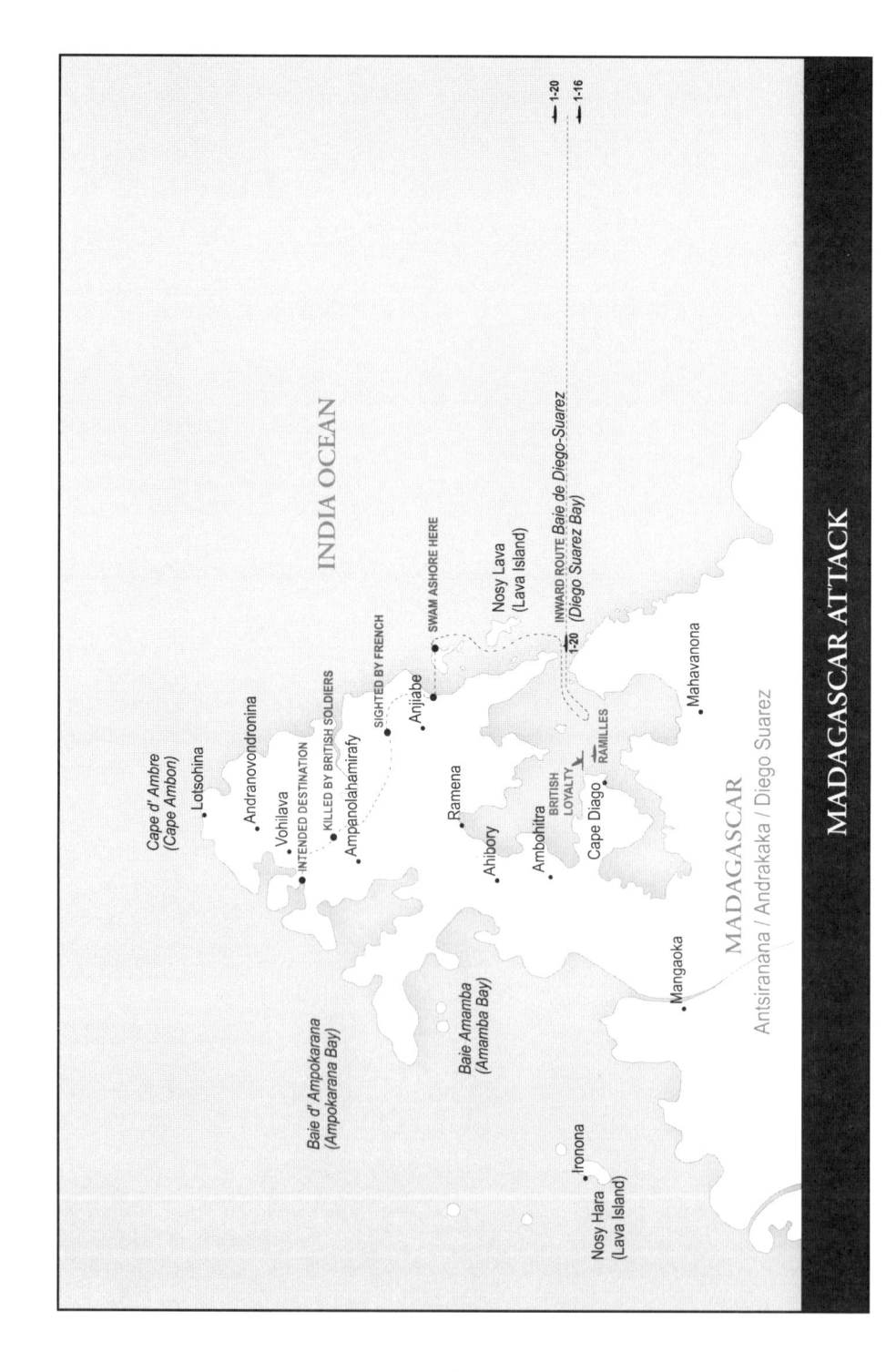

90. JAPANESE SUBMARINE RAIDERS 1942 *A Maritime Mystery*

While there were plenty of Japanese spies and sympathisers in Australia during WWII, the direction of the radio transmissions was more likely an aberration of RDF technology of the day. Due to radio's ability to travel "over the horizon", RDF makes a particularly good navigation system for ships and aircraft at long distances from land. It works by pointing a directional antenna in "various directions" and then listening for the direction in which a radio signal comes through most strongly. However, at sea level this technology can suffer from anomalies of radio propagation, where the signals may be arriving at the antenna from multiple directions, perhaps because they are reflecting off nearby buildings, hills, or metal structures from nearby ships inside the harbour. This can result in false directional readings. Without triangulation from other sources, RDF intercepts can be misleading and sometimes the reciprocal of the true bearing. It is more likely that the strongest signal reaching *Chicago's* antenna was a reflection bouncing off Sydney's hilly terrain and the true direction of the Japanese transmissions was somewhere off the coast.

Returning to the Third Submarine Company, after receiving Sasaki's final attack order, Vice-Admiral Daigo telegraphed a personal message to the crews of the midget submarines to support their morale:

One chance out of a thousand at hand. Approach the enemy with the utmost confidence and calm.

Encouraged by Daigo's words, the midget submarine crews prepared to meet their destiny. Their audacious attack resulted in death for all of them; more than 4,000 miles from their homeland.

Meanwhile, events half-way around the world, had they been known, would have alerted naval authorities of the likelihood of a similar midget submarine attack on Sydney Harbour. Some 12 hours after Flying Warrant Officer Ito reconnoitred Sydney Harbour, a similar float plane from Rear-Admiral Ishizaki's Eighth Submarine Squadron in the Indian Ocean was circling the British battleship *HMS Ramillies*, which was anchored in Diego Suarez Bay, Madagascar.

The Japanese Planning Board had called for simultaneous attacks in the Pacific and Indian Oceans. The attacks were planned to occur at the same time to prevent the British Admiralty from alerting Allied forces throughout the world. Had one attack preceded the other, the Admiralty might have been able to warn the Allies to take adequate defence precautions against similar attacks.

At the end of April 1942 Ishizaki led his group to Penang, on the Malayan Peninsula, to collect their craft from the converted seaplane carrier *Nisshin*, after which the submarine squadron proceeded into the Indian Ocean. The force consisted of three midget submarine carriers (I-16, I-18 and I-20) and two seaplane carriers (I-10 and I-30). Rear-Admiral Ishizaki flew his flag in I-10.

During May, reconnaissance aircraft flew over Aden (7th), Jubiti (8th), Zanzibar, Dar-es-Salaam (19th) and Durban (20th). In Durban it was estimated that an average of 30 merchant ships a day were lying at anchor but Ishizaki, adhering to Japanese policy, was looking for naval game.

The British battleship *HMS Ramilles*. In March 1942, *Ramilles* joined the Third Battle Squadron based in the Ceylon area and in April 1942 was in the naval force tasked for the capture and occupation of Diego Suarez on the island of Madagascar. During the night of 29 May, a Japanese light aircraft circled *Ramilles* lying at anchor in Diego Suarez Bay.

At 10:30 pm on 29 May, a reconnaissance aircraft began circling the British battleship *HMS Ramilles*. Unlike Muirhead-Gould at Sydney Harbour, the captain of *Ramilles* realised that the aircraft came from an enemy warship, and an alarm was raised. *Ramilles* weighted anchor, darkened the ship and steamed around Diego Suarez Bay for some time before taking up a new anchorage.

Early in the evening of 30 May, Ishizaki led the Eighth Submarine Squadron to within 10 miles of the entrance to Diego Suarez Bay. The sea was rough with a high swell running. Two midgets were launched from I-16 and I-20, but the engines from I-18's craft failed to start. Consequently, it did not take part in the attack.

Rain squalls repeatedly enveloped the two midget submarines, hindering their navigation. Only one succeeded in reaching the entrance of the bay through the white-capped breakers – the craft from I-20.

Commanded by Sub-Lieutenant Katsusuke Iwase and Petty Officer Takazo Takada, the midget entered the bay shortly after 8:00 pm. Twenty-five minutes later the midget submarine fired its first torpedo at *Ramilles*, and an hour later fired its second torpedo at the tanker *British Loyalty*, which caught fire and sank. With their torpedoes expended, Iwase and Takada made their way out of the bay to rendezvous with their parent submarine off Cape Ambon, on the northern extremity of Madagascar. However, possibly due to a change in gravity of the craft caused by the release of the two torpedoes, they were unable to make the recovery point and decided to swim ashore.

When they landed ashore, Iwase and Takada were met by members of the Antarakee tribe who gave them food and shelter. Armed with only a revolver and a ceremonial sword, they decided to trek overland to Cape Ambon to rendezvous with the waiting submarine force. They set off on a journey that was to last for three days and end with their deaths. During the journey over mountainous terrain they met a Frenchman who, frightened by their appearance, fled into the jungle. They continued on their journey but on the third day were confronted by a group of 15 British soldiers. The sergeant in charge called for Iwase and Takada to surrender, but Takada commenced firing with his pistol. He succeeded in killing one British soldier and wounding a further four before being fatally shot himself. Iwase, an unusually small man in appearance, charged the remaining British soldiers with his ceremonial sword and was cut down by the fierce machine-gun fire that followed. Shortly after this action, the sergeant discovered the Frenchman hidden in the jungle and ordered him to fetch the local village chief. The bodies of Iwase and Takada were then stripped and buried.

The fate of midget I-16, commanded by Lieutenant Saburo Akeida and Petty Officer Masami Takemoto, has never been determined. It is assumed that they both perished with their craft before reaching the entrance to the bay.

Ramilles suffered only minor damage from the torpedo attack, which resulted in one compartment flooding. Thanks to the quick action of her crew, the British battleship avoided disaster by sealing off the flooded compartment. She was able to make temporary repairs before steaming to the port of Durban in South Africa the following day.

Meanwhile, after the attack, the rain squalls had passed over Diego Suarez Bay and the sea was occasionally illuminated by the full moon. Ishizaki surfaced at the recovery point off Cape Ambon at 10:20 pm. When he saw reflections of a fire in the sky over the bay, and also intercepted a radio message from *Ramilles* announcing the attack, he presumed the attack had been successful. For the following two days Ishizaki searched for the midget submarines and their crews along the foreshores. Finally, on 2 June, he abandoned all hope of recovering a single crewman. The Eighth Submarine Squadron then turned its attention to the destruction of merchant shipping in the Mozambique Channel where 19 vessels were sunk over the next two months.

Although the Diego Suarez Bay (GMT +3) and the Sydney Harbour (GMT +10) attacks were to occur simultaneously, local conditions and geographical time differences between the two locations hindered the sequence of events. All times being local, at 10:30 pm on 29 May, the reconnaissance aircraft from I-10 had been correctly interpreted as indicating the close proximity of an enemy unit – 46 hours and 45 minutes before the first midget submarine was discovered in Sydney Harbour. *Ramilles* was torpedoed at 8:25 pm on 30 May – 30 hours 50 minutes before the first midget submarine was discovered in Sydney.

When the attack commenced in Madagascar, Vichy French forces, which had surrendered to the British only three weeks earlier, lined the foreshores and cheered. They believed that a French submarine had penetrated the harbour to repel the British forces.

Within hours of the attack, the captain of *HMS Ramilles* informed the British Admiralty in London, unsure whether the attackers were Vichy French or Japanese. The Admiralty knew the attacker to be Japanese, but did not notify the Allied naval forces. The reason they later gave for not raising the alarm was that they would not disclose the losses sustained in case the information benefited the enemy.

Had the Madagascar attack been known in Australia, naval authorities there may have issued a warning of the likelihood of a similar threat to Sydney Harbour – particularly in view of the previous warnings that Japanese submarines were in the area and of the reconnaissance flight of an unknown aircraft over Sydney. Only after the Sydney Harbour attack did the British Admiralty issue a general alert to Allied navies throughout the world, warning that "every possible precaution is to be taken". ●

CHAPTER SEVEN
From Hyde Park to Hollywood

CHAPTER SEVEN

FROM HYDE PARK TO HOLLYWOOD

I discovered a pub so wild that taxis refused to take me to the front door. It was on the waterfront and reminded me that this was once a convict island. Women fought on the floor, tearing each other's hair out, while men emptied pints of beer over the writhing bodies. And an old man danced crazily to a jukebox, his hair matted with blood that had stiffened over the days.

Waltzing Materialism
Anonymous English writer.

Australian civilians in common with the government of the day were inexperienced in the realities of war. During these dark times, everyone had seen news photos of the devastation caused by Hitler's blitzkrieg bombers in Europe; but fear of the Japanese was much more deep rooted and intense. Rumours were circulating around the country about the horrific treatment of 16,000 Australian soldiers and nurses captured in Singapore and now incarcerated in the infamous Changi prison camp. There were stories of Australian nurses being gang raped then killed, of slivers of bamboo being forced under fingernails and of public and summary eviscerations with swords. All confirmed an impression that the Japanese were a devilish, cruel and monstrous enemy.

During the three weeks following the indecisive Coral Sea battle and aerial engagement on 8 May, it finally dawned on Australia that an invasion could be at hand.

When Japan entered the war, the Australian Government issued identity cards to all civilians over 16 years of age; air raid wardens were given steel helmets and National Emergency servicemen and women were trained in fire-fighting, first-aid and aircraft spotting. In case of possible gas attacks, respirators were stored in readily accessible places.

In Sydney the underground railway tunnel was hastily converted to an air raid shelter, with numerous entrances situated throughout the city, while civilians in the suburbs dug slit trenches in their backyards for use as bomb shelters. Sandbags were stacked against city buildings to protect them from bomb blasts and street names, hotel names and signposts were ripped down to confuse the Japanese invaders. A now weird and ghostly Bondi Beach was fortified with barbed wire and tank traps, while cliffs and headlands around Sydney were honeycombed with concrete pill-boxes, gun turrets, and searchlight and anti-aircraft batteries.

At the Sydney General Post Office the tower was dismantled and its stones numbered then put into safe storage until after the war. Frequent air raid drills were carried out in office buildings, schools and factories. A top secret "denial squad" was formed and trained to fire and demolish important factories and other industrial plants to deny the Japanese their use… an idea which came from the Russian "scorched earth" policy against invading Nazis. This unpopular squad even partially cut through steel beams which supported the roofs of some of Sydney's biggest factories to help facilitate their rapid destruction; and explosives and inflammable materials were stored within their confines to help expedite the destruction.

From the end of 1941 onwards a "brown-out", or modified blackout, was imposed, whereby lights couldn't be seen from the air but could be seen from the street. Car headlights were masked at night and dark curtains placed across exposed windows. In Kings Cross, however, lights from clubs and bars were kept blazing, as if oblivious to the outside world, and prostitutes continued to ply their trade with cries of "Hello Sailor".

Dread of a Japanese invasion expressed itself in a brittle gaiety which seemed to overtake everyone. The advent of the American GIs raised Australians' hopes of defeating the Japanese and had the effect of lifting morale generally. Sydney office and hotel buildings were taken over by a wave of khaki to accommodate administration staffs and servicemen on leave or passing through Sydney in transit to other areas.

It should be remembered that Sydney was a front line city under benign occupation by American troops. There were more than 80,000 US servicemen in Australia at this time. But their wartime "invasion" of Sydney had its compensations. It cosmopolitanised what had been an isolated and provincial town, dreamily locked up in its own rather puritanical past. The social and sexual ramifications of the American invasion were immense, and have been made public in a number of classic books. John Hammond Moore wrote in his book *Over-Sexed, Over-Paid and Over Here*:

> The GI was a novelty, something new and different, and most welcome. Compared with the Australian soldier, he was beautifully dressed, well paid and often possessed an aura of mystery and romance. This was a dream come true for a generation of Australian females nurtured on Hollywood legends… and most important, with the cream of Australian manhood overseas, the GI was here in the flesh, both available and willing.

A more personalised version appears in Dymphna Cusack and Florence James' wartime classic *Come in Spinner*. This, the most famous novel of wartime Sydney, was first published in 1951 and has seldom been out of print since. One of the novel's heroines, Guinea, reminisces:

> Ah yes, the great days of '42… when the American forces first spread over the country in a wave of superbly tailored beige-pinks, olive drabs and light khakis; a wave that bore on its crest orchids, nylons, exquisite courtesy, Hollywood lovemaking and a standard of luxury that had never before been experienced outside the ranks of the privileged socialites…

The affluent Yanks were paid twice the amount of their Australian counterparts and soon acquired a reputation as big spenders. They handled money recklessly, offering a handful of assorted Australian notes in payment for prized cartons of Camel and Lucky Strike cigarettes, local orchids, black market liquor, perfume and nylon stockings – commodities which were now becoming a status symbol and a way of life. The smooth-talking Yanks got preferential treatment from shopkeepers, barmaids and taxi drivers, and Australian girls who accepted their orchids at night would often sell them back to the florist the next day at half price.

A satirical poem, wittily directed at the Americans at the time, was published in *Australia's Yesterdays* by Cyril Pearl. Entitled "The Passionate (US) General to His Love", it went:

> Come live with me and be my bride,
> And you'll have orchids five feet wide,
> Unrationed robes from Saks to swathe in
> And Chanel No 5 to bathe in.
> With sheer stockings by the mile on
> You'll be my serpent of the Nylon…
> We'll take a flat at Darlinghurst
> Big enough for Randolph Hearst;
> At breakfast, as we sip our bourbon,
> I'll tell you how I met Miss Durbin;
> And when I'm back in U.S.A.,
> I'll send you a cable on Mother's Day!

Apart from these erotic reveries, and on a wider level, Canadian, Archibald Shaw, indicated the Australian/American situation to US Military Intelligence officers on his return to North America in May 1942, after five years in Sydney. In his report, reprinted in *Over-Sexed, Over-Paid and Over Here*, he noted how favourably received the American soldiers were. They seemed better behaved and better educated than their Australian confreres. He made the comment that in Australia he has never seen an American soldier drunk. He then added rather perceptively:

> The great system [amongst the Australians] is beer, beer and more beer. I think it is an organised thing from the higher-ups. It is directed toward keeping the working class down – by getting them to spend their money recklessly and not allowing them to be educated outside of their work. There are lots of dog races every night, horse racing every week, lotteries every week and plenty of beer…
>
> Unions are very strong. They are controlled by the government, I know that. Another great system in Australia is not to create, but to get by. That is the heritage of the people – to copy someone else. There is a lack of originality, and besides it is much easier to copy someone else.
>
> The Australians are not worried about the war. It is hard to get them down to brass tacks. The captain of our ship told me that there were about 65 ships in the harbour at Melbourne, but there was a day's holiday just the same and no one was working. No one is interested in working – it is just a question of using up time.

A devastating indictment of Australian workers' attitudes to the war at this time can be seen in an excerpt from a confidential report by an American war correspondent to US Army Intelligence.

Although these attitudes astonished the Americans, they will come as less of a surprise to an Australian reader. The American journalist commented that Australians refused to work in the rain and took time out for their tea. The heavy looting which occurred at all docks, he regarded as a national disgrace. He added the "longshoremen" weren't searched as they left the docks and consequently got away with "a lot of stuff". He wrote incredulously: "A laborer can be caught, convicted and sentenced, serve his time, at the expiration of which his union will accept him for work at the same job where he was caught looting."

Perhaps one of the more sinister aspects of the American "invasion" was the racial conflict between white Americans and black GIs. Blacks were relegated to their own clubs by white Americans who requested that Australian newspapers not publish photographs or stories of black Americans being entertained by white hostesses. On one occasion white Americans wrecked a Sydney dance hall when the Australian manager refused to exclude black Americans, but the story was not allowed to be published at the request of the American High Command.

The influx of the Americans also allowed black markets to flourish at a time when the government was attempting to shorten drinking hours at hotels and reduce the production of beer. Sly grog shops flourished but, despite vigilant policing, there seemed to be an inexhaustible supply of alcohol in Sydney nightclubs and restaurants. The price of a bottle of "black" beer was five shillings, whereas its legal price was only one shilling and seven pence. Australian whisky sold for three pounds and scotch for five pounds. One American admitted to buying 84 pounds of alcohol in one week.

Sir Paul Hasluck reflected on this problem in his official history of Australia during World War II, when he rather sniffily wrote: "Wartime experience makes it clear that beer and betting meant more than anything else in life to a considerable number of Australians."

It was not unusual to see an Australian drinker stagger outside a pub, put his fingers down his throat, throw-up and then go back inside for another pint. This compulsive obsession with drinking overflowed into cricket, football and horse races, and women came a poor third to such "male" activities. With the arrival of the GI, women suddenly found themselves the centre of attention and Australian men complained that, in addition to the Americans killing Phar Lap, they also stole their women. Hyde Park and the Domain, Sydney's panoramic harbourside parklands, became popular havens for the explosion of young lovers.

The headland of Mrs Macquarie's Chair was crowded with couples spooning and necking in the moonlight. This famous lovers' retreat was made more exotic by the scent of magnolias wafting up from the Botanical Gardens. At this idyllic place of fraternisation under the Moreton Bay figs, which was for many an oasis, the only reminder that a war was being waged was the imposing silhouettes of Allied warships congesting the harbour. •

CHAPTER EIGHT
DEFENCES UNPREPARED

CHAPTER EIGHT
DEFENCES UNPREPARED

Writing in *Life* magazine on 8 June 1942, Cecil Brown, an American newsman not enamoured of the Australian war effort, told of a Japanese freighter that left Sydney late in November 1941. As the vessel was departing, an officer on deck shouted to an Australian wharf-labourer, "We'll be back!"
"And we'll be waiting for you," replied the dock worker.
"Oh, no you won't," the Japanese officer retorted. "We'll come on a weekend and you'll be at the races."

Over-Sexed, Over-Paid and Over Here,
John Hammond Moore.

Port Jackson is one of the finest natural harbours in the world, a fact which was realised by the first white men who sailed on it in 1788. A naval man such as Captain Arthur Phillip was enraptured about it, which is clearly shown in an account recorded in *Voyage of Governor Phillip to Botany Bay*, edited by J. J. Auchmuty:

From an entrance not more than two miles across, Port Jackson gradually extends into a noble and capacious basin; having surroundings sufficient for the largest vessels, and space to accommodate in perfect security, any number that could be assembled.

The prize for the intrepid Japanese was the Allied warships that lay in the harbour; and the objective of the mission was to sink the majestic and imposing heavy cruiser *USS Chicago*, the principal strength of "MacArthur's Navy", which, in daylight hours, lay athwart Garden Island.

From Ito's reconnaissance flight the Japanese knew there was a concentration of Allied shipping in Sydney Harbour at the time, almost of Pearl Harbor proportions in both naval and commercial capital ships.

In all, there were over 40 wartime vessels which comprised three heavy cruisers, one light cruiser, two armed merchant cruisers, one destroyer tender, one destroyer, three corvettes, three minesweepers, one minelayer, one submarine, two anti-submarine vessels, 10 channel patrol boats, 12 naval auxiliary patrol boats, two examination vessels, and the barracks vessel, *HMAS Kuttabul*.

Among the cruisers were *HMAS Canberra*, *HMAS Adelaide* and the Australian armed

The destroyer tender *USS Dobbin*, a Pearl Harbor survivor.

The light cruiser, *HMAS Adelaide*. She is armed with seven 6-inch and two 4-inch AA guns. Two 6-inch guns amidship have been replaced by depth charge throwers.

The Sydney boom defences, looking from George's Head towards Green Point. The anti-submarine net was located at the narrowest point of the inner harbour entrance, between George's Head, on Middle Head, and Green Point on Inner South Head. The single line steel anti-submarine net was supported between piles.

JAPANESE SUBMARINE RAIDERS 1942 *A Maritime Mystery* .105

Commodore (later Rear-Admiral) G. C. Muirhead-Gould DSC RN,
Commodore-in-Charge Sydney and Principal Sea Transport Officer, NSW.

106. JAPANESE SUBMARINE RAIDERS 1942 *A Maritime Mystery*

merchant cruiser *HMAS Westralia*. In addition to these major ships, the British armed merchant cruiser *HMS Kanimbla*, as well as numerous other fighting ships from all the Allied navies of the Pacific were present. According to Ito's report, a further two destroyers were in the Cockatoo dockyard under repair.

It is a measure of the misguided confidence of harbour authorities that a collection of the largest, most valuable war ships in the Pacific was clustered together around Garden Island, making a devastatingly vulnerable target – many of them with their engines shut down! The last fact is significant because the *USS Chicago*, on deciding to leave Sydney at 10:30 pm, was unable to raise sufficient steam to get underway until four hours later – that is, shortly before 3:00 am on 1 June.

Probably the most interesting group of vessels in the harbour that night was the channel patrol boats assigned to the harbour's defences. Many of these boats had been requisitioned, rented or lent to the navy by wealthy Sydney businessmen as their contribution to the war effort. Mostly luxurious motor launches, they were manned by fulltime Royal Australian Navy personnel. The best known boat which bore a naval commission was *HMAS Sea Mist*. After the war it was brought by Sydney radio station, 2GB, and lent to the popular Jack Davey as part-payment of his remuneration. This group of boats, known popularly as "The Hollywood Fleet", was moored at Farm Cove.

The channel patrol boats were assisted in their duty of defending Sydney Harbour by a flotilla of 12 naval auxiliary patrol boats which were nicknamed "Nappies" or "Nap-Naps". The officers and men of the NAP were ineligible for active military service in the permanent forces due to either age or disability. Most notable of the NAP vessels was *HMAS Lauriana*, volunteered by her owner Harold Arnott of biscuit fame.

The historical record shows there was some measure of animosity between Muirhead-Gould and his staff officers, as well as from many patrol boat personnel. The CPB and NAP, rather like a "McHale's Navy", had a relaxed and free-ranging approach which clashed with Muirhead-Gould's traditionalism. In turn, he was considered pompous and dogmatic.

A British naval officer in his fifties, Muirhead-Gould suffered from a heart condition. He had been posted to the Royal Australian Navy as Commodore-in-Charge of coastal defences of New South Wales, including Sydney Harbour, but seemingly resented being in Sydney because he had been forced to accept a posting that was unfamiliar to him. He was considered by his subordinates to be a bombastic officer, too concerned with protocol and, further, he was unpopular because he was British. His staff considered him gruff and uncommunicative. Among those who survived the war, the most charitable estimate of him was that he was a conscientious Royal Navy officer.

It should be remembered that anti-British sentiment in Australia was at its height after the fall of Singapore, the widespread belief being that Britain had sold Australia short in defence terms. Muirhead-Gould's junior officers, in longstanding larrikin tradition, would often call him "Gold", and out of hearing range they would call him "Manurehead". There is little published information about Muirhead-Gould, but shortly before the Sydney Harbour attack, he gave a rare newspaper interview:

> They told me I strained my damned heart during the First World War. I had the choice of going to Trincomalee or Sydney and I plumped for Trincomalee, not because I disliked Sydney but because I thought I would have more chance at Ceylon of getting to sea again. The damned doctor told me that the country was so hilly in Ceylon that I would delay the recovery of my heart. Here now I have to climb a hundred bloody feet twice a day from the waterfront to my front door.

Muirhead-Gould's attitude towards the CPBs and NAPs was one of disdain. He regarded the men who manned them as "weekend sailors" who had entered the service only for the duration of the war and who lacked professionalism and traditionalism. For their part, the personnel of these motor boats considered they were unselfishly contributing to the war effort.

The first rumblings of ill feeling began in August 1941, when Mr P. E. Scrivener was appointed Squadron Commander of the NAP. This appointment was not favoured by Muirhead-Gould's staff officers.

Scrivener made it his business, at first, to get on well with the Commodore, as he was then ranked, and cultivated a close friendship. It was Scrivener who first devised the idea of the NAP. With the help of Muirhead-Gould, Scrivener's scheme to establish an auxiliary patrol boat flotilla using volunteer reserves was submitted to the Australian Naval Board for consideration. In June 1941, the Minister for the Navy agreed in principle to its conception and a month later approval was given to the formation of the NAP. Muirhead-Gould appointed Scrivener as the New South Wales State Skipper.

By August, a rift began to appear in the relationship between Muirhead-Gould and Scrivener when points of divergence emerged about the running of the NAP. At separate interviews on 25 August 1941, Muirhead-Gould made the following statements to a newspaper:

> Mr Scrivener is the only man appointed to the Naval Auxiliary Patrol and staff will be chosen by myself. Mr Scrivener's instructions are to confine his activities to recruiting for the present…

And…

> I propose to retain a very close interest in the NAP and take a personal hand in its direction.

In reply, Scrivener made the following comments:

> The Commodore's function will be to instruct me that he requires certain jobs. It will be my responsibility to provide them, but the whole of the domestic matters of the NAP will be directed and managed by myself.

The Australian Naval Board drafted the requirements and conditions of service for the NAP on 2 October and directed that the state skippers were responsible to the district

Naval Officer for the training and discipline of NAP personnel. It was made clear, however, that the navy accepted no obligation to bear the cost or responsibility for the formation of the NAP, or to render any compensation for any vessel damaged or destroyed as a result of its service. The Naval Board did undertake to alter the shape and design of these vessels at their own discretion, eventually arming some of them with small, hand-held depth charges and Vickers machine guns.

With the formation of the NAP, personnel from the Voluntary Coastal Patrol (VCP) and the National Emergency Service Yachtsmen Auxiliary (NESYA) flocked to enroll. Within 10 days, over 450 men were accepted and 125 boats offered for service. By January 1942, the New South Wales Squadron consisted of 332 vessels with a maintenance expenditure of over 35,000 pounds a year, which was met by the owners. Twelve of these vessels were assigned to Sydney Harbour.

When Japan attacked Pearl Harbor, the threat of a similar attack on Sydney Harbour was considered a likelihood and an anti-submarine boom net across the harbour entrance was suggested by the British Admiralty. The Admiralty wanted a good naval base with adequate facilities in case a part of Britain's Eastern Fleet had to be transferred to Sydney. They stipulated the need for facilities to cope with the rapid repair for all classes of vessels, particularly battleships. Replying to the Admiralty's demands, the Australian Naval Board sent the following report to London at the end of December 1941:

> Sydney suitable for a main base when anti-submarine defences completed. In case of necessity, Sydney suitable for heavy ships on completion of temporary anti-submarine defences, early March.

The boom net was designed in January 1942, and pile driving for "dolphins" (that is, pylons to support the net) started the same month. The location of the net was between George's Heights on Middle Head and Green Point, the narrowest point of the inner harbour entrance.

Although completion and operation of the boom net was scheduled for early March 1942, it was not completed until July, due partially to industrial unrest.

The boom consisted of a single line of steel mesh net, supported between two dolphins. The boom gates were to be of a similar mesh, supported by barrels, and it was envisaged that the ferry steamer *Kuramia* would be converted for use as the gate vessel.

On the night of the attack, however, the boom net was still under construction. The centre position had been completed, but there were still gaps of 960 feet at the western end and 900 feet at the eastern end. Work was proceeding to the final stages with the construction of the gates. Work had stopped for the day and two Maritime Services watchmen, James Cargill and William Nangle, remained in charge of the barges during the night to prevent unauthorised persons interfering with the equipment and to safeguard it in the event of bad weather.

In addition to the incomplete boom net, eight indicator loops (cables to detect metal) were placed across the floor of the inner and outer harbour entrances to warn of enemy submarines attempting to enter the harbour. The technology at the time was considered very new, and few personnel were trained in its operation. These loops recorded a stylograph signature in a similar manner to an electrocardiograph that monitors heart beats and prints them on a continuous roll of paper.

The loops across the harbour bottom consisted of thick insulated electrical cable which, when plugged into the electricity grid, generated their own magnetic field. The magnetic properties of either a submerged or surface vessel would alter or disrupt the magnetic field around the cable, initiating a signature at the Indicator Loop Station, located on South Head. If the signature could not be visually identified, then the alarm could be raised. The control room was manned by one officer and two naval ratings 24-hours a day. In the event that the Loop Station was unable to verify any signature, the duty officer had a direct telephone link to the Garden Island Operations Room from where a general alarm could be raised.

The control and maintenance of the Indicator Loop Station came under the administration of Acting-Captain H. M. Newcombe, a Royal Navy officer who had been sent from England in late 1938 to start the little known anti-submarine shore establishment located at Rushcutters Bay. On the night of 31 May 1942, two of the six outer indicator loops across the heads were not functioning, but both inner loops – one at 15 fathoms and the other at 7 fathoms – were operational. Over previous days, the underwater cables were being tested and were not all permanently manned by operators. Newcombe later recalled that on the night of the raid, conditions were extremely good for recording "perturbations", and distinct readings were registered on one of the inner loops.

Adjacent to the Indicator Loop Station was the Port War Signal Station, which was manned by Lieutenant Commander C. J. W. Woods, a reserve officer. It was the responsibility of the duty officer to keep Rear-Admiral Muirhead-Gould informed of the movements of all ships of war, auxiliary vessels, suspicious craft and aircraft, whether Allied, neutral or hostile; to communicate intelligence, however obtained; and to act as a means of communication between Muirhead-Gould and ships at sea, including transmitting his orders and general information. According to Muirhead-Gould's official report to the Minister for the Navy, on the night of 31 May the radio transmitter at the Port War Signal Station was out of action.

The harbour was also lit by a network of navigation lights which assisted shipping to negotiate the harbour channels. Because of the high density of shipping movements in Sydney Harbour, these lights remained permanently switched on at night – despite a Naval Board directive that they be extinguished in defended ports, but capable of being switched on for short periods when ordered.

At Farm Cove, Lieutenant Reginald Andrew spent the first part of the evening familiarising himself with his new command and studied the recognition light signals used at night for identification purposes. He had joined *HMAS Sea Mist* only two days earlier after completing six weeks' training at Flinders naval base in Victoria.

Andrew was descended from eight generations of sailing ship captains. Early in the war he learned of the exploits of the torpedo patrol boats in the North Sea, the Atlantic and the Mediterranean. He enlisted in the Royal Australian Navy Voluntary Reserves (RANVR), hoping that he might be transferred to England to join these boats. But having finished his training, he was ordered to Sydney where he was given command of the

Channel patrol boat *HMAS Sea Mist*.

Lieutenant Reginald T. Andrew, commanding officer of channel patrol boat *HMAS Sea Mist*.

channel patrol boat, *HMAS Sea Mist*, assigned to the harbour's defences. On 31 May, five of his crew had gone ashore for the evening, leaving only the coxswain, motor mechanic and signalman aboard in the event that *Sea Mist* was called out unexpectedly.

Andrew decided to retire early so he would be fresh to commence his assigned patrol the next morning, but was woken shortly before 11:00 pm by the sound of gunfire on the harbour and went up on deck to investigate. After the gunfire died down, he thought it was another naval exercise and returned to bed. He was abruptly awoken again at 3:10 am the following morning by an excited Lieutenant in a speedboat shouting: "I think you'd better get underway, there're subs in the harbour." ●

CHAPTER NINE
THE ATTACK COMMENCES

CHAPTER NINE

THE ATTACK COMMENCES

Luck was certainly on the side of the defenders, and was undeserved in the early stages when inactivity and indecision were manifested.

Royal Australian Navy, 1942-1945,
G. Hermon Gill.

Outside the harbour, the Third Submarine Company manoeuvred towards the harbour entrance as darkness was enveloping the sea. The majestic cliffs of North Head guarding the harbour approaches, and the beams at Hornby and Macquarie Lights on South Head, were clearly visible. Beyond the entrance the navigation light at Dobroyd Point was visible, and Middle Head was outlined in the failing light.

Lieutenant Matsuo joined Commander Ageta in the control room of I-22 and joked with the crew. Earlier in the day he had shaved his head in preparation for his mission, and the crew took delight in his new appearance. Ageta invited Matsuo to look through the periscope. The harbour was approximately one nautical mile wide and six miles long, with scores of complicated channels. Water depths varied considerably and the winding waterways would make the speedy passage of the midget submarines difficult.

Ageta considered Matsuo to be a capable midget submarine commander with quite a task ahead of him. After the Pearl Harbor operation, he realised that the chances of survival for Matsuo and his crewman, Tsuzuku, were remote. He also realised the danger to which I-22 was exposed in approaching so close to the harbour, and moved out to sea to make the final preparations for launching the midget submarine.

Petty Officer Tsuzuku carried out the final checks on the craft and placed bottles of mineral water, whisky and concentrated food in the control room. The food consisted of soda biscuits, dried fish, pickled plums, peas, soft chocolate and special caramels, and had a combined nutritional value of one meal – all that was required for their mission. Matsuo examined the Admiralty chart and photographs of Sydney Harbour that had been taken from Australian periodicals. The Admiralty charts were marked in Japanese characters, "Confidential – General Staff February 1942".

Matsuo collected his operational orders including the callsign list of the submarine force and a checklist of operational abbreviations for use between the craft when in close proximity to the enemy. The abbreviations were necessary because the midget submarines could risk being on the surface for only short periods. From the reconnaissance report,

Matsuo noted the boom net and the two incomplete openings, the western opening the larger of the two. All these items he carefully placed in the small control room of the craft.

According to Japanese ritual, Matsuo and Tsuzuku changed into fresh uniforms sprayed with perfume. As a final gesture to the crew of I-22, Matsuo addressed them over the piping (boat's address) system and thanked them for assisting him during the voyage south. Clutching a new ceremonial sword inscribed with his name, given to him by his father at their last meeting in Kure, Matsuo entered the craft through the "traffic sheath" and carefully hung the sword in the control room. Having been preceded by his crewman, Matsuo closed the hatch sealing them from the parent submarine. Once again, I-22 headed towards the harbour where, approximately seven miles east of the entrance, he launched the midget submarine. Shortly after sunset, at 5:21 pm, Matsuo started his engines and sped away from I-22.

Similar procedures were carried out in I-27 and I-24 with the midget submarines launched at 5:28 pm and 5:40 pm, respectively. In the meantime, I-29 and I-21, now without their seaplanes, took up positions north and south of the harbour entrance so they would be in a position to observe enemy shipping movements. Captain Sasaki recorded that everything was normal and that the harbour was bathed in reflections from the foreshore lights.

The submarine carriers monitored the progress of the midget submarines on hydrophones until their drones could no longer be heard. Once they had faded, the carrier submarines proceeded to the recovery point off Port Hacking, 20 miles south of Sydney Harbour, to wait for the midgets' return. While Captain Sasaki's initial attack order indicated the midget recovery point was off First Point, Broken Bay, north of Sydney, this was later changed to Port Hacking because there were no known battery defences along the southern coastline.

From a working chart recovered from Matsuo's craft after the raid, four minutes after slipping away from I-22, he fixed his first position at 260 degrees from Outer South Head Light, 7.2 miles. Later fixes put the midget submarine 253 degrees 4.1 miles, 247 degrees 3.6 miles, and 260 degrees 1.7 miles from Outer South Head Light, but no times were recorded.

Another well-known mariner had sailed exactly the same route as Matsuo 172 years earlier. Captain James Cook sailed *HMS Endeavour* from Botany Bay on 16 May 1770. He headed north and came across a harbour, where he took his bearings on the same points of land as Matsuo. Cook wrote the following account from his circumnavigation of the world in 1773:

> We set sail from Botany Bay with a light breeze from the north-west. Soon after coming to southwards, we steered along the shore north-north-west and at noon our latitude by observation was 33 degrees 50 minutes south. At this time we were between two and three miles distance from the land and abreast of a bay or harbour which I called Port Jackson.

The position Cook described was the same as Matsuo's last plotted position, which placed him 33 degrees 50 minutes south, between two and three miles distance from the land at North Head. Ironically, Matsuo was using a chart originally surveyed by James Cook.

While the remainder of the submarine force had departed for the recovery area, Sasaki remained off the harbour entrance to watch the enemy's initial reaction. At 4:00 am the following morning, he telegraphed Vice-Admiral Daigo that visibility was good and that the lighthouses at the entrance to the harbour were on. He reported that about the time of the midgets' entrance into the harbour, at approximately 7:00 pm, there were no signs of abnormalities, but at 8:00 pm he observed searchlights moving uncontrolled within the harbour. According to Sasaki, the searchlights continued to strobe the harbour for 30 minutes and judging from this reaction he presumed the midget submarine attack had commenced but did not know the results.

Sasaki's report of searchlights moving about the harbour at random was in fact army batteries along the cliff tops testing their searchlights, as was the practice when changing the duty watch.

Lieutenant Chuma and Petty Officer Ohmori were the first to enter the harbour. At 7:55 pm, a crossing was recorded at the Indicator Loop Station on South Head, which was identified as the Manly ferry. This was followed four minutes later by another signature on the inner loop, also a ferry. Two minutes later, at 8:01 pm, a distinct but smaller signature was recorded but its significance went unreported.

Chuma's craft was discovered by Maritime Services night watchman, James Cargill, a fiery, red-headed Scotsman and an alert man. Cargill had seen service in the Merchant Navy as well as the Australian Army, and was aware of the necessity for vigilance while the boom gates were being constructed. His report of the incident is now held in the Maritime Services Board archives and is contained in a letter addressed to Rear-Admiral Muirhead-Gould, marked secret and dated 3 June 1942.

> At about 8:15 pm I noticed something unusual between the nets and the west channel pile light. I then called my mate, W. Nangle, and asked him what he thought it was. We thought at first it was a fishing launch with no lights and knowing that that was not allowed, I went in the rowing boat to investigate. The obstacle was about 50 yards away. I went right up alongside and found it was a steel construction about four to five feet above the water, which looked like two large cylinders with iron guards around them. I went straight away to No 14 patrol boat [sic], which I saw about 80 or 100 yards away, and reported the result of my investigations to the officer in charge of the boat. He asked me what I thought it was and I told him that I thought it was a submarine or a mine and I suggested to him that he should come and investigate. He said that he could not go any closer. I then suggested he send a man with me and I would take him to it in the rowing boat. I then rowed almost alongside the obstacle, which had by this time come higher out of the water, and he said it was a submarine and asked me to put him back aboard the patrol boat as quickly as possible, which I did. The officer in charge of the patrol boat took my name and told me I could go back to my job. It would then be about 10:30 pm.

In an interview with the author in 1982, Cargill said the submarine commander may have seen him moving about in his boat. Earlier in the evening he had noticed a derrick swinging dangerously on the crane barge at the western end of the net and sculled his punt to the barge to secure the loose guys attached to the derrick before sculling back. Forty years after the attack, I asked him to recount his memory:

8.00pm No.12 STUD 28 EMF   INNER 1   31-5-42   **8.00pm**

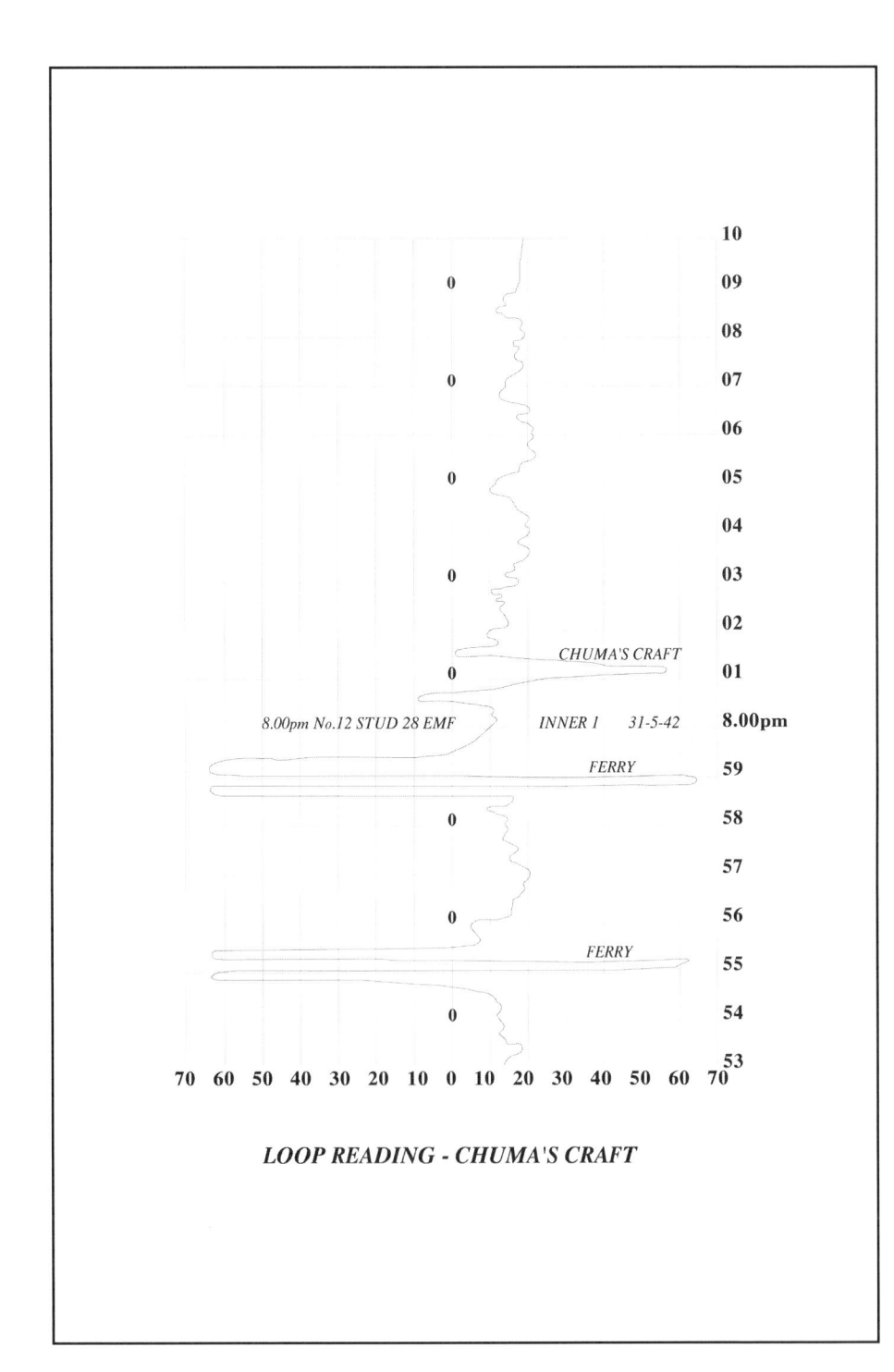

CHUMA'S CRAFT

FERRY

FERRY

LOOP READING - CHUMA'S CRAFT

He tried getting through the gate on the bottom and hit the pile light inside the channel. He must have gone astern as he got one of the big rings of the net around his propeller. He struggled a long time then blew the submarine up. The metal went 40 feet aloft. How lucky we were. The pile light saved Sydney.

Cargill recounted that all inward shipping went down the Eastern Channel, including ferry boats, while the deeper Western Channel was used for outward shipping and large draught vessels. According to Cargill, the submarine was caught inside the boom net defences near the West Gate when it became entangled.

It's plausible Chuma planned to sink a large outward bound vessel in the western channel, before misfortune overtook the midget submarine. The priorities of the midget submarine commanders were to carry out a successful attack, then to protect the crews of the mother submarines. Sealing the harbour's major shipping channel would allow the midget submarines to return to their parent submarines in relative safety.

If this was Chuma's plan, it could have resulted in a serious disruption to Allied naval and merchant shipping in the south-west Pacific. Dockyard facilities within the harbour may have been inaccessible and rendered useless for a considerable length of time. Damaged naval and merchant shipping would have had to be diverted to Simonstown, South Africa, the nearest dockyard large enough to cope with such vessels.

It's also possible Chuma's craft passed through the West Gate and simply hit the pile light before becoming entangled in the boom net. Despite the modifications to the midget submarines following the Pearl Harbor attack, their crews still had difficulty controlling them.

The official account of Chuma's discovery varies from Cargill's account. According to Rear-Admiral Muirhead-Gould's preliminary report of the attack on Sydney Harbour, he wrote that the watchman "took some time to collect a friend and to communicate this vital information to the channel patrol boat on patrol". In his official report of 16 July, he records that *HMAS Yarroma* was not informed by Cargill of the object until 9:30 pm, but the channel patrol boat would not approach fearing the object was a magnetic mine. Cargill also confuses *Yarooma* for *Lolita*, "No 14 patrol boat" which he saw about 80 or 100 yards away.

According to the chronological narrative, *Yarroma* (No. 51 patrol boat), reported a "suspicious object in net" to the Garden Island operations room at 9:52 pm and was told to close and give a full description. At 10:10 pm, *Yarroma* reported the "object was metal with serrated edge on top, moving with the swell." *Yarroma* was ordered to give a fuller description and at 10:20 pm a stoker from *Yarroma* accompanied Cargill the short distance back to the object caught in the net, more than two hours after the initial discovery. At 10.30, *Yarroma* reported: "Object is submarine. Request permission to open fire." Five minutes later, *Yarroma* reported the submarine had exploded.

A more emboldened Cargill expounded on the events of that night in interviews with the *Sydney Morning Herald* in 1945 and, again, in 1957. From these interviews it can be seen that a good deal more occurred during this crucial period than Muirhead-Gould mentioned in his report.

Channel patrol boat, *HMAS Lolita*. Note the Vickers .303 machine gun forward and depth charge canisters aft.

Channel patrol boat, *HMAS Yarroma*. Note the .303-inch Vickers machine gun aft and depth charge canisters on the stern.

120. JAPANESE SUBMARINE RAIDERS 1942 *A Maritime Mystery*

In newspaper accounts, Cargill suggested that the patrol boat should follow him in his boat to investigate, and he sculled alone towards the object. He was more than surprised to find that *Yarroma* had picked up anchor and made her way towards a nearby pylon from where it examined the mysterious object from a distance with a searchlight. He told Cargill he thought it looked like naval wreckage, but Cargill replied it was not. Cargill reported the object was thrashing backwards and forwards, attempting to pull clear of the net and he advised *Yarroma's* commander that he "had better hurry up or we will have no navy left". Sub-Lieutenant Eyres advised Cargill that it would be dangerous to go any closer, because there were depth charge canisters on his deck and he feared that the object may be a magnetic mine. Muirhead-Gould later wrote that the actions of *Yarroma* were "deplorable and inexplicable".

At 9:52 pm, more than an hour and a half after Cargill first discovered the object, and over an hour after he reported his findings, Eyres notified the Operations Room at Garden Island of a "suspicious object in the net". *Yarroma* was ordered to "close and give a full description". Able-Seaman Pat Doyle on *Yarroma* recounted many years after the war that the channel patrol boat was unable to raise the Port War Signal Station or the Garden Island Operations Room by radio for some time after Cargill's initial report.

At 10:20 pm, *Yarroma* signalled *HMAS Lolita* by Aldis lamp to "come over". Under the command of Warrant Officer Herbert S. Anderson, *Lolita* was patrolling the East Gate opening, unaware of the activity at the western end of the boom net. Anderson immediately closed *Yarroma* and was informed of the suspicious object caught in the net and ordered to investigate. Anderson manoeuvred *Lolita* to within 5 yards of the object, with her stern facing the submarine so as to cover it with the patrol boat's machine gun.

Anderson described the "baby submarine" as being about three feet out of the water with the periscope clearly visible. The stern appeared entirely submerged and it was struggling to extricate itself from the net. Unlike Eyres, Anderson realised the urgent necessity for action and ordered his crew to "standby depth charges".

The coxswain of *Lolita*, Able-Seaman James Nelson, vividly recalled the anxious moments leading up to the attack. In an interview with the author he related how the channel patrol boat first examined the object with the Aldis lamp, after which both he and Able-Seaman James Crowe immediately identified it as a "baby submarine". The periscope was rotating and the beam of their searchlight reflected from the periscope glass. At that time the Dutch submarine *K-9*, which had a very similar sort of net cutter on the bow, had been working with the Australian navy. Both Nelson and Crowe thought it might have been the *K-9* returning to harbour, but the size of the submarine caught in the net disturbed them. Nelson recalled that the decision to attack was made by Anderson because there was every chance the submarine would break free of the net. Anderson ordered Nelson to send a short visual message to the Port War Signal Station – "Have sighted a submarine. Intend to attack."

Lolita carried out two depth charge attacks, but the charges failed to detonate because the water depth was too shallow. When the first charge failed to detonate, Nelson and Crowe rigged three elliptical floats to a second charge, which they hoped would delay its descent in the water, enough to cause the charge to prematurely detonate. The charge could only be detonated by a combination of depth and pressure and they reasoned that

Warrant Officer Herbert S. Anderson, commanding officer of channel patrol boat *HMAS Lolita*.

Courtesy Harold F. Anderso

Able-Seaman James Nelson, coxswain aboard *HMAS Lolita*.

Courtesy James Nelson

by delaying the descent, enough water might enter the pressure chamber to trigger the detonator. However, this charge also failed to explode. Nelson and Crowe rigged a third charge in a similar manner but as *Lolita* was making her run, the submarine exploded. The blast was so big, loud and forceful that it lifted the patrol boat out of the water before she heeled violently over to port. Nelson said later that *Lolita* was fortunate not to get blown to pieces along with the submarine.

When a large oil patch appeared on the surface, it left no doubt in Anderson's mind that the submarine was destroyed. In his report, he recorded that the midget submarine exploded at 10:35 pm. After informing Eyres of what had happened, Anderson resumed his patrol at the East Gate opening while awaiting instructions; but none came.

NAP flotilla leader, L. H. Winkworth, in *Lauriana*, was at the harbour entrance when Chuma's craft self-destructed. He recorded in the vessel's running log that he saw an orange-coloured flash roar 40-foot above the sea, followed by a delayed explosion which sounded to him like a depth charge. Immediately afterwards, searchlight beams from concealed crevices at George's Heights and rock faces near Lady Bay converged on the boom net area. Visibility at this time was fair, although the night sky was still cloudy. Winkworth watched the searchlights and the channel patrol boats scurrying along the boom net and waited for instructions from the Port War Signal Station; but none came.

When the submarine exploded, the anti-submarine vessel, *HMAS Yandra*, also on patrol at the harbour entrance, sped towards the scene of the explosion to investigate, while *Lauriana* waited off Inner North Head and *Allura* patrolled off South Reef. *Yarrawonga* had gone off duty earlier for an hour's rest and Winkworth ordered the auxiliary vessel back on patrol.

Before the explosion, Muirhead-Gould had been dining with officers from *USS Chicago* at his official residence in Elizabeth Bay. Following *Yarroma's* initial report of a suspicious object in the net, he was unconcerned, aware that seaweed and other debris had clogged the net over previous days. He took no immediate action and, instead, decided to wait for *Yarroma's* complete report. Following *Yarroma's* more alarming report of a metal object with serrated edge on top, he suggested to Captain Bode that he should return to his ship and proceed to sea with *Perkins*. At 10:27 pm, he issued a general alarm for all ships to "take anti-submarine precautions" and closed the port to outward shipping. Eight minutes later, the midget submarine exploded.

Muirhead-Gould had once been reported saying that he hoped the defences of Sydney Harbour would not have to be put to the test. His forebodings were now realised when he issued a general alarm:

> Presence of enemy submarine at boom gate is suspected. Ships are to take action against attack.

The explosion resounded through the harbour suburbs, shattering the stillness of the night. With the explosion, Sydney had received its first practical confirmation of the close proximity of the enemy. But getting the alarm out was another thing. Muirhead-Gould writes in his report of the great congestion in signal traffic through the Port War Signal Station overlooking the harbour approaches.

It is evident that Port War Signal Station is not capable of, and was never intended to cope with, such a situation. It was impossible for the Operations Room at Garden Island to communicate with these boats direct, and the only alternative method was by boat. In order to ascertain exactly what was happening, I had myself to go down to the boom and interview officers on the spot and return with the information to Garden Island.

Muirhead-Gould highlighted that channel patrol boats and naval auxiliary patrol boats were not fitted with R/T transmitters, and they had no signalmen, which complicated visual communications. He also reported that "the R/T set at Port War Signal Station was out of action at the time of the incident". As a result, the general alarm had to be conveyed by word-of-mouth by the duty staff officer at Garden Island from a boat scurrying around the harbour to alert the defences. Each vessel had to be informed individually, and many of those vessels that did have R/T transmitters had switched their sets off for the night. Some vessels were unaware of the alarm until the following morning.

Meanwhile, a second submarine had penetrated the harbour defences, crossing the inner indicator loop at 9:48 pm and, as yet, remained undetected. ●

Lolita, she was cruising round just by the Eastern Gate,
When a message flashed from *Yarroma* read Come immediate.
Lolita dashes over there at a terrific rate—
There's something in the bloody net,
Will you please investigate?

Perhaps it's just acoustic mine or just a baby sub,
But whate'er it turns out to be I'm sure it's not a pub.
We'll just go in and have a look – we'll be the bloody mug.
And if it really is a mine there is no need to relate
That we will surely go aloft to see the pearly gate.

Then as we backed towards the net we gave our eyes a rub,
There laying in the net so nice was a darling little sub.
Said the sub commander full of fun,
I really think my time has come,
I think that I have been sold a pup,
That CPB will blow me up.

I'll not stop here while he has fun,
I'll beat *Lolita* to the gun.
The Jap he carried out his plot
And bloody near *Lolita* got.
The boys they cursed so full of wrath,
The dirty bastards seen us off.

Warrant Officer H. S. Anderson, June 1942

CHAPTER TEN
SYDNEY'S WILDEST NIGHT

CHAPTER TEN

SYDNEY'S WILDEST NIGHT

The story that the only casualty inflicted by *Chicago's* gunfire was a lion in the famous Sydney Zoo, and that Captain Bode was requested to provide a new one out of lend-lease is the invention of an Australian humorist.

Rear-Admiral Samuel Eliot Morison, USN,
Pulitzer prize winning author.

At 9:48 pm, Lieutenant Katsuhisa Ban and Petty Officer Mamoru Ashibe, in midget I-24, crossed the 7 fathom inner loop at the harbour entrance. As with Chuma's craft, a signature was recorded at the Loop Station but went unreported.

Rear-Admiral Muirhead-Gould's records in his official report that: "There was a regrettable failure on the part of the Loop Station watchkeepers to identify the unusual crossings at 8:01 pm and 9:48 pm. Crossings at these times were noticed by watchkeepers but disregarded."

The following morning, when the loop signatures were examined by Muirhead-Gould, he reported that the crossing at 9:48 pm was caused by a tug and barge crossing the inner loop area and, therefore, the Loop Station "fully justified itself, though, naturally I must deplore the fact that the human element failed".

Acting-Captain H. M. Newcombe, responsible for the Loop Station, recounted after the war that personnel were lacking in concentration caused by the long hours they were forced to spend looking at the loop equipment that constantly fluctuated with the frequent shipping movements.

After crossing the inner loop, Ban and Ashibe successfully made their way down the harbour, undetected, towards Man-of-War Anchorage, while Lieutenant Matsuo and Petty Officer Tsuzuku remained lurking at the harbour entrance. At 10:52 pm, *HMAS Lauriana*, one of four naval auxiliary boats patrolling the harbour entrance, noticed a "whip" or "flurry" on the water ahead. Flotilla Leader, L. H. Winkworth thought it may have been a paravane wire running across troughs of waves. A few minutes earlier he had observed a blackened vessel coming into the harbour and the silhouette was similar to a minesweeper. Winkworth instructed Skipper Harold Arnott and the lookout on the bridge to watch for the wire and minesweeper in case it changed course, and he ran forward to the searchlight on the bow. Winkworth recorded the object "seemed to be on

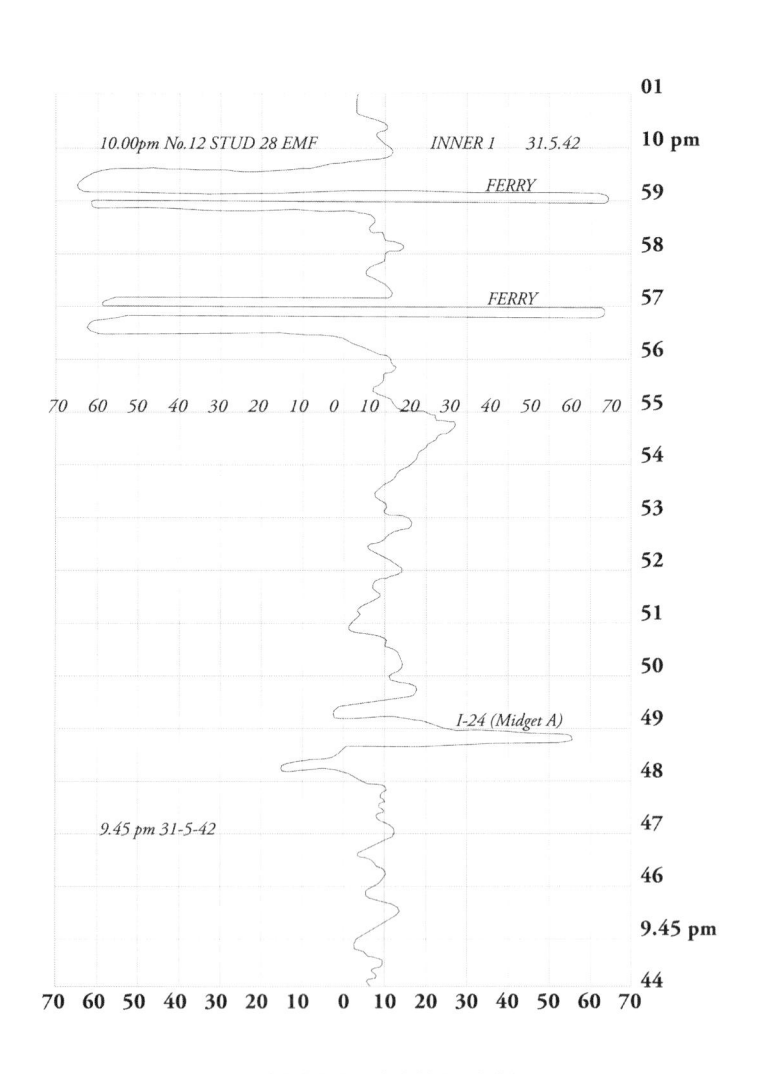

*SCHEMATIC INDICATOR LOOP
SIGNATURES*

130. JAPANESE SUBMARINE RAIDERS 1942 *A Maritime Mystery*

the same course, but heading towards the eastern channel".

In his report of the incident, Winkworth recorded that the searchlight picked up an object 60 to 80 feet away, about two points on the port bow. The searchlight operator switched the light off momentarily then on again and the conning tower was clearly seen. The submarine appeared to be almost stationary as the seas washed over the conning tower. The searchlight remained on the submarine as *Lauriana's* speed carried her past. When the angle made it impossible, the operator turned the searchlight towards the Port War Signal Station to raise the alarm, but he failed to illicit a response.

> Immediately on sighting the sub, I called to the skipper "sub" and flashed "L's" and "A's" to Port Waugh [Port War Signal Station] and the direction of channel boats at the boom net... Skipper meanwhile had made the turn to starboard, and came back over the ground, but our searchlight did not pick up any other sign of the sub. Mr Kent [bridge lookout] states that the sub submerged immediately our searchlight was flashed on the conning tower on the second occasion. No replies were received from our signals, but concluded that our signals must have been noticed.

Winkworth recorded that he was at a loss to understand why the Port War Signal Station and the Army battery near Hornby Light did not pick up *Lauriana's* visual signals.

> Had we had Verey lights or rockets we could have immediately illuminated the area for the batteries to open fire when we first sighted the sub, and had we had our promised depth charges, we could have certainly sent the sub to the bottom, or rammed him had we been given an alert earlier in the evening. When coming up on the sub, we were not sure whether it was a wire from a paravane which we were approaching, or something flapping on the top of the water. The sub's course was apparently towards the eastern channel, and on our approach he slackened speed and submerged. One of our crew states that he was moving out again when he went below [the surface].

Matsuo's craft was not seen again until 10:54 pm when it was sighted 400 yards ahead of the anti-submarine vessel, *HMAS Yandra*, and steering the same course at five to six knots. Three cables [one cable equals one-tenth of a nautical mile] from Hornby Light at Inner South Head, Matsuo altered course to port to make another attempt to proceed down the eastern channel. *Yandra* altered course to intercept in an attempt to ram the submarine because of "insufficient freedom of action to use full speed in order to carry out a depth charge attack", limited by the number of other surface craft in the vicinity.

At 10.58, the submarine appeared to submerge a little and was hidden from the bridge by *Yandra's* bow. The ship's commanding officer, Lieutenant J. A. Taplin, felt a slight impact on the bridge and the submarine was seen to break the surface on the starboard side aft, alongside the hull. As *Yandra* continued on course, the submarine was seen to list to starboard about 15 degrees with the bow out of the water at about the same angle. It was then seen to submerge while turning to starboard when about 100 yards astern of *Yandra*.

At 11:03 pm *Yandra* again sighted a conning tower 600 yards away. Taplin altered course to bring the submarine on an ahead bearing. *Yandra's* report of the incident records

HMAS Yandra's plotted tracks during the midget submarine mellee at the harbour entrance.

Starboard view of the cargo vessel *HMAS Yandra* before being taken up by the RAN for service as an an auxiliary anti-submarine vessel.

the "submarine was not seen by the gun's crew at this range, and when eventually it was seen, the gun would not depress sufficiently to fire".

One minute later *Yandra* obtained an anti-submarine ASDIC contact 400 yards away. The anti-submarine vessel went to maximum speed and commenced her run in to attack. Six depth charges were set to detonate at 100 feet. Two minutes later, the submarine was seen to submerge but the ASDIC equipment returned instant echoes at a range of 150 yards. At 11:07 pm, *Yandra* fired a pattern of six depth charges. The force of the explosions resulted in the instantaneous failure of *Yandra's* steering gear, ASDIC equipment, degaussing gear, and phone communications aft where the switchboard had fractured. Using hand steering gear from aft, *Yandra* steered to seaward until the primary steering gear and ASDIC equipment had been restored.

The force of the depth charge explosions lifted the nearby 60-ton *Lauriana* clear out of the water. Winkworth later recounted that they actually felt the launch airborne for a moment before landing with a tremendous thud.

At 11.32, *Yandra* re-entered harbour and carried out an anti-submarine sweep in the vicinity of her depth charge attack, but there were no further sightings of the midget submarine. It was presumed that *Yandra's* depth charge attack had been successful. Matsuo's craft was not seen again until 5:00 am the next morning.

According to records obtained after the war, the midget submarines had a wide turning circle. In the event of an attack, their commanders were expected to flood the forward ballast tank and submerge to at least 200 feet or deeper, and then to proceed on a course at right angles to its previous course. Ordinarily, the forward ballast tank was flooded to stabilise the craft after the torpedoes had been fired, but in the frantic moments after his discovery at the harbour entrance, it seems possible the submarine may have collided with the sea bottom during its rapid descent, damaging the craft's nose guard. It seems more than likely Matsuo and Tsuzuki waited patiently on the seabed before making their belated entry into the harbour at 3:01 am the next morning.

At the same time as Matsuo's craft was first detected at the harbour entrance by *Lauriana*, Lieutenant Ban's craft was sighted near Man-of-War Anchorage. At 10:52 pm, Ensign B. Simonds aboard *Chicago* sighted a conning tower "close aboard to starboard" and emptied his .45 automatic weapon at the conning tower. When about 500 yards off the starboard bow, lookouts on the heavy cruiser illuminated the conning tower with searchlights, and Lieutenant-Commander H. J. Mecklenberg, the senior officer aboard, ordered the ship to General Quarters. Guns from *Chicago* and the Australian corvette, HMAS *Whyalla*, were trained on the object. However, the order to open fire from *Whyalla* was not given for fear of hitting the Manly ferry and other small craft in the vicinity. *Chicago* was not so reticent and Mecklenberg gave the order to commence firing.

In an interview with the author in 1982, *Chicago's* Gunnery officer, Lieutenant William Floyd, said the ship's gun crews were already on alert following a reconnaissance of the naval anchorage area by an unidentified aircraft a few days earlier. When he learnt no action had been taken by his anti-aircraft personnel, he "laid down the law".

Naval Auxiliary Patrol (NAP) boat Flotilla Leader, L. H. Winkworth, aboard *HMAS Lauriana*, discovered midget submarine I-22 attempting to enter the harbour at 10:52 pm, but his visual signals to raise the alarm went unnoticed.

Courtesy L. H. Winkworth Estate

I directed that for the next 24 hours, everyone was to remain on their feet, alert and ready to take action immediately. Fortunately, this degree of alertness was attained during the day and the rest of the ensuing evening… The ship received a report that something had crossed the sonic range … This report was relayed by the Officer-of-the-Deck to the officer in sky-control. The sky-control personnel [who operated the searchlights] began searching to see if they could pick up anything in the harbour and some little time later, they saw what they believed to be the conning tower of a submarine.

Lieutenant George Kittredge, a junior-grade gunnery officer, remembers sighting the conning tower aft of *Chicago's* beam, between the heavy cruiser and Bradley's Head. He had the impression the hatch was open with a Japanese officer wearing a white hat looking out with a large pair of binoculars, an image he says haunted him for many years after the war.

On sighting the submarine conning tower, Kittredge jumped into the "pointer seat" of the new rapid fire anti-aircraft gun on the starboard wing of the bridge and commenced firing. About the same time, the two 5" guns starboard side aft began to fire, but they couldn't depress far enough and the shells ricocheted to the other side of the harbour.

When *Chicago* opened fire, pandemonium broke loose on the harbour. Newspaper accounts after the attack reported the Manly ferry had left Circular Quay with 27 passengers aboard when large calibre bullets threw spouts of water high into the air around her. The captain of the ferry said he saw a conning tower directly in front and immediately went hard astern. His passengers, lining the railings, were given a front row seat of the battle with red tracer bullets seemingly hurling straight towards them. The naval firing was so intense that the captain of the ferry reportedly spent a few anxious moments trying to determine the direction of the shells. The passengers thought a naval exercise using blank shells was in progress. Miraculously, no one was injured.

Launchmaster I. J. Warren, employed by Stannard Brothers, was proceeding down harbour in the dockyard boat *Nester* when four red balls of fire appeared to be heading straight toward him. They passed over and disappeared into the water beyond his launch.

On hearing the air raid siren, hotels and restaurants quickly emptied, while citizens wearing pyjamas rushed to parks, headlands and vantage points to get a better view. The main reaction was one of curiosity rather than alarm. Unable to hear or see any aircraft, many thought it was just another military exercise.

Marie Kuliffay lived in a first floor apartment in Pitt Street with her Hungarian refugee husband who had already experienced the terror of air raids in war-torn Europe. She recalled how her husband was asleep when the air raid alarm sounded while she sat reading in an armchair. Her husband leapt out of bed and into his trousers then dragged her out of the building. Outside, the street lights were extinguished and the road filled with people looking up into the sky. No one seemed alarmed and they all calmly proceeded to the Wynyard underground railway station, the nearest bomb shelter, grumbling and cursing the defence authorities for initiating another air raid exercise. Some people had become so used to air raid exercises that they merely rolled over in their beds, annoyed their sleep was interrupted, while others who lived on the harbour foreshores went to higher ground so they could get a better view.

Although most residents did not believe Sydney was being attacked, the defence authorities clearly knew otherwise. At 11:10 pm, the Australian corvette, *HMAS Geelong*, berthed inside *Whyalla* on the north-west corner of Garden Island, fired at a suspicious object in the direction of Bradley's Head. Four minutes later Muirhead-Gould ordered: "All ships to be darkened."

Rear-Admiral Muirhead-Gould records in his report that some comments had been made that ferries were allowed to continue to move about the harbour unrestricted and that he had instructed all naval vessels to display normal lights, in the hope of confusing the enemy. He wrote that he felt the more vessels moving about the harbour, the better the chances of keeping the submarine submerged until daylight; but at 11:14 pm he ordered all ships to be darkened. However, the floodlights at Garden Island remained on for more than an hour before they were eventually extinguished.

At 11:36 pm, Rear-Admiral Muirhead-Gould and his Chief Staff Officer proceeded down the harbour in a speed boat. With the congestion of signal traffic through the Port War Signal Station, and non-existent or inadequate radio communications with harbour defence vessels, he decided to interview officers "on the spot" to ascertain exactly what was happening. He boarded *Lolita* patrolling the East Gate at midnight. An account of Muirhead-Gould's interview with the crew is given by *Lolita's* coxswain, Leading Seaman J. Nelson:

> Rear-Admiral Muirhead-Gould addressed the skipper on boarding *Lolita* with the words, "What are you fellows playing at? What's all this nonsense about a submarine?" He interrogated the skipper and myself about the signal we sent to the Port War Signal Station. Gould seemed rather sceptical and treated the whole matter in a light-hearted manner. He then asked the skipper why he had thought it was a submarine that was caught in the net. He told him that myself and Crowe knew what submarines looked like. Gould asked me what I based my judgment on. I told him that I had sighted submarines when I was in the Mediterranean. I also told him that Able-Seaman Crowe was a World War I submariner who knew about submarines and had identified this one as a small one. Gould then asked the skipper: "Did you see the Japanese captain of the submarine? Did he have a black beard?"… As he proceeded to leave *Lolita*, he quipped: If you see another submarine, see if the captain has a beard as I would be most anxious to know." At that stage the echo of a tremendous explosion and gunfire reached us and all hell broke loose up harbour. The Admiral said: "What the hell was that!" Anderson replied: "If you proceed up harbour, sir, you might find your Japanese captain with a black beard."

Shortly before 12:30 am on 1 June, Lieutenant Ban surfaced again off Bradley's head, and fired two torpedoes at *Chicago*. The first passed narrowly ahead of the heavy cruiser moored at No 2 Buoy in Man-of-War Anchorage, continuing on to pass under the Dutch submarine *K-9* and *HMAS Kuttabul*, permanently moored alongside the wharf on the south-eastern side of Garden island, before detonating against the sea retaining wall. The resulting explosion deflected upwards and outwards, ripping through the wooden barracks vessel as if she were a matchbox. The explosion also splintered the Navy dive boat and severely damaged the Dutch submarine, which had been berthed outside of the former ferry vessel and sheltered to some extent from the main blast. The explosion sank *Kuttabul*, killing 21 Australian and British naval ratings and injuring another 10.

The second torpedo passed astern of *Chicago* and ran aground on Garden Island below the high water mark, but it failed to detonate. The torpedo was discovered later that morning at low tide. Lieutenant-Commander L. E. C. Hinchliffe, the Officer-in-Charge of maintenance on Muirhead-Gould's staff, examined the torpedo and found the warhead completely broken off and the yellow entrails of explosives clearly visible.

Meanwhile, at Man-of-War Anchorage, Captain Bode had returned to *Chicago* shortly before all ships were ordered to be darkened. Lieutenant-Commander Mecklenburg recounted after the war that Bode doubted that a submarine had been seen by the ship's crew and ordered the ship to secure from General Quarters and preparations to get underway. At the same time, USS *Perkins*, which had been screening the heavy cruiser, was ordered back to her buoy in Man-of-War Anchorage by Captain Bode.

> The captain went to his quarters and Lt Varviorsky [Officer-of-the-Deck] and I went up to the ship's bridge and waited. In approximately an hour we spotted two torpedo wakes approaching the ship. The *Perkins* also reported the wakes. Both torpedoes missed *Chicago* and *Perkins*, but destroyed the *Kuttabul*. The captain reached the bridge at the time *Kuttabul* exploded. He immediately commenced operations to get underway and ordered the *Perkins* underway. He sent me to Garden Island in the captain's gig to request instructions from the admiral. The admiral was well aware that there were submarines in the harbour and suggested that I should tell my commanding officer to take US forces to sea. When I returned to the mooring, the *Chicago* was underway and proceeding out of the harbour. The ship stopped and picked up the gig and I went to the bridge and informed the captain of the admiral's orders.

Commander George Chipley, the senior Engineering Department officer on *Chicago*, best described the heavy cruiser's reaction to the midget submarine attack and the urgency of putting to sea. Following a late inspection of the machinery spaces he stopped in the officers' mess for a cup of coffee when he heard shouts on the quarterdeck above him, then pistol shots, followed by the general alarm and disjointed words on the public address system about a submarine. He ran to the main engine control room and soon reported both engine rooms and all four fire rooms manned and ready.

> Ours was a veteran crew, many with years of service on *Chicago*, and all tested by six months war cruising and combat. The senior officer on board was Lt-Commander H. J. Mecklenburg, ship's communications officer … He gave me the order to do what we were doing already, preparing to get underway. Fires were lit under the seven cold boilers and the fire room crews used high rates of oil and air flow to raise steam pressure rapidly. I went up on deck to look at the stacks and I could see large volumes of persistent white smoke pouring from both stacks.

Chipley gives credit to the engineers for saving *Chicago* by producing a mass of visible white smoke that streamed astern of the ship in the moderate south-westerly wind, contrasting vividly with the low, dark clouds, giving the illusion that the heavy cruiser was underway and moving towards the Harbour Bridge.

Photograph of Lieutenant Katsuhisa Ban, *Circa* 1941, commander of midget submarine I-24.

138. JAPANESE SUBMARINE RAIDERS 1942 *A Maritime Mystery*

The Japanese midget sub commander knew that we had sighted him, that we would want to get under way and be prepared to manoeuvre, and the appearance of our smoke in the wind must have deceived him as to our speed, which was zero. The sub aimed its torpedoes as though we were moving and passed under our bow, meaning close ahead and not under the hull.

Muirhead-Gould's chronological narrative records the floodlights on Garden Island, where work was being carried out on a new dry-dock, were extinguished at 12:25 am, around the same time Lieutenant Ban fired his two torpedoes at the silhouetted *Chicago*.

Lieutenant Wilson, the duty officer at Garden Island, gives an account of the difficulties he had in extinguishing the dockyard lights in G. Hermon Gill's official history, *Royal Australian Navy 1942-1945*:

> ... the admiral ordered me to get the dockyard lights out. They were on tall masts lighting the whole area. I could not raise the dockyard by telephone so the admiral sent me off on foot. Paul Revere had a more comfortable trip than I did. I ran at full speed across a rough and rocky dockyard road into the dock and through the work sheds. As I went through I shouted to all and sundry, "Get out fast, the port is under attack". Some delay occurred finding the engineer responsible, and with authority to put the lights out. When I found him, he found it hard to believe, and spoke of the difficulty with hundreds of men in the dock, many below sea-level. I left him in no doubt of the admiral's requirements, and he sent word to evacuate the dock and prepared to turn off the main switches. I ran back and it was only a few minutes after I had reported that the torpedo exploded under *Kuttabul*...

After firing his torpedoes, Lieutenant Ban's midget submarine was not seen again. This period was the height of Sydney's wildest night. ●

CHAPTER ELEVEN
KUTTABUL SINKS

CHAPTER ELEVEN
KUTTABUL SINKS

> Confronted with the evidence of their one night of warfare, Sydneysiders can count themselves lucky the attack wasn't more successful.
>
> This Fabulous Century,
> Peter Luck.

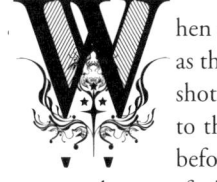

When the torpedo exploded against the sea wall, the impact lifted *Kuttabul* as though she were on top of an enormous wave. A huge column of water shot 60 feet into the air. Wooden pylons buried deep in the seabed next to the barracks ship were torn out and hurled over waterfront buildings before landing on a nearby road. Half *Kuttabul's* wooden helm was blown away, and empty fuel drums and steel boilers on the wharf were tossed about like corks. The explosion broke *Kuttabul* in two pieces and severely damaged the Dutch submarine *K-9* moored outside of *Kuttabul*. On settling into the water, the after section of the barracks ship sank rapidly, having been completely wrecked by the blast. The forward section remained afloat for about half an hour before it, too, sank, after which only the funnel and the roof deck, littered with splintered woodwork and broken glass, were visible. The explosion caused a small fire on the wharf.

Built in Newcastle, *HMAS Kuttabul* belonged to the Sydney Ferries Fleet until the opening of the Sydney Harbour Bridge, when the company was forced to lay off 17 ferries. *Kuttabul* was one of Sydney's largest ferry vessels. After periods of idleness and use as a harbour show boat, she was requisitioned by the Navy on 26 February 1941 to serve as a barracks ship for sailors in transit to other ships and shore establishments. She was permanently berthed on the south-east side of Garden Island. Many ferries were given Aboriginal names beginning with "K" and the name of *Kuttabul* meant "wonderful".

When *Kuttabul* sank, there was pandemonium. Rear-Admiral Muirhead-Gould writes in his report that the force of the explosion extinguished all the lights on Garden Island and the telephones went out of order; but came back into service four minutes later.

It was 12:30 am on a Sunday night and most people were asleep. The explosion was heard for miles around and violently shook thousands of houses and apartments along the waterfront. Picture frames fell from walls, books toppled from shelves and crockery rattled in cupboards. Some people thought there was an earthquake, while others feared an air raid was in progress. Few realised the harbour was under attack by Japanese submarines.

In the congested harbour, ship alarms and air raid sirens echoed continuously around

HMAS Kuttabul was requisitioned by the Navy to serve as a barracks vessel.

HMAS Kuttabul in her former hey-day as a harbour show boat.

the harbour. The sirens caused men to leap out of their hammocks and rush to gun turrets. Orders and curses filled the air and night was turned into day by the many searchlights now sweeping the harbour waters.

Naval ratings from British, New Zealand, Dutch and Australian navies were asleep on the *Kuttabul* and *K-9* when the torpedo exploded. Earlier in the evening, they were awakened by the sound of gunfire on the harbour. Able-Seaman Ernest Higgins, from Lorne, Victoria, recalled the "buzz" was that there was at least one Japanese submarine in the harbour; but most sailors thought the special steel netting strung across the harbour would prevent them from coming further.

> When I was told there were Japanese subs in the harbour I laughed like the others, and said it was bloody stupid; so I went back to my hammock and woke up two days later in a Sydney hospital. I was told later that I was fished out of the water with a lot of other bodies and put on the wharf. An American doctor from *Chicago*, trying to get back to his ship, saw me move and accompanied me in an ambulance to hospital.

When the torpedo exploded, Higgins, along with Stocker Lester Jamieson from Geelong and Able-Seaman Leslie Bland from Western Australia, were quartered together, above the water line. Only Higgins survived the blast. Nineteen-year-old Bland had only recently returned from six months' active duty overseas and was awaiting a transfer to the gunnery school in Victoria when he was killed in Sydney Harbour. He had been orphaned at an early age when his parents were killed in a motor accident, and he had lived with his grandparents before enlisting in the Navy.

Higgins suffered severe spinal, head and facial injuries and remained in hospital for three months before he was able to resume active service; ironically, as sentry on Clarke Island guarding the two midget submarines later recovered from the harbour floor.

Earlier in the night, Stoker Bill Williams had heard gunfire and had gone up on deck to watch the "fireworks" where he overheard someone say there was a sub scare. After the commotion died down he returned to his hammock and went back to sleep.

> I remembered going to sleep in my hammock on the lower deck and next waking up in a Sydney hospital. I had been blown into the water and picked up by Leading Stoker "Lockey" Peterson, a crew member of a passing officer's motorboat. Apparently, they thought I was dead but when the medical officer arrived he realised that I was still alive.

Able-Seaman Charlie Brown had joined *Kuttabul* six weeks earlier to await his posting to the Australian light cruiser, *HMAS Hobart*. On this night he had been rostered for sentry duty and watched the commotion on the harbour before being relieved at midnight. Billeted on the lower deck forward, Brown recalls he was the last on the outboard hammock line, with himself and Able-Seaman Eric Davies, the only Australians among a group of New Zealand sailors. Brown jumped into his hammock at 12:10 am and 20 minutes later was struggling for his life in the water.

Charlie Brown remembers a colossal orange ball of fire before being thrown, head first,

Able-Seaman Charlie Brown joined *HMAS Kuttabul* six weeks earlier to await his posting to the Australian light cruiser, *HMAS Hobart*.

Courtesy C. Brown Estate

Able-Seaman Neil Roberts of Sydney was sleeping aboard *HMAS Kuttabul* on the upper deck when the converted ferry was sunk in Sydney Harbour from a torpedo fired by a Japanese midget submarine.

AWM P02534.001

between a row of wash basins and through the ship's side. Davies was thrown upwards onto the next deck, escaping with only minor cuts to his hands. Charlie Brown was not so lucky. He vividly remembers a huge amount of wooden debris being thrown on him, and struggling to free himself before eventually starting to drift away. He remembers being in the water for a long time for everyone to get down to the wharf area and start searching. Apparently, one of his hands was spotted flailing out through the debris and he was dragged out.

Charlie Brown suffered extensive head injuries and was heavily bruised and scarred from his head to below the waist. In an interview with the author in 1988, he said that the *Kuttabul* disaster was particularly unfortunate for the New Zealand sailors, who had recently been saved from their sinking ship off Western Australia. They were all killed in the blast.

Charlie Brown eventually made it to *HMAS Hobart* and survived a second torpedo while cruising off the Solomon Islands. The *Hobart* wasn't sunk, but he told the author the two incidents didn't do anything for his nerves.

The only New Zealand survivor was Able-Seaman Colin R. Whitfield, who had climbed out of his hammock to go on duty when he heard a terrific explosion.

> Bits of ferry flew around me, and I thought that we were being bombed. Having heard that a table was good protection, I found one and ducked under it, but pieces of ferry kept flying about just the same. I called out to my mate, "Where are you Snowy?", but there was no answer. Then I waited a while and when I went to move I found that my legs were useless. Somehow, I got downstairs and found that the water was up to my knees. The next thing I remember is someone helping me on to a jetty and being carried into the sick bay. There was no panic.

Eighteen-year-old Able-Seaman Neil Roberts was on sentry duty at "Kuttabul Steps" until midnight. When his relief failed to arrive, he went to wake him. In an interview with Animax Films in 2005, he recounted that when his relief finally arrived he offered Roberts his hammock, which was located on the upper deck. He accepted the offer and a few minutes later had dozed off, still fully dressed accept for his shoes and webbing.

When the explosion came, Roberts found himself in water and caught in a stairwell. Swimming underwater, he eventually found the exit and made his way to the surface and climbed the sea wall where he was met by a bewildered rating wanting to know if any of the officers were alive. (There were no officers billeted on the barracks vessel.) Roberts was taken to a Sydney hospital suffering from shock and emersion. He said later that the decision to sleep on the upper deck saved his life.

Bandsman M. N. Cumming and another rating had returned to the barracks ship only five minutes earlier and thought the ship had been hit by a bomb. Cumming escaped with only minor cuts. After regaining his sensibilities, he stripped and repeatedly dived among splintered timber and jagged glass to recover trapped men from the wreckage. He succeeded in rescuing three critically injured ratings.

Ordinary-Seaman L. T. Combers, who was below decks in the engineers' quarters, was suddenly and violently thrown upwards. He punched his way out through a window and then heard a cry for help. On seeing a trapped seaman sinking with the wreckage, he dived into the water and pulled the rating clear, dragging him to a nearby motor launch.

Wreck of *HMAS Kuttabul* the morning after the attack. Channel patrol boat, *HMAS Miramar*, can be seen on the far right.

Petty Officer J. Littleby would normally have been in the Petty Officers' quarters which were completely demolished by the blast. Fortunately, he had accepted the invitation of a mate to sleep in a small motor boat moored nearby. When the torpedo exploded the boat was flung out of the water and a wall of water enveloped and flooded the motor boat. Fittings were blown out of sockets and the fuel tanks were ruptured. Still afloat, Littleby manoeuvred the craft alongside the stricken *Kuttabul* and rescued several naval ratings, some badly injured and all suffering from shock. Littleby pulled away from *Kuttabul* just as the forward section settled on the seabed.

Twenty-five year old Able-Seaman Frank Rudd was about to settle in for the night when the torpedo exploded. In June 1982, he recounted in Melbourne's *Sun-News* that the torpedo had hit the sea wall astern of the depot ship, "exploding and ripping the bottom out of the ship". He said *Kuttabul* went down like a stone: "With the blast, many were thrown overboard and we just had to scramble ashore the best we could."

Stoker Norman Robson was only 19 years old. He had joined the navy seven months earlier and had only recently joined the *Kuttabul* to await a warship posting. He was due to go home on leave the following morning. Early that evening he wrote a letter to his friend, Terry Crowe, after which he proceeded ashore to post it. When he returned to *Kuttabul*, he turned in for the night. He died instantly as the explosion ripped through the ship. A few days later Crowe received the letter in which Robson had written: "You can never tell with this place. Anything might happen."

Petty Officer Leonard Howroyd of Penrith had swapped duty so he could meet his wife the next day, but lost his life that night.

Ordinary-Seaman David "Boy" Trist of the Royal Navy had survived the sinking of the British battleship *HMS Repulse*, which had gone down the previous December off the Malayan coast, only to die six months later in *Kuttabul*.

Able-Seaman F. Kirby, also of the Royal Navy, had escaped injury from the bombing of *HMS Cornwall*, but met his death in Sydney Harbour.

Within minutes of the explosion, Captain A. B. Doyle and Commander C. C. Clark arrived on the scene and searched the vessel for any men who might have been trapped. They did this in darkened and hazardous conditions and assisted a number of men who had been shocked and stunned by the suddenness and force of the explosion.

When daylight arrived, the full extent of the damage was apparent. Leading Seaman diver W. L Bullard recorded that he was amazed to find *Kuttabul* on the bottom with only the funnel and wheelhouse out of the water and that the dive boat, which had been moored near the barracks ship against the sea wall, was nowhere to be seen. Bullard writes in his report that a motor launch was requisitioned and naval stores supplied replacements for the heavy gear left in the diving boat a few days earlier. The dive team was back in business and underwater by 9:15 am.

> I will never forget the scene when we arrived on the sleeping deck of the sunken ship. The sun was shining through a gaping hole in the deck head, giving a green glow to the still water. Blankets and clothing were scattered round the deck. Hammocks were still slung with their occupants as if asleep. There were two men sitting on a locker leaning towards each other as if

Royal Australian Navy servicemen make up the mourning party for the funeral of their shipmates.

The bugler stands to attention after sounding the "Last Post", while a naval guard of honour fires three volleys at the funeral of the *Kuttabul* victims. A sombre Muirhead-Gould (far-right) watches the proceedings.

they had been having a yarn before turning in. There was not a mark on any of them of any kind. The blast from the explosion must have killed them instantly.

The 21 naval ratings who died on *Kuttabul* were victims of a war which had suddenly overtaken them before they had a chance to meet it.

It was some days before all the Allied seamen were recovered from the splintered wreck. On 3 June the bodies of eight sailors were buried at Rookwood Cemetery with full naval honours. More than 200 sailors from all ranks formed a mourning party led by a sombre Muirhead-Gould. The ceremony was simple with no addresses, and the service was read by three chaplains of various denominations, after which a naval guard of honour sounded the "Last Post" as the flag-draped coffins were lowered into the ground.

Later that day, the *K-9*, then a unit of the Royal Netherlands Navy, was towed up harbour for repairs. Launched in 1922, the 210-foot long submarine was in the East Indies, now Indonesia, when Japan entered the war. Following the Japanese advance on Java, she escaped to Fremantle. The Dutch submarine was subsequently based in Sydney and later commissioned into the Royal Australian Navy as an anti-submarine training vessel; however, she became an expensive liability requiring constant servicing. The hull was scrapped in 1944 and used to carry diesel oil. She was lost in a towing accident at Seal Rocks in June 1945 when she became stranded on Fiona Beach. Classified by the NSW Heritage Council as a "Significant Historic Shipwreck", the *K-9* is now buried under beach sand and is only exposed on rare occasions. ●

THOSE WHO DIED ABOARD HMAS KUTTABUL

Stoker II	John	Samuel	Asher
Able Seaman	Leslie	William	Bland
Stoker	William	Richard	Boundy
P/Leading Stoker	Sydney	William	Butcher
Stoker II	Leslie	Joseph	Dennison
Stoker	Arthur	William	Francis
Stoker	John	Edward	Gannon
A/Stoker	Jack	Albert	Gardner
Stoker II	Frederick	Arthur	Glanford
Engine Room Artificer	Walter	George	Gordon
Petty Officer	Leonard	Walter	Howroyd
Stoker II	Lester	Richard	Jamieson
Stoker II	Kenneth	Francis	Killeen
Able Seaman	Frank	-	Kirby
Stoker	Jack	Edmund	Numan
Stoker II	Norman	Leslie	Robson
Able Seaman	Arthur	James	Smith
Stoker II	Herbert	Arthur	Smith
Ord Seaman	David	-	Trist
Ord Seaman	Raymond	Owen	Venning
Stoker II	Thomas	Joseph	Watson

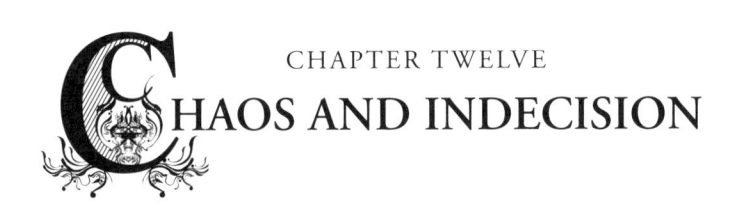

CHAPTER TWELVE
CHAOS AND INDECISION

CHAPTER TWELVE

CHAOS AND INDECISION

... the distinction between heroism and villainy begins to blur, and it is not easy to distinguish between errors of omission or of commission.

The Day The Admirals Slept Late,
A. Hoehling.

In the confusion that followed the sinking of *Kuttabul*, searchlights pencilled the harbour, seeking an invisible enemy. The anti-submarine vessel *HMAS Bingera* slipped her moorings at Man-of-War Anchorage and began to patrol between the anchorage and Bradley's Head, while *Yarroma* and *Lolita* covered the West and East boom gate openings, respectively. NAPs *Lauriana*, *Allura* and *Yarrawonga* were ordered to assist at the boom net area while *Yandra* continued to criss-cross the harbour entrance between North and South Head. The minesweeper *Goonambee*, which had already weighed anchor from Watson's Bay, patrolled along the western channel.

At 1:10 am, forty minutes after *Kuttabul* had sunk, Muirhead-Gould notified all ships: "Enemy submarine is present in the harbour and *Kuttabul* has been torpedoed." Muirhead-Gould's worst fears had been realised.

Small motor launches scurried around the harbour at high speed in an attempt to keep the submarine submerged while the American ships *Chicago*, *Dobbin* and *Perkins*, the Australian cruisers *Adelaide*, *Canberra* and *Westralia* and corvettes *Whyalla* and *Geelong*, and the British converted troop carrier *Kanimbla*, prepared to go to sea.

At 1:58 am, another crossing was recorded on the inner indicator loop. It was thought this crossing was a third submarine entering the harbour. However, Lieutenant Matsuo and Petty Officer Tsuzuku, in Midget I-22, were still lurking at the harbour entrance. The next day, Muirhead-Gould and a visiting American electrical expert, Professor L. A. Rumbaugh, analysed the loop signature and came to the conclusion that this was an outward crossing. The outward crossing was that of Lieutenant Ban and Petty Officer Ashibe making good their escape from the harbour after firing both their torpedoes.

Muirhead-Gould's draft report [undated] concerning this crossing suggests he was unaware of this signature until much later when he writes: "There was some lack of co-ordination between my operations staff, the Loop Station, and shore defences."

The inefficiencies of the Loop Station were highlighted as early as January 1992 when Acting-Captain Harvey Newcombe advised Muirhead-Gould he was not satisfied

2.00 pm No.8 STUD 28 EMF 2L *INNER* *1-6-42* **2.00 pm**

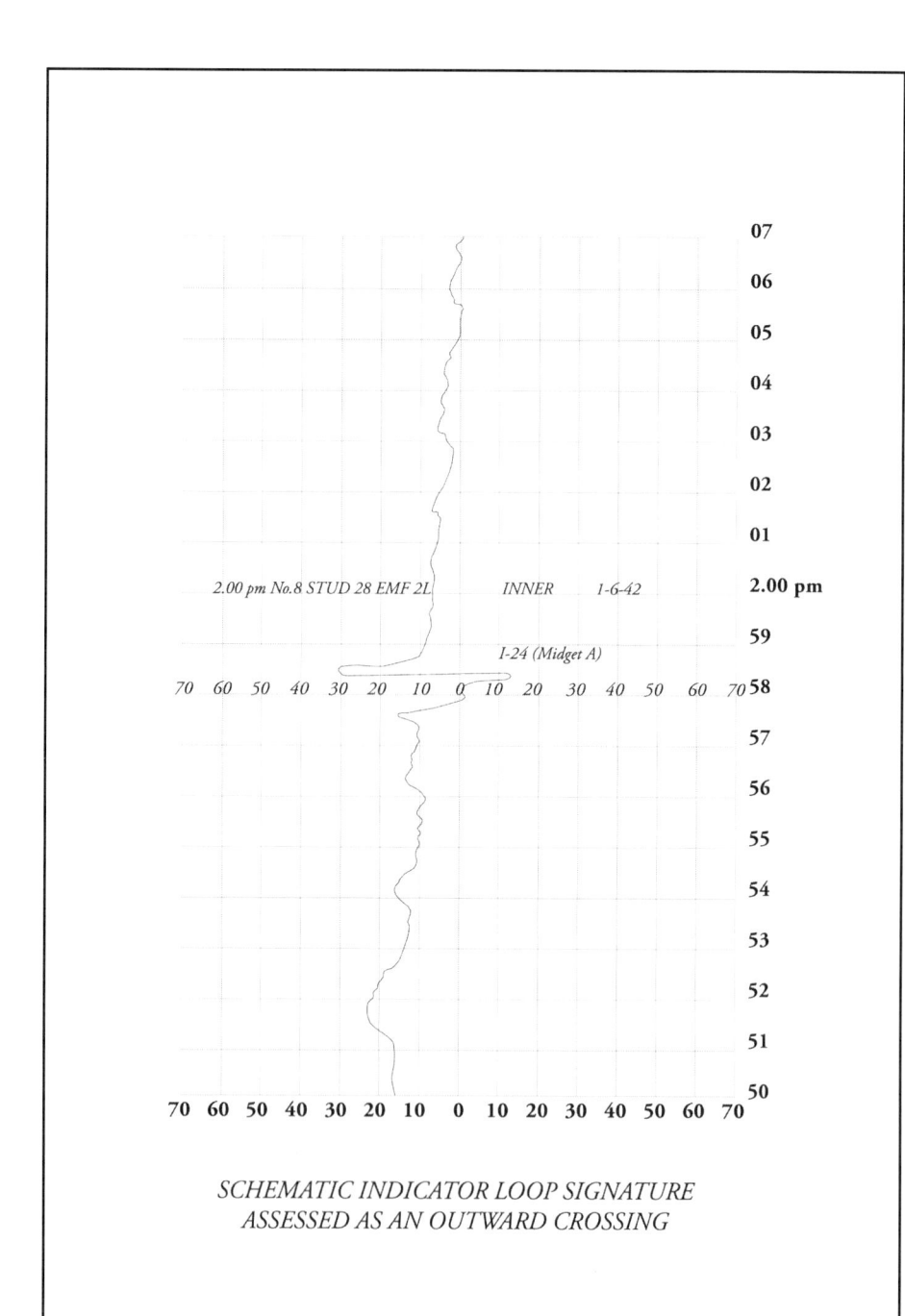

I-24 (Midget A)

*SCHEMATIC INDICATOR LOOP SIGNATURE
ASSESSED AS AN OUTWARD CROSSING*

with the watch-keeping scheme at the Loop Station. Many years after the war he recounted the detection equipment had not been properly manned, and some equipment was out of action. In fact, four of the outer loops were operational but not fully tested and, therefore, unmanned.

At 2:14 am, *Chicago* slipped her moorings at Man-of-War Anchorage and proceeded to sea, passing through the West Gate opening, which was now illuminated by searchlights, at 2:56 am. A few minutes later, the heavy cruiser sighted a periscope almost alongside, too close for the heavy cruiser's guns to bear. At 3:00 am *Chicago* notified Garden Island: "Submarine entering harbour". One minute later, a signature was recorded on the inner loop. Lieutenant Matsuo and Petty Officer Tsuzuki, who had waited patiently on the seabed, were now making their entry into the harbour through the West Gate.

Meanwhile, at Farm Cove, several off-duty patrol boats were still at their moorings, either unaware of the commotion on the harbour, or without adequate crews to proceed on patrol. Most had switched their R/T sets off for the night. Although Muirhead-Gould's report records the channel patrol boats at Farm Cove were ordered to patrol the vicinity of Bradley's Head and the boom gate area at 2:30 am, Lieutenant Wilson later recounted to the official naval historian that the CPBs were unable to see visual signals from Garden Island.

> Channel Patrol Boats were anchored in Farm Cove on the other side of Macquarie's Point, and they were unable to see visual signals from Garden Island. Long delays occurred sending messages by launches … Very few CPBs carried depth charges … All concerned in the port did as well as communications, craft, and armaments permitted. They should be applauded … Though records show that the four "stand off" CPBs in Farm Cove were not ordered to proceed until 2:30 am on 1 June, I am sure they were away and in the vicinity of the Heads before midnight on 31 May.

Channel patrol boats *Marlean* and *Toomaree* had slipped their moorings at Farm Cove shortly before midnight to see what all the commotion was about, while *Esmerelda*, *Leilani*, *Steady Hour* and *Sea Mist* were still at their moorings, unaware of the activity on the harbour. In an interview with the author in 1978, the commanding officer of *Sea Mist*, Lieutenant R. T. Andrew, said the order didn't reach Farm Cove until 3:10 am when he was awoken by the sound of a speedboat and a frantic cry, "I think you'd better get underway. There're subs in the harbour." He immediately relayed the news to Acting-Flotilla Leader, Lieutenant A. G. Townley on *Steady Hour*, who instructed him to patrol between Bradley's Head and the West Gate. Townley also ordered the depth charges to be set to 50 feet.

Sea Mist was the first to slip her moorings at 3:15 am followed by *Steady Hour*, which proceeded to the West Gate near George's Heights. *Leilani* was unmanned and unable leave her moorings. *Esmerelda*, with her engines unserviceable, was also unable to proceed.

Andrew recounted he was starved of information and unfamiliar with his new command in a darkened harbour. As he groped his way towards Bradley's Head, he memorised the current recognition signals while manoeuvring between a multitude of ships, hoping that the patrol boat would not be mistaken for the enemy and riddled with bullets.

SCHEMATIC INDICATOR LOOP SIGNATURES

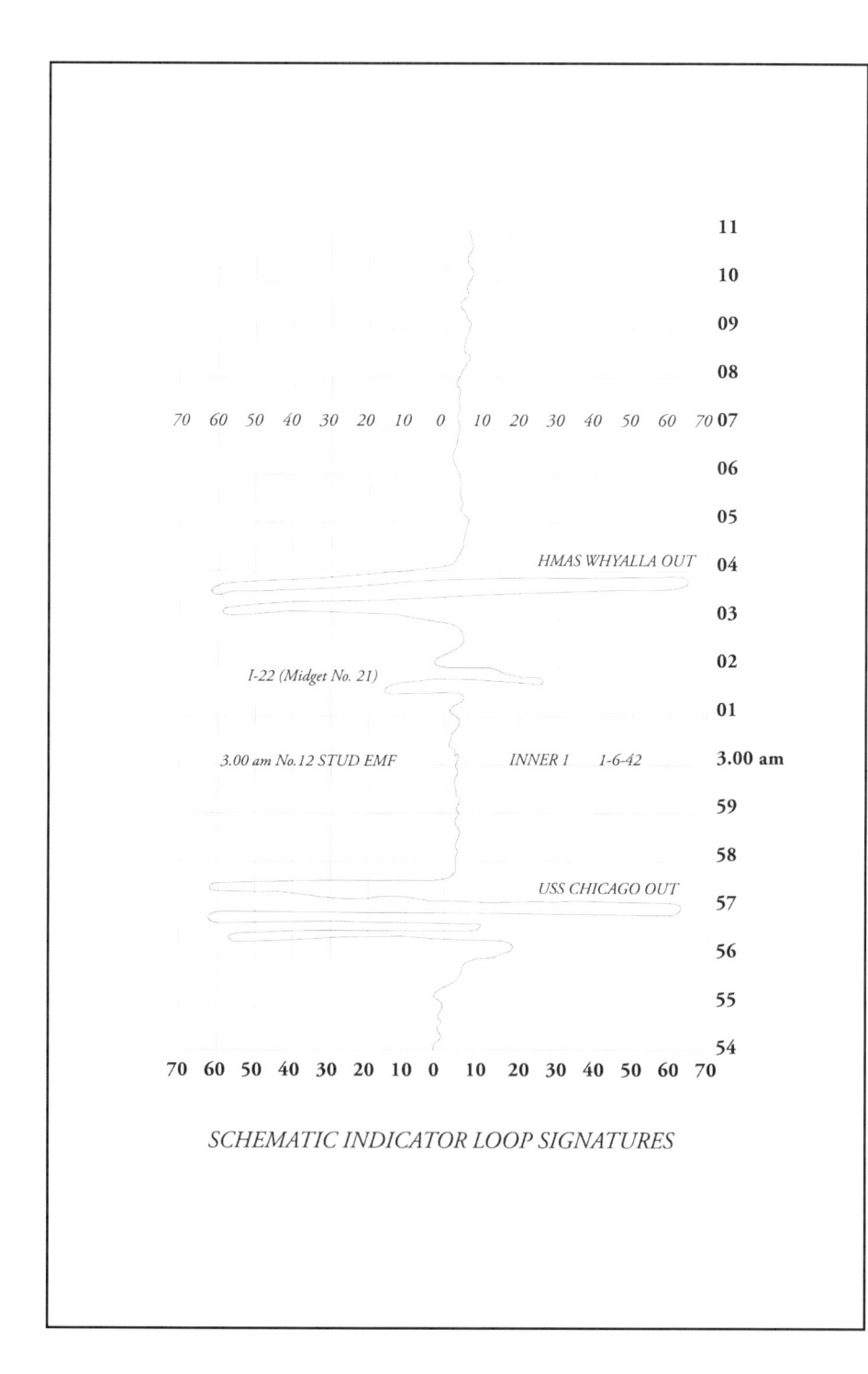

Arriving at Bradley's Head, *Sea Mist* began her patrol to the West Gate, keeping to the main channel and running parallel to the darkened shoreline. Andrew instructed his coxswain to remove the sea lashings securing the depth charges.

Hereafter, a period of quiet followed during which the Indian corvette, *HMIS Bombay*, left the harbour and *Bingera* moved to Farm Cove to carry out an anti-submarine search in the vicinity of the heavy cruiser *HMAS Canberra*, which was on "four hours notice" to raise enough steam to proceed to sea.

Suddenly, at 3:50 am, the harbour was again awakened when the British armed merchant cruiser, *HMS Kanimbla*, which was on 12 hours notice, sighted a periscope in Neutral Bay. Illuminating the periscope with searchlights, the merchant cruiser opened fire. *Bingera* raced over from Farm Cove to assist but the periscope had already disappeared. Although *Bingera* criss-crossed the vicinity for the next hour, no further contact was made.

The mood of the harbour was jittery and the slightest indication of a submarine was pounced on. On patrol in the western channel, minesweeper *Goonambee* flashed *Sea Mist* to investigate a suspicious object in Taylor Bay. The CPB made a thorough search of the bay but failed to confirm *Goonambee's* sighting and resumed her patrol.

There followed another peaceful interlude until 4:40 am when lookouts on *Canberra* reported an unconfirmed sighting of torpedo tracks from the direction of Bradley's Head. At the same time, the minesweeper *Doomba* reported an ASDIC contact off Robertson Point. The minesweeper signalled nearby *Bingera* for assistance and both vessels launched a determined search of the area. Once again, the submarine eluded them and no further contact was made in that area.

Shortly before 5:00 am, *Sea Mist* was heading down the western channel from the West Gate when Lieutenant Andrew saw a dark object off Taylor Head, approximately half way between the channel patrol boat and the shoreline. Turning to starboard, he headed towards the object, instructing the boat's signalman not to illuminate the object. Drawing closer, they both saw a midget submarine on the surface, the conning tower protruding some three feet above water. Continuing in a starboard turn, *Sea Mist* ran between the submarine and the shoreline until they were both pointing towards the West Gate. Andrew told the author it was a shattering experience to find a submarine on the surface and it caught him very much off guard and far from ready to deal with the situation.

Lieutenant Andrew continued turning in a tight circle and called for the Verey pistol and flares to be brought up from the wheelhouse. He observed that the submarine was starting to dive while the channel patrol boat was still turning on the arc. The patrol boat arrived over the swirling water where the craft had now disappeared. Firing a red flare into the sky, Andrew ordered a depth charge dropped over the stern. At the same time, he pushed the throttle wide open to clear the area in the five seconds before the charge detonated.

The detonation was devastating, followed by a huge wall of water which the 62-foot *Sea Mist* rode like a surf boat. A column of water shot skywards and, looking up, Andrew thought the stars would be extinguished. He returned to the vicinity of the depth charge explosion to assess the results of his attack and heard the whirring of propellers churning

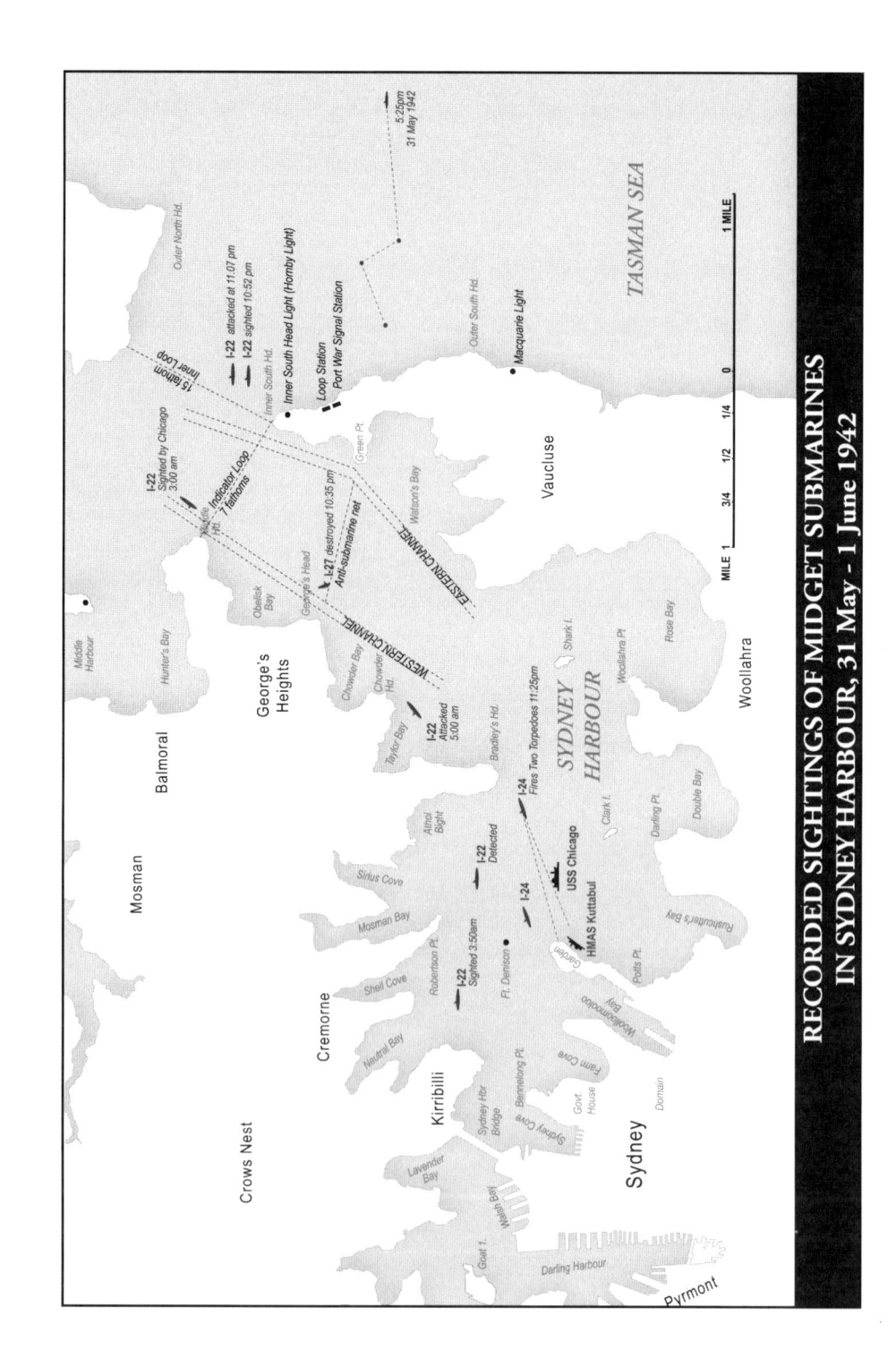

160. JAPANESE SUBMARINE RAIDERS 1942 *A Maritime Mystery*

The coaster *HMAS Binger*a, which was commissioned into the RAN as an auxiliary anti-submarine vessel during WWII.

HMAS Steady Hour swinging on its anchor in Farm Cove, Sydney Harbour. The CPB was armed with a .303 inch Vickers machine gun aft, depth charge throwers and up to six depth charges.

JAPANESE SUBMARINE RAIDERS 1942 *A Maritime Mystery* .161

through the water before he saw the submarine slowly rising upwards out of the sea. As it continued to rise, two contra-revolving propellers became visible within a metal cage. The force of the detonation had forced the craft upwards, and it now lay exposed and inverted, thrashing helplessly on the surface.

Realising the necessity to press home the attack, Lieutenant Andrew turned *Sea Mist* and once again found himself between the midget submarine and the shoreline. He ordered the coxswain to set a second depth charge to 50 feet and called for another flare. Suddenly, there was a cry from the stern. Andrew's first impression was that another two submarines were astern of the patrol boat.

> I had time to note that a second submarine seemed to be in the process of diving, but the aspect was peculiar. The submarine was not moving forward and the conning tower was boiling with escaping air. It was slipping below the surface and then I realised it was sinking.

Although Andrew insisted later that he saw three submarines in Taylor Bay, he could only have seen one. Nonetheless, with the realisation that there might be more than one submarine in the vicinity, he decided to demolish the inverted craft as quickly as possible. Firing another flare into the sky, he ordered the coxswain to release a second depth charge. Andrew said later that the release point was so close he could easily have stepped off the bridge and on to the hull of the submarine.

As the flare mushroomed downward, bathing the vicinity in red light, *Sea Mist* desperately tried to clear the area to avoid the detonation. The crew braced themselves and waited for the tremendous upheaval that would follow. When it did, *Sea Mist* was dealt a crippling blow. At once, her 10 knots were reduced by half and the stoker reported one engine had stopped. With the patrol boat's speed reduced to five knots, Lieutenant Andrew considered it unlikely he could carry out another attack and safely clear the danger zone in time.

Andrew said after the war that he was concerned when he was ordered to set his depth charges at such a shallow depth. As he explained: "When I encountered the submarine, I only had four to five seconds to clear the area after dropping my charges, and at my maximum speed of 10 knots, it did not give me much of a safety margin."

After surveying the damage to *Sea Mist*, Andrew realised his boat was virtually disabled. He flashed *Steady Hour* for assistance and, although nearby, the CPB did not respond. *Sea Mist* limped closer to *Steady Hour* so Andrew could converse by megaphone. Flushed with success, but disappointed at not being able to press home the attack, he was ordered to return to Farm Cove.

The flares fired from *Sea Mist* were seen by a number of vessels in the harbour, including *Lolita* who came racing to the scene along with *Yarroma* and *Goonambee*. The coxswain of *Lolita* described the scene as a "swarm" of small naval vessels, but the CPB was ordered by *Steady Hour* to "stand-by".

At this time a North Shore ferry appeared from nowhere and *Lolita* attempted to head it off before it entered the "danger area". Only under threat of machine gun fire across the bow did the ferry master finally divert his course. Ferry masters later criticised the patrol

Stern view of *HMAS Sea Mist*, showing four depth charge canisters lashed to her deck.

boats which, they said, had been running all over the harbour indiscriminately dropping depth charges. In all, there were 17 charges dropped.

From 5:10 am until 8:27 am, *Steady Hour* and *Yarroma* searched the vicinity for the midget submarine. At 6:40 am, *Steady Hour* dropped two charges and at 6:58 am *Yarroma* picked up an ASDIC contact and dropped one charge. At 7:18 am *Yarroma* made a second attack, and at 7:30 am *Steady Hour* reported that her anchor had caught up in the submarine and that light oil and large bubbles were clearly visible. *Yarroma* carried out a third and final attack at 8:27 am where oil and air bubbles continued to rise.

Rear-Admiral Muirhead-Gould recorded in his preliminary report that although he thought *Sea Mist's* claim of three submarines sounded "fantastic" at the time, he considered it was possible.

> Members of her crew drew a most convincing sketch of the stern cage of the submarine which they claim to have seen. At this time, no one was aware that these submarines had tail cages. It's unfortunate that all efforts to locate this submarine have failed.

Muirhead-Gould recorded that he considered *Steady Hour* was responsible for sinking this midget submarine. He added that *Yarroma* and *Sea Mist* were equally concerned in the submarine's destruction and therefore, to some extent, *Yarroma* had made up for her previous indecision.

It seems more likely Matsuo's craft was crippled by *Sea Mist* at 5:00 am on 1 June. An examination of the wreckage after the attack revealed it was unable to fire its two torpedoes. The torpedoes were protected by metal caps that were pushed off before firing and an attempt had been made to fire one torpedo; however, the metal cap had jammed against the damaged nose-guard.

It's plausible Lieutenant Matsuo's craft was sighted by *Kanimbla* off Robertson Point at 3:50 am, and again by *Doomba* who reported an ASDIC contact off Robertson Point at 4:50 am. A conning tower was sighted by Mr Robert Dulhunty from his balcony in Mosman. The sub seemed like it was at the bottom of his garden in Little Sirius Cove. Mr Dulhunty and his father, also Robert, are probably the only civilians to have opened fire on the midget submarine. The 24-year-old accountant at the time fired two shots at the conning tower with his .22 rifle, and his father fired off another two rounds before the conning tower disappeared.

Unable to fire his torpedoes owing to damage sustained to the submarine's nose guard earlier in the night, Matsuo and Tsuzuki may have been caught while trying to escape the harbour when sighted in Taylor Bay by *Sea Mist*. When first discovered, Lieutenant Andrew reported the submarine was pointing towards the West Gate. What seems like hurriedly drawn charts (*Appendix D*) recovered from the midget submarine after the Sydney raid supports the notion Matsuo had planned his escape from the harbour along the western channel. ●

CHAPTER THIRTEEN
CENSORSHIP AND THE PEOPLE

CHAPTER THIRTEEN

CENSORSHIP AND THE PEOPLE

The greatest tragedy that could overcome a country would be for it to fight a successful war in defence of liberty and lose its own liberty in the process."

Robert Gordon Menzies,
Former Prime Minister of Australia (1939-1941 and 1949-1966).

The first newspaper stories of the Japanese attack did not appear in Sydney until the late editions on 1 June 1942. According to *Daily Telegraph* journalist, John Hector, two articles were filed immediately after the attack, including his own, but neither article ran for censorship reasons.

The duty censor officer in Sydney on Sunday 31 May was 35-year-old Tulla Brown who remembers the Navy imposed an embargo on press cover for several hours, thus, news of the attack did not make the morning editions.

By fortuitous circumstances, Tulla Brown was the only press censor working when most of the harbour action was on and for some hours afterwards. The press censorship operated on overlapping rosters, usually four or five censors on duty at any one time. The shift of which she was part worked from 6:00 pm to 2:00 am on every night except Sunday. Because Sundays were quiet, the shift was from mid-afternoon until 11:00 pm.

In a letter published in the *Bulletin* in 1982, Tulla Brown wrote that Sundays from 11:00 pm were not only unusually quiet nights for submissions, they were also notable for lack of late night or all-night transport. Because her transport was the all-night Watsons Bay tram, she was scheduled on alone until 2:00 am. She said that had she been one of a team instead of alone on duty, she would not have had such vivid recollections of that dramatic night.

Tulla Brown recalled that one of the censors who had signed off at 11:00 pm had rang her from Circular Quay before 11:30 pm, telling her that "things are popping down here" with some sort of naval action and warning her to be ready for a very busy night.

> I then promptly telephoned and awakened the chief censor in Canberra, believing, rightly, that he in turn would need to ring the Prime Minister, asleep or awake, as press submissions on a subject so much involved with security would certainly be flowing in.

She recalls their talk led to a mutual feeling that if people near the Quay, or living where they had harbour-side views and were hearing and seeing gunfire, as well as hectic searchlight activity and explosions, that it was important to quickly formulate censorship directions to allow for speedy publication. She wrote the concern was that delays would heighten public alarm.

> The chief censor made very subtle private "soundings" of his own by telephone to confirm what he had heard from me, and I from my home-going colleague, before disturbing Mr Curtin. He took the same view as my chief and I had reached.
>
> Of course, the service view had to be determined. I was directed to try to reach Rear-Admiral Muirhead-Gould on the telephone. This was a fruitless exercise. I tried many times but never got past a junior RAN officer at Garden Island, telling me with increasing embarrassment that the Rear-Admiral was not yet available and was, in fact, "patrolling" around the harbour. At some later stage came the rumour, probably from the press, which was then ringing me incessantly, that the Rear-Admiral was "tootling" around vantage points on his motor-scooter, then a novelty in this country. That was perhaps the only laugh of the night.

Tulla Brown wrote that she was directed by the chief censor not to make any reference about harbour events, and that she had to keep in touch with the censorship offices in Brisbane and Melbourne, with the latter obliged to keep in contact with points west and south.

> One of my outstanding memories of the night is the harrying I was subjected to from the *Daily Telegraph* once it was realised that there was "only a woman" on call at our office. I guessed it was hoped that I might panic under the stress of repeated telephone calls and blurt out some information they did not have. First a sub-editor on what was probably a reasonable inquiry. But then, relentlessly at short intervals, the chief sub-editor, the news editor, an unremembered executive, and finally the formidable Brian Penton, then at the top of that paper's hierarchy.

Daily Telegraph journalist John Hector recounted to the author that some eight weeks earlier, Penton had been told "by the highest authority in Australia" that a Japanese attack on Sydney Harbour was expected. This prediction resulted in a 20 pound wager between Penton and Hector. Hector quite emphatically recalls attempting to file this information sometime before the attack, but censorship prevented the story being published. If true, Hector's strong recollections point to a national government that knew more than it was letting on.

Sir Paul Hasluck in his book, *The Government and the People*, describes nine newspapers which were banned by the government by means of censorship power; and the daily newspapers complained of continuous and needless delays of publication because of censorship.

Hasluck goes on to say that "censorship probably went furthest beyond the normal practices of Australian democracy". He further records that: "Censorship acted as the handmaiden of all government departments with their wartime activities."

When Curtin became Prime Minister in October 1941, censorship was intensified. Such was the power of censors at that time that it caused Robert Menzies to comment:

> The greatest tragedy that could overcome a country would be for it to fight a successful war in defence of liberty and lose its own liberty in the process.

Menzies and Curtin themselves were censored on several occasions after issuing press statements, by what Hasluck calls blundering and over-zealous individual censors.

Tulla Brown recalls that the big expansion of the censorship apparatus started almost immediately after General MacArthur's arrival in Australia in early 1942 until mid-November.

> This was the period of very big events, of which, of course, we were aware, as we were aware of their crucial significance. These included the battles of the Coral Sea and of Midway, the New Guinea and island campaigns… We were required to follow the MacArthur communiqués on non-local military actions and work in tandem with his military censors. I must confess that these pro-American "boys", who ignored specific credit to the Australian forces, were often as unpalatable to the Australian censors as they were to our war correspondents who were restricted by them. They sourly called General MacArthur "God".

In the weeks following the Sydney Harbour raid, there were demands from some sections of the press for an official inquiry; but none came. The Curtin Labor War Cabinet was deeply concerned about the defeatism of the population and could ill-afford another Royal Commission into the handling of defences so soon after the Darwin attack. ●

CHAPTER FOURTEEN
ATTACK POST-MORTEM

CHAPTER FOURTEEN

ATTACK POST-MORTEM

So, by a combination of good luck and aggressive count-attack, an extremely well-conceived enemy operation succeeded only in underlining to the embattled Australians their front row seat in the Pacific War.

Lieutenant-Commander J. B. Wilkinson, USNR.

Unlike the Darwin aerial attack some five months earlier, Japanese preparations for submarine attacks on South Pacific bases commenced almost four months beforehand, in February 1942 when Japanese reconnaissance aircraft flew over the major cities on the Australian eastern seaboard. The fact that these flights took place didn't become known until after the war.

David Jenkins records in his book, *Battle Surface*, that a pre-dawn reconnaissance flight over Sydney occurred on 17 February when 30-year-old Warrant Flying Officer Nobuo Fujita piloted his "Glen" float plane over the low cliffs at La Perouse, south of Sydney, at a height of 8,000 feet and flew across Botany Bay. He then headed to Parramatta with the city and the harbour on his right. Coming down to 3,000 feet, he had a clear view of the Sydney Harbour Bridge. Despite the brownout, he reported many lights, including the lights at the Garden Island Naval base and the Macquarie lighthouse with its 1.4 million candle power light. The pilot counted 23 ships at anchor in the harbour. Fujita recounts that he fully expected the air raid sirens to sound and the anti-aircraft guns to open fire, but he went undetected, crossing North Head on his return to I-25 waiting off the coast.

The official Japanese War History records preparations for a midget submarine attack in the South Pacific commenced on 10 May when Operation MO (Port Moresby operation) was deferred. The basic structure of the plan was:

1. After MO Operation, I-21 and I-29 will detect the proposed points for the attack at Sydney, Auckland and Noumea.

2. The aircraft will ascertain the position of the enemy's main vessels, then for the attack all the submarines will assemble at the attacking area.

3. The time of the (midget submarine) dispatch is set between within one hour from

sunset or within one hour from the moonrise. After the attack, the crew will be retrieved before the following morning. If the retrieval of the crew is not completed within the planned time, then the retrieval will continue for three nights.

4. Immediately before and after the attack, aircraft reconnaissance will be made.

Prior to the main Coral Sea engagement, two American aircraft carriers were sighted around Tulagi, in the Solomon Islands, but the Japanese failed to relocate them and it was presumed they had left for South Pacific bases. Vice-Admiral Daigo ordered I-21 to Suva and I-29 to Noumea with their reconnaissance seaplanes to search for them. At the same time, he ordered I-22, I-24, I-27 and I-28 to make their way to Queen Carola Harbour in the Solomon Islands to collect their midget submarines from the Japanese carrier, *Chiyoda*.

According to the historical record, I-29 arrived off Noumea on 4 May to watch for enemy movements but failed to recognise any powerful navy vessels in the area. Unknown to I-29, the *Yorktown* force, which included *Chicago*, *Perkins* and the fleet oiler, *Tippercanoe*, had sailed from Noumea a few days earlier to rendezvous with the *Lexington* force in the Solomon Sea and I-29 failed to make contact with them.

On 5 May, while patrolling between Noumea and Brisbane, I-29 sunk the large American cargo ship, *John Adams*, and two days later the Greek cargo ship, *Chloe*.

In the meantime, I-21 had arrived off Suva Harbour but was unable to locate any powerful naval vessels. Captain Sasaki then proceeded to Auckland Harbour, but fog prevented aerial reconnaissance of that harbour.

The first warning presaging an attack on Allied forces in Australian waters came on 16 May 1942 when the Russian merchant steamer *Wellen*, on passage to Newcastle, was fired on by I-29, 30 miles east of that port. The submarine surfaced almost alongside the steamer and fired off seven rounds before submerging again.

Although Rear-Admiral Muirhead-Gould temporarily closed Newcastle and Sydney ports to merchant sailings, he considered the submarine attack was that of a lone submarine that had already left the area. Twenty-four hours later, he re-opened both ports to merchant shipping. However, I-29 continued to lurk off Newcastle and Sydney, looking for the greatest concentration of Allied naval vessels.

On 23 May, I-29 launched her seaplane for a dawn reconnaissance over Sydney Harbour. Although it was prohibited for aircraft to fly over the harbour, the flight went undetected. When the pilot reported battleships and cruisers dotted about the harbour, Captain Sasaki made the decision to attack Sydney Harbour.

On 26 May and again on 29 May, the defence authorities received two more warnings of Japanese submarines operating in Australian waters when the New Zealand naval authorities intercepted Japanese radio transmissions, first 700 miles and then 40 miles east of Sydney. Japanese chatter was also heard on *Chicago* and reported to the duty officer at the Garden Island Operations Room. The source of these chatter was the Third Submarine Company now converging on Sydney. Why these warnings were ignored is inexplicable. A plausible explanation was the fear by MacArthur of alerting the Japanese to the fact that they had broken their codes.

Another warning of an impending attack on Sydney Harbour came in the early hours of 29 May when an unidentified aircraft was sighted over Man-of-War Anchorage. Unlike *HMS Ramilles* in Diego Suarez, and the Gunnery Officer on *Chicago*, Muirhead-Gould failed to recognise the implications.

It's a moot point that the official account by G. Hermon Gill records this reconnaissance taking place on 30 May, which was based on Muirhead-Gould's 13-page official report. Muirhead-Gould records that: "A reconnaissance of Sydney Harbour, especially the Naval Anchorage area, was carried out by one biplane single float plane at approximately 0420K/30 May."

In an interview recorded in Sydney's *Daily Telegraph* (29 May 1957), the Japanese pilot, Susumu Ito, on a visit to Sydney, recounted that he flew over Sydney Harbour on the night of 29 May 1942. Captain Sasaki, who survived the war, also records in the official Japanese War History that the reconnaissance flight took place on 29 May:

> I-21, after arriving in bad weather from Auckland on the 28 May in the evening off Sydney Heads, dispatched the aircraft for pre-attack reconnaissance on the 29 May at 0247 hours [3:47 am Australian time].

While G. Hermon Gill relies on Muirhead-Gould's chronological narrative to record the official history, he also writes that, "… little significance appears to have been attached to the sighting". This ambiguity is reflected in Muirhead-Gould's report where he records: "The attack was possibly preceded by aerial reconnaissance, which may have been carried out on 29, 30 and 31 May." From these remarks, Muirhead-Gould was uncertain which day the unidentified aircraft was sighted over the harbour.

If Muirhead-Gould was uncertain which day the reconnaissance took place, an eye-witness account was published in *Smith's Weekly*, a sensationalist tabloid of the day, on 13 June 1942.

> … two or three nights previously, an aeroplane flew over Sydney. It came from the direction of the sea, with lights showing, and subsequently, with lights out, flew between the Allied warships and Garden Island.

Years later, Lieutenant P. F. Wilson recounted his memory of the incident in a letter to G. Hermon Gill:

> The first sighting was made by the army artillery battery at George's Heights, Middle Head, who was lulled into a sense of false security by the plane's American markings and type. They reported the sighting by telephone to me, adding "there is no cause for alarm as it is an American Curtiss falcon float plane". I was quite aware that *Chicago's* planes were on its deck and that no other American cruiser was anywhere in the vicinity …

Chicago's Gunnery Officer, Lieutenant Commander William Floyd, told the author in 1982 that he was ordered by Captain Bode to investigate the incident.

> ... my investigations disclosed that a Japanese plane had been observed flying down the harbour shortly after daylight ... The only person in the *Chicago* that saw this plane was the Officer of the Deck. He happened to be an aviator and he identified it as a Japanese plane.

The *Chicago* never filed an official report of this incident, or the raid itself, with the Australian Naval authorities.

On 30 May, the British Admiralty was informed of the Japanese raid in Madagascar. Had the Admiralty issued a worldwide warning at this time, rather than 18 hours after the first midget submarine was discovered in Sydney Harbour, a similar attack may have been anticipated in Australia. The reason the Admiralty gave for not raising the alarm was that they didn't want to disclose their losses in case the information benefited the enemy. The Australian authorities adopted a similar position immediately after the Sydney raid by censuring newspapers and public radio broadcasts to deprive the enemy of information. In the meantime, wild rumours had already begun sweeping Sydney, gleaned from stories told by eyewitnesses.

Paradoxically, at no time during the war were there as many ships in Sydney Harbour as there were on the night of 31 May. Since the defences of the harbour were in turmoil, one could easily wonder why the midget submarine attack did not succeed. Unlike the actions of naval authorities at Pearl Harbor and Washington, Australian authorities held no official inquiry into the Sydney Harbour attack. Only one 13-page report was submitted by the Naval Officer in Charge of Sydney Harbour to the Australian Naval Board. Captain H. M. Newcombe later told the author that he thought he would have been summoned before an inquiry as the officer-in-charge of the Indicator Loop Station; but he was not.

Marked "Secret", Muirhead-Gould's report did not become available for public viewing until 1972, 30 years after the Sydney raid, and only then after arduous battles with custodians of official records.

It took more than two hours from when Cargill first discovered the object caught in the boom net at 8:15 pm, to when Rear-Admiral Muirhead-Gould issued his first "general alarm" at 10:27 pm for all ships to take anti-submarine precautions and closed the harbour to outward bound shipping. By this time, a second midget submarine had already penetrated the harbour and remained undetected for more than half an hour. In his preliminary report he wrote:

> Great difficulty has been experienced in making any sort of chronological plot. A great many ships and boats and, therefore, people were concerned in these operations, and all were so busy that they had no thought for recording actual time of incidents.

In his draft conclusions, Muirhead-Gould attributes the delay to valuable time wasted by James Cargill "who took some time to collect a friend and to communicate this vital information to the CPB on patrol". The delay was also caused by non-existent or poor communications between harbour defence vessels, the Garden Island Operations Room, and the Port War Signal Station.

In his official report, Muirhead-Gould recommends Cargill to the Notice of the Naval

Board for his "vigilance and initiative in his personal efforts to report a suspicious circumstance to the proper authorities". Cargill was awarded 40 pounds and Nangle, who assisted Cargill, was awarded 10 pounds.

Many years after the attack, Cargill said that there have been many stories told about the net across the opening of the harbour, but he discounted most of them. In 1982, he drew a "mud map" of his recollections at the boom net that night. Cargill remembers the midget submarine running into a pile light inside the western channel, before going astern and becoming entangled in the steel boom net.

Cargill's recollections point to the enormous difficulties the submarine crews experienced controlling their craft. A collision with the seabed is also thought responsible for the damaged nose guard on Lieutenant Matsuo's midget submarine sunk in Taylor Bay.

James Cargill died in Randwick in 1986 at the age of 96 years and his ashes scattered off South Head, his passing attracting a brief paragraph in the local newspaper.

Muirhead-Gould directly attributes the failure of the Loop Station to the human element, but considered the loop system fully justified itself. He records in his draft conclusions that he "… cannot greatly blame the operators concerned because no one had ever before experienced the effect of a midget submarine crossing a loop, nor had anyone, in Sydney at any rate, ever seen a midget's signature".

In his preliminary report, Muirhead-Gould records Chuma's craft was in the harbour for two hours before the loop anomaly at 8:01 pm was interpreted as a crossing, however, its significance was not recognised at the time, "owing to the ferry and other traffic over the loops".

After the war, Acting-Captain Newcombe, responsible for the Loop Station, recounted that four of the six outer loops were in operation, but the detection equipment was unmanned owing to manpower shortages. The shortage was exasperated by insufficient personnel trained to operate this new, specialised underwater detection equipment.

Muirhead-Gould records that the floodlights on Garden Island were extinguished at 12:25 am and five minutes later the torpedo exploded. In G. Hermon Gill's account, the official naval historian records the lights were extinguished at 11:25 pm and the torpedo exploded five minutes later.

It's more likely Muirhead-Gould ordered the floodlights extinguished at 11:14 pm when he ordered all ships to be darkened, before he proceeded down the harbour to interview officers at the boom gate. Lieutenant Wilson's account that it took some time to find the dockyard personnel responsible for switching off the floodlights supports the notion that the dockyard floodlights were extinguished only minutes before the torpedo exploded beneath *HMAS Kuttabul*.

The long delays to communicate orders from Muirhead-Gould to harbour defence personnel is evident throughout the raid and was the major factor contributing to the general confusion on the harbour. No more so is this evident than the time it took to alert the off-duty channel patrol boats moored at Farm Cove, hidden from Garden Island by Mrs Macquaries Point. Although the off-duty CPB's were fitted with an R/T set, they had been turned off. From when Muirhead-Gould issued his order for these vessels to proceed to sea at 2:30 am on 1 June, it took another 40 minutes before the order reached nearby Farm Cove, more than two and a half hours after *Kuttabul* had been sunk.

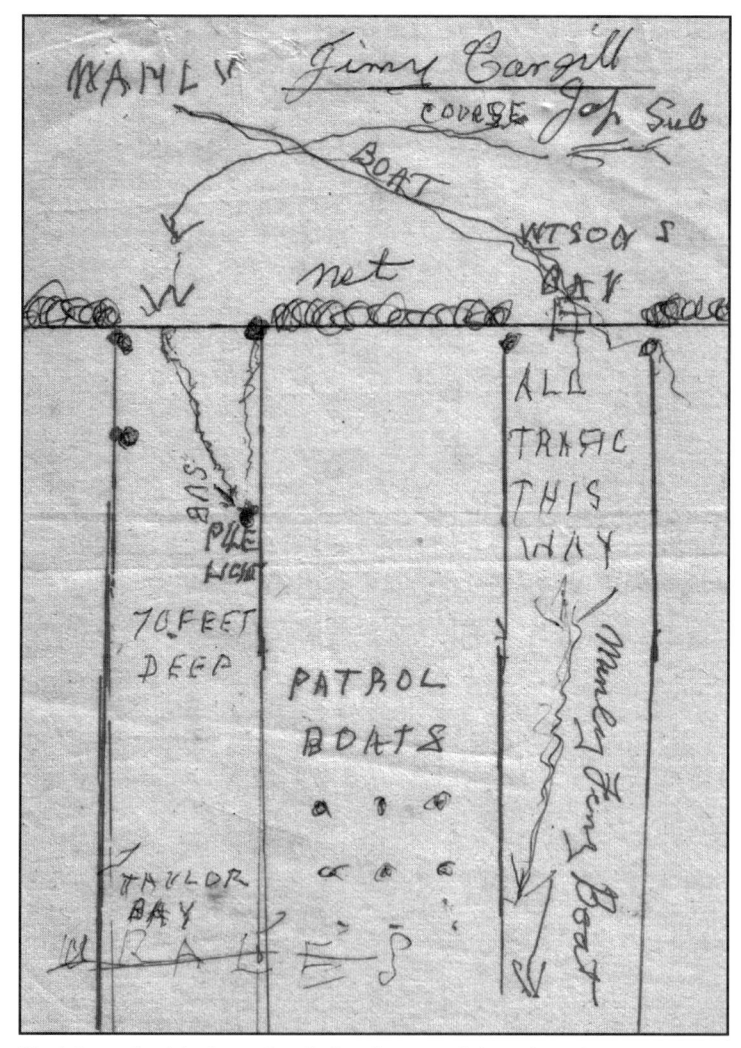

Hand-drawn sketch by James Cargill. Cargill recounted the midget submarine ran into a pylon light inside the western channel, before it went astern and became entangled in the steel boom net.

The Sydney Harbour raid has the distinction of being the only Australian action devoid of military honours. Muirhead-Gould records that from a preliminary examination of the evidence, he considered *Steady Hour* was responsible for sinking the midget submarine in Taylor Bay and that, "further investigations show that *Yarroma* and *Sea Mist* were equally concerned in this attack". He considered that for *Yarroma's* part in the sinking, the CPB had redeemed herself, to some extent, for her earlier failures.

In the final analysis, *Sea Mist*, not *Steady Hour*, should be considered responsible for sinking the third submarine at 5:00 am. Although Matsuo had a reputation for calmness in a crisis, it is unlikely he would have stayed in the vicinity when he was first discovered, unless the midget submarine was no longer operational following initial attacks by the patrol boat. Another 90 minutes passed before *Steady Hour* dropped the next depth charge. From then until 8:27 am, *Steady Hour* and *Yarroma* dropped a further five depth charges in the same vicinity where the midget submarine was eventually recovered.

Although Muirhead-Gould concedes in his draft conclusions that while *Sea Mist's* claim of three midget submarines sounded fantastic at that time, he records in his draft report that members of her crew drew "a most convincing sketch" of the stern cage. He writes: "At this time, no one was aware these submarines had tail cages."

Following the Sydney raid, the Naval Board sent their congratulations to *Steady Hour, Sea Mist* and *Yarroma*. CPB Flotilla Leader, Lieutenant-Commander E. Breydon, who did not take part in the attack, added his own congratulations and said that their action had brought great honour to the CPB flotilla. Rear-Admiral Muirhead-Gould sent his personal congratulations to *Lolita, Yandra, Bingera* and *Whyalla*:

> I congratulate the officers and men upon their vigilance and efficiency in the successful engagement against the enemy on Sunday 31 May and Monday 1 June. The weary months of patrolling have proved worthwhile.

Soon after the Sydney raid, Lieutenant Andrew was posted to Cairns as Ullage Master, which involved garbage disposal and exterminating bugs and rodents. He later served at Madang, New Guinea, as Boat Officer and saw out the war as Beer Officer. After the war, he worked as a storeman in Mosman before he retired to Port Stephens, NSW, where he died from a heart attack in 1984. Lieutenant Townley, who came from a prominent Tasmanian family, went on to become Minister for Defence in the Menzies Government. He died in 1963 soon after approving the purchase of the controversial F111 aircraft for the Australian Air Force.

In the days following the Sydney raid, little information emerged from the Australian Naval authorities, and MacArthur's headquarters in Melbourne issued few details. Wartime censorship imposed by the Curtin Labor government substantially reduced the amount of information released immediately after the attack. The only statement from Rear-Admiral Muirhead-Gould came from his secretary, Mr E. A. Lucas, who said: "If you wish to make any inquiry on that (attack), you must address it to the secretary of the Naval Board."

The lack of information was highlighted by the Allied Air Command which went on record as saying Naval Intelligence officers had "compiled meagre official reports of Sunday night's action in the harbour", and more detailed reports may have assisted them

James Cargill photographed in 1982. He was awarded 40 pounds for his "vigilance and initiative in his personal efforts to report a suspicious circumstance to the proper authorities."

Photo Steven L. Carruthers

Warrant Officer Herbert S. Anderson (left), commanding officer *HMAS Lolita*, and Lieutenant Athol G. Townley, commanding officer *HMAS Steady Hour*, and family.

Courtesy Harold F. Anderson

in their air search for the parent submarine. At that time, it was believed only one large submarine had towed the midget craft to the harbour entrance.

Susumu Ito vividly recalled the immediate days after the attack while waiting off the coast to recover the midget submarine crews. He remembers the submarine force lying deep during the day to avoid the many aircraft and surface ships searching for them.

The Minister for the Navy, Mr Makin, visited Sydney shortly after the attack and met with Rear-Admiral Muirhead-Gould. Makin later announced that no inquiry would be necessary, stating that:

> A thorough investigation has been made into the circumstances of the Japanese midget submarine raid and this has proved the defences are up to the mark. It must not be forgotten that the defences are not yet complete.

In Parliament, Makin reassured the Australian public with the following speech:

> When Japan entered the war, we were well prepared. The completeness of these preparations was made apparent in the attack on Sydney Harbour. The form of attack was one difficult to counter, as the enemy used midget submarines, able to make an entry through channels denied to a larger ship. That this attempt was instantly detected and that the counter measures were so prompt and so effective, reflects the credit on those responsible for the harbour defences.

USS Chicago and *HMAS Canberra* sailed from Sydney in July 1942 for the Guadalcanal landing. On 9 August, *Chicago* and *Canberra*, as well as three US heavy cruisers, *Quincy*, *Astoria* and *Vincennes*, took part in the battle for Savo Island. They were all sunk accept *Chicago*, who failed to go to the aid of *Canberra* when she was on fire and dead in the water and still being shelled by a Japanese heavy cruiser within easy range of *Chicago's* guns. Captain Bode shot himself six months later when facing court martial for that failure.

In August 1942, *Chicago* returned to Sydney for temporary repairs and left for the last time in September. After a complete refit near San Francisco, the heavy cruiser was sunk by five torpedoes from Japanese land-based aircraft in the Battle of Rennell Island near Guadalcanal on 30 January 1943.

The conduct of Rear-Admiral Muirhead-Gould was unremarkable, at best. Earlier in the evening he had dined with Captain Bode and some of his officers at Tresco and no doubt his drinking had some influence on his tardiness and silly comments when he took his barge down the harbour to the boom net to interview officers on the spot at midnight.

In 1944, Muirhead-Gould returned to England and was later transferred to Germany as Flag Officer, Wilhelmshaven. This was changed later to Flag Officer, Western Germany, to indicate better the scope of his command, which included all naval forces in the British zone west of the Elbe, and Hamburg. On 11 May 1945, he landed on the small German island of Heligoland in the North Sea and accepted its surrender. He found the island devastated by bombing and almost uninhabitable. Muirhead-Gould died from a heart attack in Germany in 1946.

Had there been more casualties in Sydney Harbour that night then this audacious attack would have earned greater significance in Australia's military history. Because there

The heavy cruiser, *USS Chicago*, photographed from the heavy cruiser, *USS Wichita*, on 29 January 1943, just prior to the Battle of Rennell Island. In the distance is the US heavy cruiser *Louisville*. Sailors in the foreground at work on a paravane.

was no official investigation, the Sydney Harbour attack has loomed large in Australian folklore, the more so because of the mysterious disappearance of the midget submarine from I-24, crewed by Lieutenant Ban and Petty Officer Ashibe.

For more than half a century, numerous theories have arisen to try and shed light on the whereabouts of the missing midget submarine. The one thing most maritime historians and authorities agree on is that the submarine escaped the harbour soon after 1:58 am on 1 June 1942 when an outward crossing was recorded on the inner indicator loop.

In the early years following the Sydney raid, many believed the missing submarine still lay undiscovered somewhere in the harbour. However, there have been many fruitless searches of the harbour by the Royal Australian Navy and private organisations using modern-day technology such as side scan sonar.

A popular search area immediately after the attack was Taylor Bay, based on *Sea Mist's* report of three submarines in that location. However, there have been extensive searches of this area, first by hard-hat Navy divers who would train there, and later by Navy and recreational scuba divers adopting various grid searches. The area has also been extensively searched using magnometers and sophisticated side-scan sonar.

There are two wrecks in and off Taylor Bay - *SS Centennial* and *SS Currajong*. One or the other has often been mistaken for the missing midget submarine. In the early evening of 23 August 1889, the 66-metre *Centennial* was rounding Bradley's Head when she collided with the collier *Kanahooka*. Laden with coal and 80 passengers and crew, the iron-screw steamer sank in three minutes in 23 metres of water with the loss of only one life. The 70-metre *Currajong* was rammed by the *Wyreema* on 8 March 1910 just off Bradley's Head. Today, the *Currajong* is recognised as one of the most intact shipwrecks in NSW. It is illegal to dive this wreck, as well as unsafe owing to the many vessels, large and small, that pass overhead. The wreck lays in 18 to 26 metres of water. The *Currajong* was the focus of a publicity stunt in 1980 to promote submarine burgers at a nearby harbour restaurant.

In the early years, Navy divers trained in different locations throughout the harbour, including the deep waters inside Bradley's Head and Middle Harbour. Infrequent dredging operations inside the harbour have also failed to uncover submarine wreckage.

Until the early 1980s, Sydney Harbour was a popular commercial fishing ground, with trawlers plying the harbour from one end to the other, dragging their nets for prawns and white bait. Many of these fishermen kept records of underwater obstructions to avoid damaging their expensive nets. Most have been investigated and eliminated as submarine wreckage.

The most popular theory by Japanese historians is that Lieutenant Ban and Petty Officer Ashibe escaped the harbour and the midget submarine now lays in deep water somewhere east of North Head. Other historians believe the submarine lays somewhere between Sydney Heads and the recovery area off Port Hacking.

In 1982, a coastal survey was made from South Head to Coogee, down to 70 metres depth and out to around four miles off shore. The survey located nine objects that met the profile of a midget submarine. Most have been investigated and found to be rocky outcrops or other wreckage. This search area represents only a fraction of the area between Sydney Harbour and Port Hacking with water depths beyond safe diving limits for recreational divers.

Today, modern-day satellite communications and depth sounding equipment allow offshore commercial fishermen to locate fishing grounds quickly, as well as to pin-point underwater obstructions with a high degree of accuracy. They too keep good records, including latitudes and longitudes obtained from satellite fixing; however, there are far too many sites of interest along the NSW coast to mount any serious sub-sea investigation.

In November 2005, producers from Animax Films and Foxtel presented what seemed to be compelling evidence of the final resting place of the missing midget submarine from I-24. Their documentary showed the results from a number of technical surveys, including seabed profiling, magnetometer readings and side scan sonar tests which all pointed to an object measuring the same dimensions as the midget submarine. Located 14 nautical miles north of Sydney Harbour, the object was buried below the sand off the seaward side of Lion Island, inside the entrance to Broken Bay. However, the Heritage Office, responsible for managing shipwrecks in NSW, found no evidence of the midget submarine after a series of in-depth tests at the site. The tests found the site was covered in just three metres of sand, not enough to conceal the 24-metre long midget submarine.

The film-makers put forward a new theory based around the discovery of an underwater object some 14 years earlier by commercial diver Mike Buesnel while laying fibre optic cable across Broken Bay, and information contained in war diaries uncovered by amateur historian, Mr Jim Macken QC. The war diaries contain numerous reports of submarine sightings in the Broken Bay area in the weeks after the Sydney Harbour attack.

According to their theory, Lieutenant Ban and Petty Officer Ashibe escaped the harbour soon after 1:58 am when an outward crossing was recorded on the inner indicator loop. Instead of turning south to rendezvous with the submarine force, or east where it was thought they may have scuttled their craft in deep water, they went north, presumably to act as a decoy to draw the enemy away from the carrier submarines waiting off Port Hacking to the south. It is thought the midget submarine travelled over the surface, reaching Broken Bay around dawn. They theorise the crew set the midget submarine to periscope depth to continue to act as a decoy before they committed suicide.

Thereafter, over the next several weeks, they believe the buoyant craft drifted with the strong currents in Broken Bay as it was washed up and down the Hawkesbury River, occasionally bobbing to the surface when it was sighted by Navy and Army personnel manning defence installations. It was also seen by fishermen in the area.

While researching his book, *Pittwater's War*, Jim Macken uncovered war diaries in the Australian War Memorial archives that suggested the midget submarine may have headed to the Hawkesbury area. On 8 July, more than a month after the Sydney raid, a submarine was reported near Brooklyn on the Hawkesbury River. A partially exposed submarine was also spotted stranded in the mangroves around midday on 9 July, but vanished before searchers arrived. Numerous other sightings followed and planes and patrol boats were sent to search the area, all without result. It was thought with all the sightings that an attack was imminent on the Hawkesbury River Bridge, which was fortified with mines and an anti-submarine net was positioned along its length. The last sighting of a submarine was in Broken Bay near Lion Island on 1 August 1942. Respected amateur historian Jim Macken still believes their is a high probability the midget submarine lays somewhere in Broken Bay. ●

Chapter Fifteen
Campaign of Destruction

CHAPTER FIFTEEN

CAMPAIGN OF DESTRUCTION

Defeat of Germany means the defeat of Japan, probably without firing a shot or losing a life.

President Franklin D. Roosevelt

Outside Sydney Harbour, the submarine force proceeded to the recovery area to await the return of the midget submarines while Captain Sasaki remained off the harbour entrance to record the enemy's reaction. Having observed searchlights sweeping the harbour in an apparently random manner, he proceeded south of Sydney to join his force for the recovery phase.

Commencing from a point four kilometres off Cape Banks, south of Sydney, four large submarines spread out at four kilometre intervals in a line running to the east. Sasaki made his way six kilometres further south to collect any midget craft which might overshoot the recovery area unnoticed.

The plan was for the parent submarines to first recover the crews, and then sink the midget submarines. The rationale was that it would take too long to recover the craft and expose the submarine force to unnecessary danger.

At 1:05 am on 1 June, a large submarine was sighted by the Sydney trawler *San Michele* five miles off Port Hacking. A naval intelligence report at the Australian War Memorial records: "Submarine steaming south at slow speed. Probably parent submarine of midgets." However, the report didn't reach the Garden Island Operations Room until 3:40 am, at a time when the harbour defences were in turmoil.

The Third Submarine Company waited throughout the night but none of the craft returned. In his 4:00 am report to Vice-Admiral Daigo on 1 June, Sasaki concluded:

> Although the visibility was extremely good, and circumstances suited for retrieval, we received no communication from SSBs [midgets]. We are still standing by for retrieval without any trace of our SSBs.

At dawn, Sasaki ordered his force to disperse and submerge for the day and to rendezvous again the following evening. The submarine force reassembled at the recovery area in the evening of 1 June while I-21 and I-29 searched along the shoreline in the slim hope that the crews had abandoned their craft and were stranded somewhere along the coast. Under the cover of darkness, Sasaki also conducted a search around the outer entrance to Sydney Harbour.

While searching the coastline, Captain Sasaki intercepted a radio broadcast issued by General MacArthur's headquarters in Melbourne.

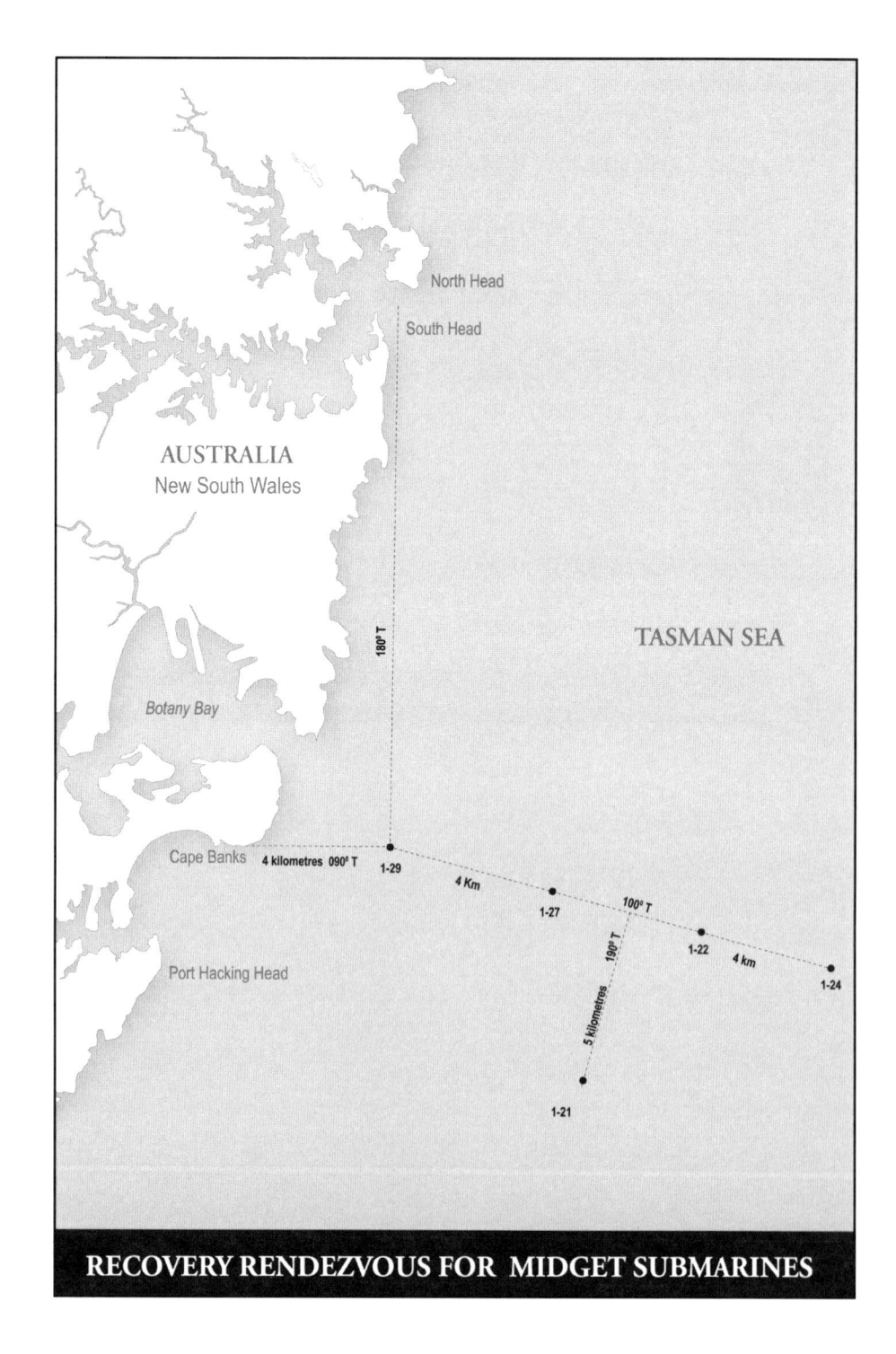

RECOVERY RENDEZVOUS FOR MIDGET SUBMARINES

188. JAPANESE SUBMARINE RAIDERS 1942 *A Maritime Mystery*

In an attempted submarine raid on Sydney, three enemy midget submarines are believed to have been destroyed – one by gunfire, two by depth charges. The enemy's attack was completely unsuccessful. Damage was confined to one small harbour vessel of no military value.

As dawn approached the submarine force again dispersed until the following evening. During this phase of the recovery, a periscope was sighted at the entrance to Botany Bay by *HMAS Marlean*, a channel patrol boat on duty outside the bay. *Marlean* attacked with depth charges but the submarine escaped and moved further out to sea. Another periscope was sighted by *Whyalla*, which had been patrolling outside Sydney Harbour, but the periscope disappeared below the surface before the corvette could come to "Action Stations". A search of the area failed to re-establish contact with the submarine.

The Third Submarine Company reassembled off Port Hacking again in the evening of 2 June, but there was still no sign of the midget submarines. At dawn on 3 June, Sasaki abandoned all hope of recovering any of the crews and ordered his force to disperse. The primary objective now was to wage a campaign of destruction along the Australian east coast to "weaken the resolve of the enemy" and to disrupt supply lines. I-29 proceeded north to harass shipping off Brisbane, I-27 was ordered to Tasmania, and I-22 crossed the Tasman to New Zealand to look for targets between the North and South Islands and along the shipping routes between Fiji and New Zealand. In the meantime, I-21 and I-24 remained off the coast of Sydney for another 10 days.

After issuing these orders, Sasaki telegraphed Vice-Admiral Daigo that although the crews of the midget submarines had carried out brave attacks, they were all killed in combat after entering the harbour, information he had gleaned from MacArthur's communiqué of 1 June.

In the days after the Sydney raid, the Australian Department of Information monitored Japanese broadcasts around the clock, but picked up no public broadcast relating to the Sydney attack until 5 June.

> The Imperial Navy made an attack on Sydney Harbour with midget submarines on 31 May. We have succeeded in entering the harbour and sinking one warship. The three midget submarines which took part in this operation have not reported back.

Although MacArthur's headquarters issued a brief statement on 1 June, the first detailed reports of the raid came from American and British broadcasts. The Sydney press was particularly outraged when the initial news came from Melbourne, not Sydney. When the Minister for the Navy came under fierce fire in the House of Representatives for not allowing Sydney to release the news, Mr Makin replied: "It was thought undesirable to make an earlier announcement because enemy ships might still have been in the vicinity."

In response to the Japanese raid on Sydney, the Deputy Prime Minister, Francis Forde, made the following speech in Parliament:

> The public should not complacently count on this as the last attack in these waters. The attempted raid brings the war much nearer to the industrial heart of Australia. It should clearly

The Broken Hill Pty Ltd (BHP) cargo vessel *Iron Chieftain*. The 4,812 ton ship regularly sailed between Newcastle and Whyalla carrying coke and other materials for shipbuilding. She was armed under the Defensively Equipped Merchant Ships (DEMS) program in 1939 and carried a single 4-inch gun aft. The *Iron Chieftain* was sunk around 11.00 pm on 3 June 1942 about 27 miles east of Sydney in the general area where the coastal steamer *Age* had been shelled by a submarine only an hour earlier. Survivors reported that the ship's master, Captain Haddelsey, and the third officer, Mr Kennedy, sighted the submarine on the surface on the port side and watched it for about five minutes until the captain ordered "hard a'starboard", but before the ship could respond, a torpedo struck amidships on the port side. The *Iron Chieftain* sank in about five minutes with the loss of 12 of the crew. The names, in alphabetical order, of the men lost on the *Iron Chieftain* are: Harold Henry Bennett, Fourth Engineer Officer; Thomas Clarke, Bosun; Thomas R Glossop, Able Seaman; Marcus Gunn, Chief Engineer Officer; Lionel Haddelsey, Captain; Archibald Cook Kennedy, Third Officer; John Lander Kerr, Fireman; John Welblund Lindemann, Deck Boy, aged 17; Sidney Henry Shaw Sargent, Fireman; Sidney Francis Stafford, Wireless Operator; George Winchester Stronach, Fireman; and George Sutherland Swainson, Fifth Engineer Officer. The Japanese submarine responsible for the loss was thought to be either I-21 or I-24.

indicate the absolute necessity for eternal vigilance by all services. It should act as a new stimulus to the whole of the people to co-operate wholeheartedly on a complete war effort.

Forde's words were both true and prophetic. On 3 June, Sasaki brought I-21 to the surface 40 miles off Sydney and attacked the Australian steamer *Age* with gunfire. Unarmed, the steamer ran for safety and arrived in Newcastle the following day without further incident.

At 11:30 pm, soon after the *Age* was attacked, I-24 sank the Australian coaster, *Iron Chieftain*, which was on passage from Newcastle to Whyalla. *Iron Chieftain* had sailed from Newcastle at 10:00 pm but was only able to make good six knots against the heavy seas. Twenty seven miles from Newcastle Harbour, the submarine surfaced and fired a torpedo at the coaster. Laden with coke, *Iron Chieftain* sank in five minutes, taking with her 12 crew including the master and third mate who were last seen on the bridge.

One of the survivors, Naval gunner Cyril Sheraton, gave the following account of the *Iron Chieftan* attack in the *Sydney Morning Herald*:

> I was in my pyjamas and watch coat beside my gun when the torpedo struck. I tried to get my gun into action but did not have a chance. The captain and third mate were on the bridge and were watching the submarine for five or six minutes before the skipper shouted "Hard a'starboard". The torpedo struck before the ship could swing. I could see the submarine 200 yards away on the port side. As the ship sank under me, I was dragged onto a raft. After the ship sank, the submarine circled our raft and we thought that we might be machine-gunned so we lay still. The submarine finally left and we drifted in the darkness.

When news of the *Iron Chieftain's* sinking reached Sydney, Rear-Admiral Muirhead-Gould closed the ports of Sydney and Newcastle to outward bound shipping, and ships at sea were warned to "zigzag". The anti-submarine vessel *Bingera* sailed from Sydney to search for survivors and picked up some of the crew, including Sheraton. Another 25 crewmen were found 30 hours later after rowing their open boat ashore.

With Second Officer Brady in charge, the lifeboat picked up as many men as could be seen in the water. When no more survivors could be found they began to row through the heavy swell, taking turns at the oars to keep warm. After some hours the sea abated and conditions became easier. The men began singing to boost their morale, but it was a dismal attempt and ceased after a while. They continued to row in silence. Thirty hours later they arrived about a mile off The Entrance, north of Sydney. Unfamiliar with the area, Brady fired distress flares into the sky, but local fishermen did not understand their meaning. When help failed to arrive, the men rowed slowly ashore, weary, drenched and cold. The exhausted Second Officer was reluctant to surrender his charge to the police and had to be threatened with violence before he would consent to go to bed and warm up.

At dawn on 4 June, six hours after *Iron Chieftain* was sunk, I-27, en route to Tasmanian waters, surfaced and attacked the Australian steamer *Barwon* 30 miles off Gabo Island. The submarine commenced the attack with gunfire, followed by a torpedo which exploded prematurely alongside the steamer. Fragments of metal landed on the ship but there was no damage or casualties. *Barwon* was able to escape by outrunning her attacker.

Japanese decoy periscope recovered off the south coast of Sydney.

Courtesy L. E. C. Hinchliffe Estate

192. JAPANESE SUBMARINE RAIDERS 1942 *A Maritime Mystery*

At 4:45 pm on the same day, I-27 torpedoed the Australian ship *Iron Crown*, laden with manganese ore and bound for Newcastle. *Iron Crown* went down in one minute, taking with her 37 crew, including the captain. The submarine was forced to crash dive when an Australian Hudson aircraft suddenly appeared over the horizon.

Australian naval authorities became exceedingly jittery about the increasing Japanese submarine activity and frequent molesting of Allied shipping. On 4 June the Australian Naval Board decided to suspend all merchant sailings from eastern and southern Australian ports. However, merchant vessels already at sea before the Naval Board directive continued to fall victim to elements of the Third Submarine Company. In the absence of enemy warships, the Japanese naval authorities considered merchant vessels legitimate targets.

It was the Japanese Navy's policy to limit the number of torpedoes that a submarine commander could fire at a particular target. Merchant ships and destroyers were allotted only one torpedo, cruisers warranted three, and battleships and aircraft carriers were allotted maximum torpedo firepower. Since this policy reduced the chances of sinking a merchant ship, Captain Sasaki ordered his submarine force to resort to surface gunfire attacks in an effort to economise on torpedoes.

While Sasaki's submarine force waged its campaign of destruction, Allied aircraft continued to scour the sea in search of the submarine raiders. During this period there were many reported sightings of periscopes. However, to confuse the enemy, Sasaki's force released decoy periscopes along Australia's east coast. These decoys were made of long bamboo sticks, painted black, at the top of which was attached a mirror that would glint in the sunlight. Below the surface were two sake bottles lashed to the decoy periscope. The glass bottles were half-filled with sand and half-filled with diesel oil. The weight of the sand would cause the bamboo stick to float upright in the water, and the oil was to convince the enemy of a successful attack when it floated to the surface once the bottles shattered following a bomb or depth charge attack.

One of these decoy periscopes was responsible for a reported sighting by a Dutch aircraft eight miles south-east of Sydney on the morning of 6 June. The aircraft attacked and reported damaging a submarine at periscope depth when thick diesel oil was seen on the surface.

A decoy periscope was later recovered offshore by a commercial fisherman who turned it over to Muirhead-Gould's staff for examination.

Also on 6 June, 22-year-old Flight Lieutenant G. J. Hitchcock taxied his Lockheed Hudson bomber across the tarmac at Williamtown, north of Newcastle, and with only a scratch crew, took off to search for enemy submarines. The base medical officer had been invited to join the flight with the promise that Hitchcock would sink a submarine. Hitchcock's promise almost became a reality.

Flying at 2,000 feet, the air gunner, Flight Sergeant A. T. Morton, sighted a periscope 80 miles east of Sydney. Hitchcock descended abruptly to 500 feet and commenced his attack. The Hudson accidentally dropped its entire bomb load, which fell astern of the periscope. Hitchcock recalled that the aircraft received an almighty thump from behind when the bombs exploded. The Hudson circled the area for half an hour. While bubbles were seen rising to the surface, there was no oil. Hitchcock considered his attack was

Above & Below: results of the Japanese shelling of Sydney's Eastern Suburbs in the early morning of 8 June 1942.

unsuccessful, but newspaper accounts thought otherwise, crediting the Hudson with "the first Australian killing". Hitchcock told the author that the newspaper accounts had the effect of lifting morale and he and his crew became temporarily famous.

In the days that followed the Sydney Harbour attack, residents had begun to settle back into their normal daily routines. However, they were not without foreboding as they read press reports of submarine attacks on merchant shipping along the coast.

Sydney's apprehensive mood turned to panic when Sasaki's submarine force interrupted their campaign against Allied shipping and turned their attention to frightening the civil population. On 8 June, shortly after midnight, I-24 surfaced 12 miles off the coast of Sydney and fired 10 high explosive shells.

The examination vessel *HMAS Adele*, which was responsible for challenging suspicious vessels attempting to enter harbour, sighted the gunfire flashes out to sea, as did the army battery on Outer South Head which probed the sea with searchlights. Five minutes later the air raid alarm was sounded and city and coastal navigation lights were temporarily extinguished. The submarine submerged before the coastal defences could return fire.

There were no major casualties reported from this unexpected shelling, although one resident – a refugee from Nazi Germany – was terrified when a shell crashed though his bedroom wall. According to newspaper accounts, the man leapt out of bed, fracturing his ankle, and the shell failed to explode.

The remaining shells exploded in the suburbs of Rose Bay and Bellevue Hill, shattering windows and causing only superficial damage. One shell exploded harmlessly in Manion Avenue, Rose Bay, where a large crater was formed in the roadway.

The main objective of the shellfire was to destroy the Sydney Harbour Bridge, however, the Japanese also wanted to frighten the population. Although they failed in their first objective, they succeeded in the second beyond their expectations.

During the shelling, panic broke out when confused residents ran screaming into the streets thinking the air raid siren meant that Sydney was under attack by enemy aircraft. Urban Australians did not react very favourably when, later that morning, harbour front and other wealthy Eastern Suburb residents put their houses up for sale and fled to the Blue Mountains and even further inland, fearing a Japanese invasion at any moment.

A steady trickle of harbourside residents had been leaving Sydney following the Japanese attack on Sydney Harbour more than a week earlier; but with the shelling of the Eastern Suburbs, the trickle increased to a frenzied stream of panicky citizens. When every house, boarding house and hotel in the Blue Mountains was crammed, these "escapees" retreated further inland to Orange in the central-west of New South Wales. Some people fled from Sydney to the Hunter Valley – to towns like Singleton and Muswellbroook – but they were turned away when every available accommodation space had been taken. This is a good indication of how serious the belief was that Australia would be invaded by the "Yellow Peril".

Compared with Londoners during the Blitz, these Australians behaved with less than Churchillian courage. Only after the war was over did many of them sheepishly return, some buying back their houses at vastly inflated prices.

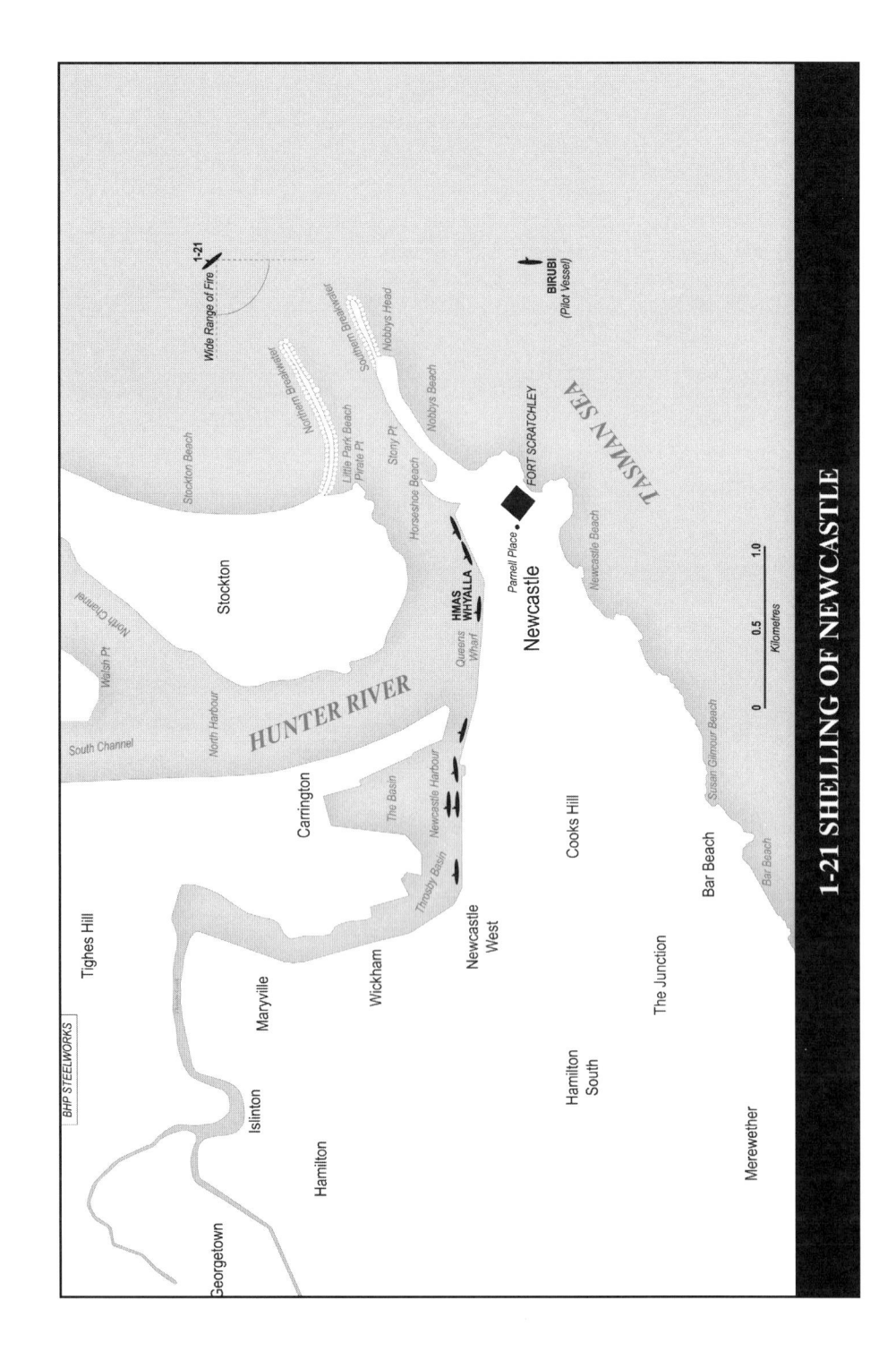

196. JAPANESE SUBMARINE RAIDERS 1942 *A Maritime Mystery*

Scenting an opportunity, poverty-stricken European refugees, many of them Jewish émigrés who had weathered far greater ordeals in Europe, had quickly moved into the area. They had shrewdly bought up the vacated real-estate at absurdly deflated prices and, after the war, many became millionaires overnight. One Eastern Suburbs real estate agent, Mr Karl Malouf, told the author that the exodus of the rich had been extensive. He remembers the harbourside suburbs of Vaucluse and Bellevue Hill were a forest of "For Sale signs." Malouf's company went on to become one of Sydney's best known realtors.

Just over two hours after I-24 shelled Sydney, I-21 surfaced three miles off Newcastle. The submarine fired 20 star shells over the industrial heart of the city, followed by six high explosive shells, only three of which exploded. Close examination of the unexploded shells later that day revealed that they had been manufactured in England in 1914! The nose sections were very rough, with some fuses bent and damaged, which explained why the majority of shells failed to explode.

The main Japanese target at Newcastle was the BHP steelworks. As with Sydney, however, the shells landed over a wide area, one shell exploding on the road behind Fort Scratchley, a coastal Army battery, and another some distance away near Nobby's Head. Two star shells also exploded above the corvette *Whyalla*, which had recently arrived in Newcastle after searching for enemy submarines off the coast.

Fort Scratchley, overlooking Newcastle Harbour, was originally built during the Russian scare of the nineteenth century and was modified and reactivated for World War II. In the early hours of the morning the duty sergeant at the Fort reported to the searchlight commander, Captain W. J. Harvey, that he could see flares in the sky and that something unusual appeared to be happening. Gun flashes were then seen and the searchlights probed the sea. At the extreme range of the searchlights, Gunner Colin Curie reported sighting a submarine. The battery commander, Captain Walter Watson, put the battery on alert and the guns were loaded ready to fire. Suddenly, Watson saw a gun flash and cried "Duck!" The shell exploded in Parnell Place, narrowly missing the observation post. Watson telephoned fire command for permission to open fire and, when he received no reply, opened fire anyway. The telephonist then reported, "Fire command says engage when ready, Sir!" Watson retorted, "Tell them I bloody-well have!" He then gave ranging corrections to his gunners and fired a second salvo.

The pilot steamer *Birubi* was at sea off Nobby's Head when the shelling began. In her haste to run for the harbour entrance and safety, the pilot vessel emitted huge clouds of thick black smoke, which obscured Watson's field of vision and he was unable to correct the range of fire. Sasaki submerged before Fort Scratchley could fire a third salvo. The pilot vessel later reported that the first salvo had fallen short of the submarine and the second had overshot.

Some remarkable escapes were made from the Newcastle shelling. Residents had heard an air raid siren shortly after midnight, followed by the "All Clear", which actually signified the end of the shelling attack on Sydney. When, an hour later, firing commenced on Newcastle, residents were confused and caught unaware.

In Parnell Place, Mrs Wilson had decided to evacuate her two young children from their home above a shop: "I thought it was only air raid drill or practice. Then I realised

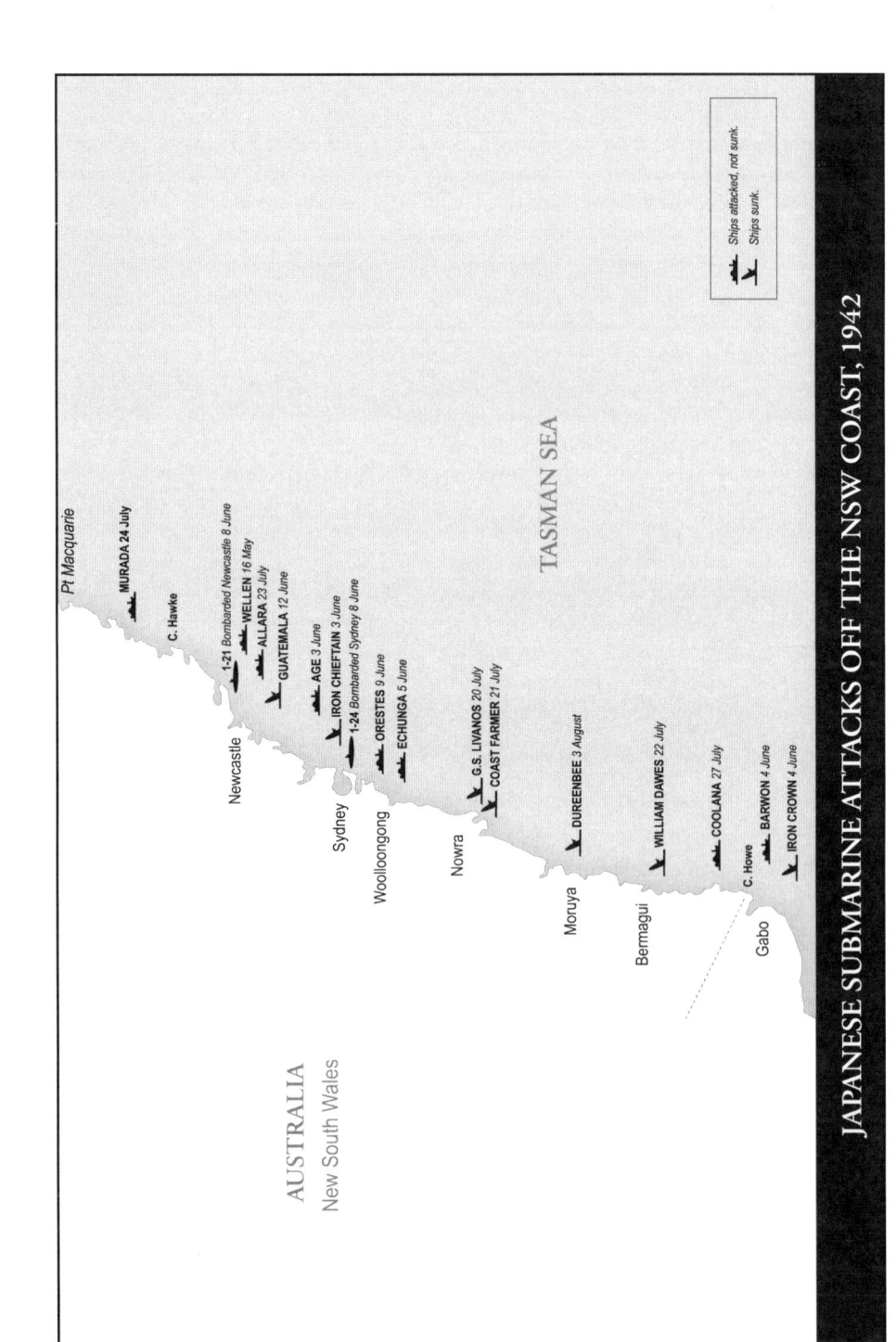

JAPANESE SUBMARINE ATTACKS OFF THE NSW COAST, 1942

Ships attacked, not sunk.
Ships sunk.

TASMAN SEA

Pt Macquarie
MURADA 24 July
C. Hawke
1-21 Bombarded Newcastle 8 June
WELLEN 16 May
ALLARA 23 July
GUATEMALA 12 June
Newcastle
AGE 3 June
IRON CHIEFTAIN 3 June
1-24 Bombarded Sydney 8 June
ORESTES 9 June
ECHUNGA 5 June
Sydney
Woolloongong
G.S. LIVANOS 20 July
COAST FARMER 21 July
Nowra
DUREENBEE 3 August
Moruya
WILLIAM DAWES 22 July
Bermagui
COOLANA 27 July
C. Howe
BARWON 4 June
Gabo
IRON CROWN 4 June

AUSTRALIA
New South Wales

198. JAPANESE SUBMARINE RAIDERS 1942 *A Maritime Mystery*

it wasn't… The shells were screaming across. The worst part was not knowing where they are going to hit."

Scooping her two children from their bed, Mrs Wilson was making her way downstairs when a shell exploded on the road outside. It was not until daylight that the young mother realised how close she and her children had come to death. She discovered shrapnel from the blast had torn through a wire mattress base where the children had been sleeping and, when she rolled back the mattress, a huge gaping hole was revealed in the wall.

There were only two casualties reported from the Newcastle shelling, both victims of shrapnel from the blast in Parnell Place. Bombardier Stan Newton had been on his way to Fort Scratchley when he was knocked unconscious by a piece of shrapnel that struck him in the forehead. Regaining consciousness, he was greeted by a surprised air raid warden. Newton then ran on to the Fort to take up his position, unaware the shrapnel was still lodged in his head.

Meanwhile, naval authorities ordered a total blackout of the Newcastle and Sydney coastal areas. *HMAS Whyalla* and the American destroyer *Perkins* were ordered to escort eight merchant ships from Newcastle to Melbourne.

Submarine bombardment of enemy cities was employed by the Japanese only on limited occasions. From the time of surfacing, often over a minute passed before the submarines could commence firing. Ranges had to be estimated from charts, and to score a direct hit was extremely difficult. The rangefinders they used were portable and inaccurate, making the whole operation a rather clumsy exercise. Also, only 20 shells could be stored at one time in the ammunition locker on the upper deck. If more ammunition was required, it had to be brought up from below, thus creating a dangerous situation, especially if the submarine had to submerge in a hurry.

After the shelling of Sydney and Newcastle, I-24 and I-21 turned their attention back to terrorising merchant ships off the coast. At 1:00 am on 9 June, I-24 pursued and shelled the British merchant ship *Orestes* 90 miles south of Sydney. Steaming independently from Sydney to Melbourne, *Orestes* presented a prime target for I-24 which chased the merchantman for five hours. During the running battle *Orestes* suffered several direct hits, resulting in a large fire. Believing the merchant vessel was doomed, I-24 broke off the attack; but *Orestes* succeeded in extinguishing the fire and made Melbourne safely the next day.

Not so fortunate was the Panamanian vessel *Guatemala*. At 1:15 am on 12 June, I-24 intercepted and successfully sank the merchant ship 40 miles from Sydney. *Guatemala* had left Newcastle in the convoy escorted by *Perkins* and *Whyalla*, but soon found herself straggling behind the convoy. The Norwegian master, Captain A. G. Bang, heard two gunshots to starboard but saw nothing. A few minutes later the second officer saw the track of a torpedo approaching the ship, which struck before he could take evasive action. The crews took to the lifeboats and *Guatemala* sank an hour later without any casualties. Soon afterwards the Australian minesweeper *Doomba* picked up the 51 crew and transported them to Sydney.

The Japanese account of the *Guatemala*'s sinking varies slightly from official Australian records. In his book, *Sunk*, Mochitsura Hasimoto records the submarine fired one torpedo

The Australian hospital ship *Centaur*, sunk by a Japanese submarine off the Queensland coast on 14 May 1943.

SUBMARINE	AREA	SHIPS SUNK	PERIOD
I-124	North Coast of Australia	1	-
I-1	West Coast of Australia	3	March 1942
I-2	West Coast of Australia	-	March 1942
I-3	West Coast of Australia	-	March 1942
I-24	Sydney	3	June-July 1942
I-27	East Coast of Australia	1	June 1942
I-22	East Coast of Australia	-	June 1942
I-29	Brisbane	-	June 1942
I-11	South of Sydney	2	July-Aug 1942
I-174	North of Sydney	2	July-Aug 1942
I-175	North of Sydney	-	July-Aug 1942
I-21	Sydney	6	Jan-Feb 1943
I-26	Brisbane	2	April 1943
I-178	East Coast of Australia	1	April-June 1943
I-177	East Coast of Australia	1*	April 1943
I-180	East Coast of Australia	2	April-May 1943
I-174	East Coast of Australia	2	May-June 1943
RO 33	North Coast of Australia	1	July-Aug 1942

* The hospital ship *Centaur* was sunk by I-177.

at *Guatemala* which detonated prematurely. The submarine then surfaced and engaged the Panamanian vessel with gunfire, but found it difficult to score a direct hit in the darkness. The submarine intercepted an SOS from the ship announcing she was under attack and asking for assistance. Eventually, one of I-24's shells hit its target, after which *Guatemala's* crew stopped the ship and took to the lifeboats. The submarine then fired a second torpedo which sank the doomed ship.

This was the last enemy submarine attack in Australian waters for about six weeks.

From the time of the Sydney Harbour raid until the sinking of *Guatemala*, the Third Submarine Company had sunk four ships with the loss of 73 lives over a period of 12 days. From mid-July until the beginning of August, three more large Japanese submarines – I-11, I-174 and I-175 – joined with I-24 to continue Japan's campaign of destruction along the coast. They succeeded in sinking another four vessels before leaving Australian waters.

Thereafter, a period of calm followed until January 1943 when I-21 returned to Australian waters and sank six ships off Sydney over the following month. Then, in April 1943, I-26 sank two vessels off Brisbane, and a further six ships were sunk between April and mid-June 1943.

When Japan lost her forward bases at Rabaul and Truk, distant operations into Australian waters were rendered progressively more difficult. By the end of July 1943, submarine operations became almost impossible.

Between June 1942 and December 1944, a total of 27 merchant ships were sunk in Australian waters with the loss of 577 lives, including the 21 sailors who lost their lives on *Kuttabul*. Of the total fatalities, 268 lives were lost in one attack when the Australian hospital ship, *Centaur*, was sunk 40 miles east of Brisbane on 14 May 1943. The *Centaur* sank in about three minutes with only 64 survivors, who spent 36 hours in the water before rescue. The Japanese submarine thought responsible for the sinking was I-177 commanded by Lieutenant-Commander Nakagawa, who was later tried as a war criminal and spent four years in prison for firing on survivors from a British merchant vessel torpedoed in the Indian Ocean. The sinking of the *Centaur* was not raised at his trial. ●

AUTHOR'S NOTE

AUTHOR'S NOTE

> General MacArthur ... was better informed about the enemy dispositions than any other military leader in history.
>
> *The Pacific War*
> John Costello

The midget submarine operations on Sydney Harbour and Madagascar, although they achieved only minor military results, had been intended by Admiral Yamamoto to play a significant role in Japan's overall naval strategy. However, his main strategy was to launch an operation on the Aleutians and Midway Island. He gambled on trapping the American Pacific Fleet, which would steam west from Pearl Harbor to repel the Midway operation and be caught unaware by Japanese submarines and carriers strategically lying in wait. But the gambit failed because the Allies were reading a large portion of crucial Japanese fleet signals and, significantly, over-the-target weather reports sent in low grade code which provided an indicator of intended area operations. Although only 20 per cent of all this traffic was deciphered, it was enough to anticipate Japan's next move in the Pacific theatre.

The bulk of the information on the secret war was gleaned from listening posts at Washington's Naval Headquarters (NEGAT), Pearl Harbor's Pacific Fleet Combat Intelligence Unit (HYPO), and MacArthur's code-breakers in Australia (BELCONNEN). Of these three intelligence units, BELCONNEN was used to the greatest advantage by MacArthur who has been described by John Costello in his book, *The Pacific War*, as being "better informed about the enemy dispositions than any other military leader in history".

Prior to the war in the Pacific, "Magic" machines had been installed in Washington and Manila, with the unit destined for Pearl Harbor diverted to Bletchley Park in order to read Japanese signal traffic. When MacArthur fled from the Philippines to Australia in March 1942, he carried with him the decoding device, which he quickly set up in his Melbourne headquarters. Code breakers attached to MacArthur's command searched continuously for patterns in the Japanese signal traffic in order to break their codes. A steady stream of intercepted information was exchanged between Washington, Pearl Harbor and Melbourne to quickly build up a directory of solved cryptograms. Within five months of the Pearl Harbor attack the highly sensitive and revealing Japanese JN25 code was sufficiently penetrated to allow MacArthur and Rear-Admiral Chester W. Nimitz in Hawaii to obtain a clear picture of Japanese disposition and intentions. Fortunately for the

Allies, at this crucial period of 1942, a planned change in the two code books that made up the JN25 code, was postponed from 1 April to 1 May, and was later deferred to 1 June because of problems associated with distributing the two new books to every Japanese ship.

The code breakers began to reap the rewards of their efforts when they deciphered Japanese intentions of a southward thrust towards Australia as early as 25 March. By April, the volume of traffic focusing on Rabaul had intensified and, coupled with coast-watcher reports of a sudden increase in the flow of planes, shipping and troops to Rabaul, MacArthur and Nimitz were able to predict that the Japanese intended to launch an offensive operation in the South Pacific in the near future. By 3 May, the entire Japanese plan for the sea invasion of Port Moresby and Tulagi had been deciphered and Nimitz deployed his meagre naval forces accordingly to intercept the Japanese threat.

"Magic" intercepts had also uncovered plans for a second offensive operation in the mid-Pacific before the main action of the Coral Sea battle had unfolded, although some confusion existed over the precise location. On 5 May, Yamamoto issued his operational plans for "Operation MI" (Operation Midway) with the aim of occupying Midway and strategic points west of the Aleutian Islands. His strategy contemplated a crushing and decisive naval engagement ending with the defeat of the American Pacific Fleet, which, he hoped, would bring the United States to the peace table and a quick end to the Pacific War.

Yamamoto's elaborate plan was to be choreographed in a series of carefully synchronised movements centred on Midway. His strategy called for the Aleutian Islands operation to precede Midway by 72 hours. The Japanese fleet then intended to lie in wait for the United States Pacific Fleet which would predictably come charging to the battle area from the west where it would be mauled firstly by a submarine force deployed across its line of advance, and secondly by a surface action from aircraft launched from four Japanese carriers.

The first deciphered signals referring to the Midway operation were intercepted on 4 March 1942; by the end of April signals were being intercepted referring to the Aleutians and that the operation would occur after the Port Moresby invasion. However, the Japanese signals used the letter indicators AF, representing Midway, and AO for the Aleutians, which confused the intelligence teams working desperately to solve the riddle.

By the end of April, MacArthur's BELCONNEN intelligence team in Australia insisted that the Japanese intended to invade Australia, and not Midway or the Aleutians as was considered by Nimitz's HYPO team in Pearl Harbour. He demanded reinforcements to meet the threat, but they were denied him because of the "beat Hitler first" global strategy. MacArthur provoked the wrath of Churchill when he persuaded Curtin to demand at least two Royal Navy carriers and first call on reinforcements on their way to the Middle East. He then leaked reports to the *Sydney Morning Herald* in late April 1942 about the forthcoming Operation in New Guinea, which sent the Chief of Naval Operations in Washington, Admiral Ernest J. King, into a rage for endangering the whole naval intelligence operation. Fortunately, the Japanese paid little attention to the newspaper speculation, which became evident when radio intercepts showed no discernable change in Operation MO that had now been extended to take in the phosphate-rich Ocean and Nauru islands after they had seized

Port Moresby. Prior knowledge of a midget submarine attack on Sydney Harbour, and a major air strike on Townsville following Operation MO, would have only strengthened MacArthur's belief that the Japanese planned to invade Australia.

Despite MacArthur's fears, intercepts soon indicated a Japanese naval force amassing at Saipan Island for an operation in the mid-Pacific, but Nimitz was at his wits' end to pinpoint the exact location of the intended offensive. Washington's NEGAT intelligence team further confused the picture when it concurred with MacArthur's predictions of a renewed southward advance. Uncertain now of where the Japanese intended to move, Nimitz's HYPO team decided to initiate a ploy to once and for all determine where Yamamoto's forces intended to strike. Instructions were relayed to the garrison commander on Midway to make an emergency radio call in plain English stating the island's water distillation unit had broken down. Naval authorities radioed back from Pearl Harbor that a water barge was on its way with emergency supplies. The ruse succeeded when, 24 hours later, intercepts were deciphered containing orders for the Japanese invasion force to take aboard extra water.

Good fortune continued to favour the BELCONNEN, HYPO and NEGAT intelligent teams until 1 June when the Japanese finally switched to their new code books; but the exact plan and time of the Midway operation had already been exposed and Nimitz carefully deployed his carrier force in ample time to successfully ambush the Japanese carriers. As a result, the tide of the Pacific War was turned sharply in favour of the Allies.

Despite the adverse outcome at Midway for the Japanese, Yamamoto continued as Commander of the Combined Fleet through the following Guadalcanal campaign, which further depleted Japan's naval resources. While on an inspection tour in the Northern Solomon Islands, he was killed in an aerial ambush by US Army Air Force planes on 18 April 1943 following a signal intercept five days earlier. Since most of his inspection trip was to be made by minesweeper, it is indicative of how precisely timed the American plan had to be. His death was a crushing blow for the Japanese Imperial Navy.

In an Australian context, in 1942 Australia found herself almost defenceless. Japanese war plans called for the seizure of Fiji and New Caledonia and carrier strikes against Australian east coast cities in July 1942. Only the miracle of Midway in June and victory in the long and terrible struggle for Guadalcanal pushed back the Japanese threat.

The Battle of Midway in June 1942 was the turning point in the Pacific War. From then on, Allied forces slowly won back the territories occupied by Japan. In 1944, intensive air raids started over Japan, and in the northern spring of 1945, US forces invaded Okinawa in one of the bloodiest battles of the Pacific War. After US military forces dropped two atomic bombs on Hiroshima and Nagasaki, Japan finally surrendered unconditionally on 14 August 1945. ●

Epilogue

EPILOGUE

> I nurtured my son just as I grew precious flowers
> So that he could dedicate himself to the Emperor.
> Now that the storm has passed
> And all the cherry blossoms have blown away,
> The garden looks very deserted.
>
> *Matsue Matsuo* Memorial poem
> presented to the Australian War Memorial
> on the anniversary of her son's death.

After the Sydney Harbour attack, naval divers were sent down into the cold harbour depths to search for the sunken midget submarines. The water was so murky that visibility was restricted to a little over three feet and it took the divers some time to find Matsuo's craft, which was lying on its keel in 75 feet of water, the two torpedoes still stuck in their tubes. An attempt had been made to fire one torpedo, which had jammed against the torpedo cap. Although the stern section had almost completely separated from the main section of the submarine, the engine was still turning slowly. On closer inspection, the divers found the hull was severely dented from depth charge bombing. After tapping on the hull and receiving no response, they presumed the crew inside were dead.

In his report of the salvage operation, Leading Seaman W. L. Bullard recorded that he heard a continual throbbing noise in his helmet when he entered the water, but thought it was caused by some boat on the surface.

> Walking and trailing heavy breast rope and air hose was hard going and the stirring up of the mud made for poor visibility. After about 10 minutes I stopped to let the water clear and have a breather, and as the water cleared I caught a glimpse of a steel wire stay about 20 yards away. I walked towards it and saw a submarine lying practically on an even keel and apparently undamaged. I put my hand on the hull, which was quite warm. Suddenly, I realised that the sound I had heard from the time I entered the water was coming from the sub and was quite loud. I thought she might take off at any minute and I hated the thought of tangling up with her if she did.

Bullard reported his findings to naval experts on the surface and it was agreed that the recovery of the midget would be difficult and dangerous. Relays of divers were sent down to hammer a ridge around the bow of the craft where a wire hawser would be placed from a floating crane in preparation for lifting the submarine. It was hoped that the hawser would grip the ridge. As darkness descended, work ceased for the day, and the following morning the dive team discovered that the engine had stopped.

The first attempt to recover the midget submarine failed when the wire hawser parted, but a second attempt was successful. The craft was raised to the surface and towed across the harbour to Clarke Island where naval authorities examined its contents. The bodies of Lieutenant Matsuo and Petty Officer Tsuzuku were recovered and taken to the city mortuary where it was revealed from a post mortem that they had died from gunshot wounds. A ceremonial sword bearing the name of Matsuo was found hanging in the control room, and a *senninbari*, or thousand stitch belt, was recovered from his body.

When a Japanese soldier was called to active duty, the women in his family often made a *senninbari* for him to take along as good luck. This term literally means "thousand-person-stitches", but is usually translated into English as "thousand stitch belt". They were usually cloth strips of a size to be worn around the head as a headband (*hachimaki*) or around the waist. A woman from the family would stand on a street corner and entreat passersbys to add a stitch each. When one thousand stitches had been collected, the belt was believed by some to have special power to protect the bearer from the hazards of battle. Matsuo's *senninbari* had been presented to him by his mother at their last meeting in Kure at the end of March 1942. The thousand stitch belt was returned to her on a visit to Australia in 1968 to pray for the soul of her son.

On 5 June the entangled stern section of Chuma's craft was salvaged from the boom net. The submarine had been blown completely into two parts and the shattered bow section had sunk to the harbour floor where divers recovered the remains of Lieutenant Chuma and Petty Officer Ohmori. Miraculously, the two torpedoes lay undamaged on the seabed. Leading Seaman Bullard reported the craft was "hopelessly fouled by her propellers in the steel mesh defence net" and he had to cut out the stern with underwater cutting gear to free the submarine.

When the bodies of the Japanese sailors were recovered it was decided to grant them a funeral with full naval honours. Their coffins were draped with the Japanese flag and placed in a chapel. It was hoped that such a civil act would spur the Japanese to similarly honour Australia's war dead overseas. The service was attended by Rear-Admiral Muirhead-Gould, the Swiss Consul-General, a member of the media and an unknown woman. Three volleys were fired into the air by a naval guard of honour, which was followed by the sounding of the "Last Post". The four Japanese soldiers were then cremated, as was the tradition of the Japanese. Their ashes were placed in a columbarium at the Eastern Suburbs Crematorium where they remained until arrangements were made by the Swiss Consul-General to have them returned to Japan.

On 13 August 1942 the ashes were formerly handed to Tatsuo Kawai, the man who had been Japanese Ambassador to Australia prior to the Pacific War. The ashes left Australia on an exchange ship carrying Japanese diplomats and civilians to Lourenco

Salvage operations of Lt Chuma's midget submarine I-27, recovered from the boom net.

The forward half of midget submarine I-22 recovered from Taylor Bay. Note the depth charge damage below the conning tower. A close-up of the stern shows how cleanly the explosion sheared through the metal. The "traffic sheath" is visible beneath the midget submarine.

JAPANESE SUBMARINE RAIDERS 1942 *A Maritime Mystery* .213

Bow section of midget I-22, showing a damaged nose guard and jammed torpedo caps.

Rebuilding of composite submarine on Clarke Island, made up from the bow section of I-22 and the stern section of I-27.

Marques in East Africa where they were transferred to the exchange ship *Kamakura Maru* for the return journey to Japan.

When the *Kamakura Maru* arrived in Yokohama on 9 October, thousands of people lined the streets to pay homage to their fallen heroes. Japanese broadcasts announced the arrival of the ashes in Yokohama and A. G. Oshigaha, a Japanese journalist, wrote in his newspaper of the deep emotion he felt at meeting the souls of Matsuo and his companions. So moved was he that he sent Rear-Admiral Muirhead-Gould a message over Tokyo radio:

> If you had been at Yokohama pier on Friday morning, you would have understood what sort of fatherland and what kind of parents have produced such fragrant and noble souls as those of the four heroes.

Matsuo and the midget submarine crews received posthumous promotions of two ranks, and Matsuo's ashes were placed in a tomb at his birthplace in Yamaga City.

Although Muirhead-Gould emerged from the Sydney Harbour attack publicly uncriticised, he came under fire for giving a decent burial to the enemy seamen. In a radio broadcast to Australians in July 1942, his words were a fitting eulogy for the dead sailors:

> I have been criticised for having accorded these men military honours as we hope may be accorded to our own comrades who have died in enemy lands, but I ask you – should we not accord full honours to such brave men as these? It must take courage of the very highest order to go out in a thing like that steel coffin. I hope I shall not be a coward when my time comes, but I confess that I wonder whether I should have the courage to take one of those things across Sydney Harbour in peace time. Theirs was a courage which is not the property or the tradition or the heritage of any one nation: it is the courage shared by the brave men of our own countries as well as of the enemy, and however horrible war and its results may be, it is a courage which is recognised and universally admired. These men were patriots of the highest order. How many of us are prepared to make one thousandth of the sacrifice that these men made?

This moving speech – the more so for having been delivered by a man who had not distinguished himself during the raid – was broadcast throughout Australia to raise war bonds.

Both Captain Hankyu Sasaki and Commander Ageta survived the war. Twenty-seven years after the war, Sasaki reflected on the treatment of the Japanese crews recovered in Sydney Harbour in an interview with Takeo Yamashita, co-author of *To Sydney by Stealth*:

> I cannot help feeling great respect and deep gratitude to the Australians who courteously buried the young martyrs of the enemy with full naval honours and sent the ashes back to Japan. It was in the middle of the war, and their civil deed without partial feeling of friend or foe was really great and humane. It gave a good lesson to all the world what true humanity and reasonable sense should be.

At the conclusion of the war it was learned that none of the carrier submarines which took part in the Sydney Harbour attack had survived the war, and only a very small number of officers and men attached to the Third Submarine Company returned to Japan. According to the demobilisation Minister, K. Nakamura, representing the Imperial Japanese Navy, all the related documents and reports received from these submarines were lost through fire or other causes.

The first submarine to meet her demise was I-22, which was sunk on Christmas Day 1942 by an American torpedo boat off south-east New Guinea. The submarine's captain at that time was Commander Chinao Naruzawa, who had not long succeeded Commander Ageta.

On 10 June 1943, the American patrol craft *PC487* sank I-24 off the Aleutian Islands, and on 4 February 1944 the *USS Charrette* and *USS Fair* sunk I-21 north-west of the Marshall Islands. Eight days later I-27 was sunk by the British destroyers *HMS Paladin* and *HMS Petard*, south-west of the Maldives Islands. Finally, on 26 July 1944, fate overtook I-29 north of Luzon Island in the Philippines in the form of the American submarine *USS Sawfish*.

When Ageta returned to Japan he was transferred to the Submarine Training School at Kure where he remained until war's end. Twenty years after the Sydney Harbour attack, he lamented the tremendous losses experienced in Japan's submarine service. He told Japanese historian Takeo Yamashita that the Midget Submarine Corps was the most courageous in the Japanese Navy because the crews repeatedly volunteered for desperate naval engagements having a good idea they would never return. Captain Sasaki gave a more "in depth" account:

> When Japan began to have a hard fight, thousands of young men devoted their lives to their country, with a belief in God's favourable wind in the sky and blessed reversal of their desperate battle by the human torpedoes in the sea. It may fairly be said that those young men took over this spirit from those who started for the attacks on Pearl Harbor, Sydney and Diego Suarez, never to return.

Of the midget submarine crews, few survived the war. Matsuo and Chuma had graduated from Kure Naval College with 219 other cadets. Of these, 80 became airmen and 50 turned to the midget submarine service. Only 100 of their fellow college graduates survived the war – less than half. Of the 20 crew who participated in the Pearl Harbor, Diego Suarez Bay and Sydney Harbour attacks, only one survived. In an interview with historian Takeo Yamashita, Captain Hankyu Sasaki described his efforts to recover the crews from both Pearl Harbor and Sydney Harbour:

> When I started for the Pearl Harbor attack and also the Sydney Harbour attack commanding the submarines, Admiral Yamamoto said to me, "Be sure to recover the crews". Although I did my best, we could recover none of the crews in either case. I am very sorry for them. But those young men's spirit, fighting spirit of bravely carrying out their duty for their country even at the cost of their lives … that is something we should value highly forever.

After the Sydney Harbour attack the Japanese Navy carried out two more daring midget submarine attacks during which they achieved their greatest results. Under the command of Captain N. Ota, I-16, I-20 and I-24 proceeded to Truk Lagoon where they embarked their midget submarines and headed for Guadalcanal in the Solomon Islands. In mid-November,

Members of the Japanese Imperial Navy Midget Submarine Attack Group who carried out simultaneous attacks on Diego Suarez Bay and Sydney Harbour on 31 May 1942. Members are shown in crews of two with the commanding officer seated in the front row and his crew member standing behind him.

Front row (L to R): Sub-Lt Katsusuke Iwase (died Diego Suarez); Lt Masaharu Oota (didn't take part in Diego Suarez attack because of engine problems, but died later when submarine sank in Bay of Biscay); Lt Kieu Matsuo (died Sydney Harbour); Lt Saburoo Akieda (died Bay of Biscay); Lt Kenshi Chuma (died Sydney Harbour); Lt Teiji Yamaki (although a member of Sydney Harbour attack group, he did not take part because of a training accident); and Lt Katsuhisa Ban (presumed killed Sydney Harbour).

Back Row (L to R): Petty Officer (PO) Koozoo Takada (died Diego Suarez); PO Daiseiki Tsubokura (died Guadalcanal); PO Masao Tsuzuku (died Sydney Harbour); PO Masami Takemoto (died Diego Suarez); PO Takeshi Oomori (died Sydney Harbour); PO Shizuka Masumoto (killed in a battery explosion accident before Sydney Harbour attack); and PO Mamoru Ashibe (presumed killed Sydney Harbour).

嗚呼忠烈真珠灣襲擊九軍神

Nine midget submarine warrior heroes from the Pearl Harbor attack. This picture appeared in the *Yomiusi Shinbun* in March 1942. Conspicuous in his absence is Kazuo Sakamaki, the only survivor who was captured. *Top to Bottom (L to R):* Shigemi Furuno, Naoji Iwasa, Masaharu Yokoyama, Naokichi Sasaki, Shigenori Yokoyama, Akira Hiroo, Kiyoshi Inagaki, Yoshio Katayama, Sadaji Uyeda.

Courtesy Japan Midget Submarine Association

sometime after dark, I-16 and I-20 launched their craft towards Lunga Anchorage. One succeeded in sinking a transport ship and an American destroyer. The other was unable to fire its torpedoes due to a malfunction and was forced to return to its carrier submarine.

One month later Ota launched two more midget submarines off Lunga Anchorage where another two transport ships were sunk by one craft. Again, the other midget submarine was unable to fire its two torpedoes and returned to its parent submarine. Like Pearl Harbor, Diego Suarez and Sydney Harbour, the two craft that fired their torpedoes in Lunga Anchorage did not return.

In anticipation of the Philippines invasion, four midget submarines were moved to the area to defend the straits in the centre of Mindanao. Positioned at the narrowest section of the straits, they achieved results which were unparalleled by their predecessors. Over a three-month period they successfully sank 14 naval vessels, including two cruisers, one seaplane carrier, five destroyers and five transport ships. The crews survived all of these attacks but when the Americans landed at Davao on 20 March 1945, they scuttled their craft and swam ashore.

Sub-Lieutenant Kazou Sakamaki in midget I-24 was captured at Pearl Harbor and became America's first Japanese prisoner of war. He was taken to nearby Bellows Field for interrogation and later transferred to a POW camp in Wisconsin, USA. Sakamaki was deeply humiliated to be taken alive as Prisoner of War No. 1. He burned himself with cigarettes in prison and demanded to be allowed to commit suicide, but his American guards declined. He returned to Japan in January 1946 when it became known that, of all the men who served in midget submarines during the course of the war, only 20 officers and men survived.

When news of the loss of life at Pearl Harbor reached Japan shortly after the attack, Sakamaki's photograph did not appear alongside the other nine which were published in newspapers and who were acclaimed as heroes and promoted two ranks posthumously for their part in the attack. However, the fact that one crewman was not accounted for raised some suspicions among those associated with the midget submarines.

When Sakamaki returned to Japan, the public became aware of his role at Pearl Harbor and many thought he should have perished along with his compatriots; however, in Japan's new age of enlightenment, he was accepted back by his family and soon became one of Japan's leading industrialist managers working for the Toyota Motor Car Company. Sakamaki went on to become a key Toyota executive and was sent overseas to Brazil to head the company's distribution centre in the Americas. In the 1990s, he joined the US speaker circuit and participated in several platform discussions about the Pearl Harbor attack and his experiences as a prisoner of war. After a lifetime of avoiding the spotlight, Kazuo Sakamaki passed away on 29 November 1999, at 81 years of age. His passion for privacy was such that his family did not release the news of his death for nearly a month.

The wreckage of his craft was recovered and transported to mainland USA where it toured 41 states during the war years before winding up on the docks in Chicago, Illinois. From Chicago, where she was when the Japanese surrendered, the midget submarine was moved to a US Naval Submarine Base at Key West, Florida, as a front exhibit for the small naval museum. Today, the midget submarine is a popular exhibit at the Nimitz Museum in Texas where it will remain until 2008.

In early 1942 when the clean-up in Pearl Harbor began, a midget submarine from I-22

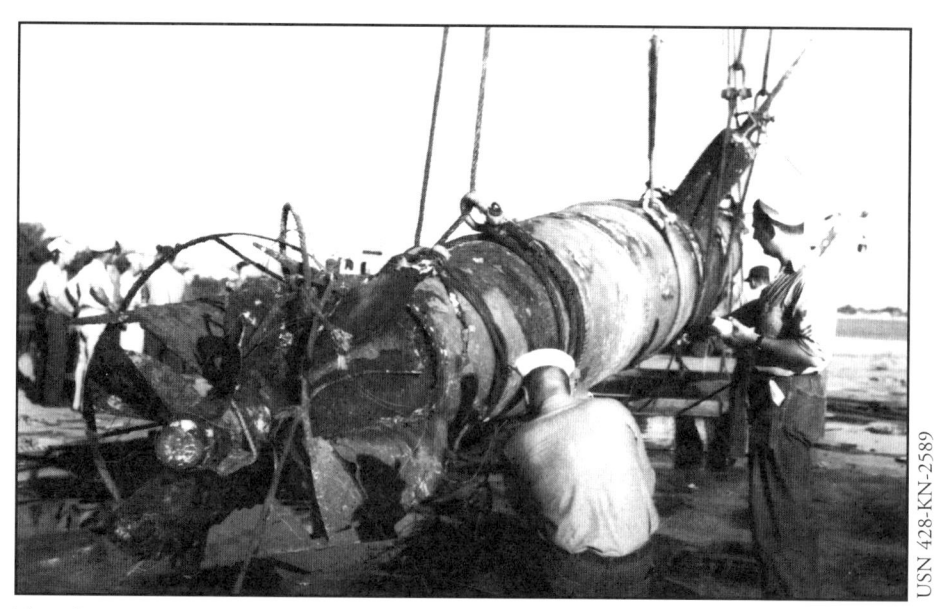

This submarine was recovered near the entrance to Pearl Harbor in late July 1960. The propellers are slightly damaged and part of the guard on the right side is missing.

Guadalcanal, British Solomon Islands Protectorate, November 1942. A Japanese midget submarine salvaged by a US Navy construction battalion (Seabees) after being scuttled by her crew during the Battle of Guadalcanal. In the background is the stranded hulk of the Japanese transport *Yamazuki Maru*.

220. JAPANESE SUBMARINE RAIDERS 1942 *A Maritime Mystery*

was recovered inside the harbour where it had been sunk by depth charges during the height of the attack. After several months in the water, both the wreckage and remains of the crew were buried in the construction of a new pier. After the war the midget submarine and her crew, Lieutenant Iwase and Petty Officer Sasaki, were disinterred and then reburied again with appropriate ceremony. The midget still lies in coral and sand fill as a permanent part of the base it attacked.

On 13 June 1960, the midget submarine from I-18 was discovered in 75 feet of water near the mouth of Pearl Harbor by Navy scuba diver, C. F. Buhl. The submarine's torpedoes were still intact. The hatch door in the conning tower was secured from the outside and no remains were found inside the submarine. What happened to the crewmen, Sub-Lieutenant Furuno and Petty Officer Yokoyama, still remains a mystery. The midget submarine was raised and, at the request of the Japanese government, returned to Japan. It now stands as a monument on the grounds of the former Japanese Naval Academy at Eta Jima.

On 8 August 2002, two deep diving submersibles operated by the Hawaii Undersea Research Laboratory (HURL) found a fourth Japanese midget submarine, which is believed to be the first midget sunk in the attack on Pearl Harbor. This was the midget submarine from I-20, crewed by Sub-Lieutenant Hiroo and Petty Officer Katayama. The discovery has been described as the most significant modern marine archaeological find ever in the Pacific since the discovery of the *Titanic* in the Atlantic. The midget submarine was found in over 1,300 feet of water about 5 miles off the mouth of Pearl Harbor. Photographs show it in an upright position on the bottom and in remarkable condition. Both torpedoes are still in place. The submarine has no apparent depth charge damage but does have shell damage on both sides of the conning tower.

The discovery of I-20 confirmed the account radioed to naval command at Pearl Harbor at 6:45 am on 7 December 1941 of a Japanese submarine trying to enter Pearl Harbor behind a cargo ship. The crew of the attacking *USS Ward* dropped four depth charges directly on the submarine. The charges were set to detonate at 100 feet, when the craft was at the surface. *Ward's* captain reported a direct hit on the conning tower with the 4-inch side gun and that the midget submarine had fully lifted out of the water following the depth charge attack before it sank.

This was the first combat action of the as yet unopened Pacific War. Unfortunately, *Ward's* coded report didn't reach the Commander-in-Chief of the US Fleet and Pacific Fleet in Pearl Harbor, Admiral H. E. Kimmel, until 7·40 am, shortly before the aerial attack began. At the subsequent Pearl Harbor investigation, some question was made of the accuracy of *Ward's* report. The destroyer itself was later targeted by the Japanese and sunk in a *kamikaze* attack in the Philippines, ironically, on 7 December 1944.

The location of the fifth midget submarine, crewed by Sub-Lieutenant Yokoyama and Petty Officer Uyeda, still remains a mystery, however, it is believed to have successfully penetrated Pearl Harbor and fired it's two torpedoes at the battleships *Oklahoma* and *West Virginia* before escaping the harbour and eventually sinking in the deep waters somewhere between Oahu and Lanai Islands.

Following the attack on Sydney Harbour, the remains of the two midget submarines salvaged from the harbour were reconstructed to build a single composite submarine.

The midget submarine was loaded onto a transporter en route between Sydney and Melbourne during an exhibition tour to raise money for the naval relief fund and is now part of the Australian War Memorial's collection.

Melbourne, Victoria, March 1943. The captured Japanese midget submarine on display with Army and Navy personnel posed in front of it.

Composite midget submarine at rest on the west lawns of the Australian War Memorial, now housed inside the building.

Items taken from the craft were put on exhibition at Fort Macquarie and then auctioned to the public. The wife of the US Consul-General and the Danish Consul-General paid three pounds each for a cartridge from the Japanese revolver. Muirhead-Gould's four-year-old grandson, who assisted in the auction, sold souvenirs to the Lord Mayor and his wife.

Following its reconstruction, the composite midget submarine was loaded on to an army transport vehicle and sent on a tour of the nation to help raise money for returned servicemen and the Red Cross. The midget submarine travelled through bush towns from Sydney to Melbourne, then moved onto Adelaide before making its final overland voyage to Canberra and its final resting place. The composite submarine is now housed inside the Australian War Memorial building, protected from the corrosive elements of weather.

When the momentum of fighting escalated in the South-West Pacific, Australians came to realise that for the first time war was knocking at their door. While the major powers were dictating global strategy, Australia had become, in General Tojo's mocking words, "the orphan of the Pacific". General Hideki Tojo was Japan's wartime Prime Minister and Commander-in-Chief of the General Staff.

However, when the security of Australia, and therefore the Pacific, was threatened, it was not long before the orphan was adopted by America. On 16 November 1942, the Australian Prime Minister expressed his concern to President Roosevelt about the "beat Hitler first" grand strategy:

> The decisions on global strategy have been taken by Mr Churchill and yourself. The Commonwealth Government has shown a ready willingness to co-operate in other theatres at considerable risk to the security of Australia. The government considers the contribution it has made entitle it to the assurance that the fullest possible support will be given to the situation in the Pacific. The simple fact is that we had no voice in the decisions. We were confronted with a *fait accompli* and we had no alternative but to accept those decisions, much as we dislike them.

Much of the information in this book has come from cautious survivors of the raid and by arduous battles with even more cautious custodians of public records. It is an indication of how officially unresolved the history of the Japanese midget submarine raid was in the years following the attack that several participants on the harbour that night were reluctant to tell their story for fear of loosing their pensions or worse, being prosecuted under the *Official Secrets Act*. The attitude of these men was a product of the quite unjustified fear of being considered unpatriotic, a feeling that was nurtured by the closed and fearful attitudes of censorship instigated by the Curtin government.

A. F. Davies, the sociologist who spent a lifetime studying Australian politics, has written: "… the characteristic talent of Australians is bureaucracy". But attitudes are changing in modern-day Australia, with people attempting to establish a national identity which has been denied them by the actions of closed and untrusting governments. From the volumes of books, films and television documentaries about World War II, it is apparent that Australians not only have a thirst for knowledge about the war but are adult enough to accept the not so glorious aspects of previous times.

It is significant that Japanese private organisations, such as the Japan Midget Submarine Association, and even the keepers of official records, are more open and

Charlie Brown, a survivor from *HMAS Kuttabul*, meets Lt Matsuo's sister, Mrs Fuji Saeki, at Garden Island in 1988. In the background (with camera) is Matsuo's niece, Mrs Kazuko Matuo.

Flag Officer Naval Support Command, Rear-Admiral A. R. Horton, and President of the Japan Midget Submarine Association, Admiral Jikyo Ishino, unveil the *HMAS Kuttabul* Memorial Plaque on Garden Island in 1988.

helpful than were any of their Australian counterparts. A Japanese organisation similar to the RSL has a fund whereby relatives of the war dead can visit the places where their loved ones were killed to pray for their souls. It was as a beneficiary of this fund that Matsuo's mother, Matsue Matsuo, visited Sydney in 1968 to throw sake and rice over the waters of Taylor Bay where her son died 27 years earlier. In her anguish at meeting the soul of her son, she was undoubtedly remembering their last meeting on the eve of his departure for Sydney Harbour.

In March 1942, Kieu Matsuo wrote his family a letter in which he said he was undertaking a dangerous new mission, which was so secret he was unable to tell them more. Matsuo had a good idea that he would not see his family again, so he asked to meet them. He wrote: "When you come, please worship for me at the Kikuchi Shrine and receive seven talismans of the shrine. It is my constant wish to go to a battle with the soul of the Kikuchi clan enshrined there". Matsuo had admired the Kikuchi clan, which had heroically fought alongside the southern ruling dynasty in Kyushu against the oppressive northern dynasty during the fourteenth century. In these battles three of the Kikuchi were killed and had become martyrs whose souls were still worshipped at the shrine. Matsuo hoped to emulate the courage of the Kikuchi martyrs, so when he met his family for the last time at Kure, it was an intensely emotional time. Matsuo's family, including his brother and sister, dined at a nearby hotel, but he declined to tell his family of the dangers of his coming mission. The next day Matsuo commenced final training on the midget submarines and two months later met his death in Sydney Harbour.

The actions of this 26-year-old hero were to give him a place in Japanese history. When Matsuo's exploits became known, thousands of Japanese youths volunteered their lives to the *kaiten* (human torpedo) units, hoping to emulate his courage and self-sacrifice. Indeed, it seems as if on that early morning under the waters of Sydney Harbour, the spirit of the Kikuchi martyrs possessed him.

Matsuo wrote his last letter to his parents on 27 May, four days before undertaking his final mission. It's clear he knew he would not return.

> Looking back on my 26 years on this earth, they are about to end without ever putting both your minds at ease, but I ask you to please approve and understand the last task I have been chosen to perform. I hereby bid a farewell, wishing you both and everyone else longevity and happiness as I feel grateful in knowing that I will undertake this mission with absolutely no regret.

In his closing words, Matsuo asks his parents to visit the parents of his crewman to tell them he is sorry. He describes Tsuzuku as a "truly brilliant man" in whom he has the greatest trust.

When the bodies of Matsuo and Tsuzuku were recovered by naval divers, the magnitude of their ordeal became clear. Realising they were doomed, Matsuo tried to set alight the submarine's self-demolition charge, but this failed when water rapidly entered the craft. The wick drowned only inches from the explosive. Rear-Admiral Muirhead-Gould writes in his preliminary report that Tsuzuku had removed his boots, perhaps in an attempt to escape the craft. However, salvage records show Tsuzuku's body was recovered from the forward compartment in the midget submarine. In a final gesture of Japanese

There are at least four different types of midget submarines in this group, though the great majority are of the standard "Koryu" type. The two boats at right in the second row appear to have an enlarged conning tower and shortened hull superstructure. The two boats at left in that row are of the earlier Type A or Type C design, similar to those used in Sydney Harbour, as are a few others further back in the group.

honour and courage, Matsuo and Tsuzuku used a revolver to commit suicide.

Was the Sydney Harbour raid a suicide mission? Teiji Yamaki, who was to take part in the Sydney Harbour attack before being injured in an explosion off Truk Lagoon, gives the following explanation to help understand the mindset of the midget submarine crews:

> The midget submarine commanders realised that they could not sacrifice the hundred crew members of the mother ship by making them wait while they returned. Therefore, the priorities of the midget submarine commanders were a successful attack first, and the safety of the mother ship second. Although they were asked to return, the commanders knew this was a mission from which they may not return.

The ritual act of self-sacrifice as a weapon of war did not appear on a large scale until the closing stages of the Pacific War with the appearance of Japanese *kamakazi* bombers. In these attacks, aeroplanes were used as flying bombs, used chiefly against American aircraft carriers. As Japan became more desperate, suicide attacks as a weapon of war became formalised and ritualised. According to eyewitness accounts by Allied personnel, the first *kamikaze* attack, in the generally accepted sense of the term, was carried out by an unknown pilot from the Imperial Japanese Army Air Force on 21 October 1944. The target was the flagship of the Royal Australian Navy, the heavy cruiser *HMAS Australia*, which was hit by an unidentified Japanese plane carrying a 200 kg (440 pound) bomb off Leyte Island. The plane struck the superstructure of the heavy cruiser above the bridge, spewing burning fuel and debris over a large area. However, the bomb failed to explode; if it had, the ship might have been effectively destroyed. At least 30 crew members died as a result of the attack, including the commanding officer, Captain Emile Dechaineux. Among the wounded was Commodore John Collins, the Australian force commander.

Towards the end of the war in the Pacific, the Japanese Navy also used both one and two-man piloted torpedoes called *kaiten* for suicide missions. Although sometimes called midget submarines, these were modified versions of the unmanned torpedoes of the time and were distinct from the torpedo-firing midget submarines used at Pearl Harbor, Diego Suarez Bay and Sydney Harbour.

Though extremely hazardous, the early midget submarine attacks were not technically suicide missions, nor were the early *kaiten* which were equipped with escape hatches; even though their pilots chose not to use them. By contrast, later *kaitens* provided no means of escape. After aiming a two-person *kaiten* at their target, the two crew members traditionally embraced and shot each other in the head. The first *kaiten* attack on American ships took place on 20 November 1944 and the human torpedo attacks continued until the end of the war. However, *kaiten* attacks resulted in sinking only two American vessels with the loss of 162 American lives, in comparison to 106 *kaiten* pilots who lost their lives, including 15 killed in training accidents.

In Japanese culture, social support for suicide missions was strong, where *seppuku* (honourable suicide) was part of *samarai* duty. It was also fostered and indoctrinated by the Imperial program to persuade, often through coercion (such as through doping), Japanese soldiers to commit these acts.

In the modern age, suicide attacks have become the defining act of political violence. Since the 1980s, the low cost and high lethality of suicide attacks have made it a favourite with guerrilla, insurgent, and especially terrorist groups, notably in the Middle East and Sri Lanka. The Tamil Tigers were, as of 2000, "unequivocally the most effective and brutal terrorist organisation ever to utilise suicide terrorism" (according to Yoram Schweitzer of the Institute for Counter-Terrorism in Israel). On 7 January 2006, Tamil Tigers sunk a Sri Lankan gunboat in a suicide attack with the loss of all 15 crew. The Israeli-built Dvora-class gunboat was on a routine patrol outside Trincomalee Harbour, a main base for the island nation's navy.

Since 2001, suicide bombings have been used frequently by Islamist militants, mostly in the Al-Aqsa Intifada and the Iraqi insurgency. The 11 September 2001 attacks in New York used hijacked airplanes to become the largest and most destructive individual suicide bombings.

Throughout history suicide attacks have taken various forms and have been encouraged by the lionisation of those who laid down their lives for causes they deemed righteous. There are numerous examples, from Samson's suicidal destruction of a Philistine temple (as recounted in the Book of Judges) to the legendary Swiss hero Arnold von Winkelried, and the Japanese *kamikaze* and *kaiten* pilots of World War II. The first modern suicide bombing involving explosives deliberately carried to the target either on the person or in a civilian vehicle and delivered by surprise was is in 1981; perfected by the factions of the Lebanese Civil War and especially by the Tamil Tigers of Sri Lanka. By 2006, suicide bombings as a tactic had spread to dozens of countries. Those hardest hit were Lebanon during its civil war, Sri Lanka during its prolonged ethnic conflict, Israel and the Palestinian Territories since 1994, and Iraq since the invasion in 2003. What the Western World considers as the protagonists, are countries with strong cultural and religious beliefs; not unlike the *Samarai* duty in Japanese culture during WWII.

Returning to the Sydney Harbour attack, intelligence reports and summaries by MacArthur's intelligence team for the months of May and early June 1942 are conspicuous by their absence in the National Archives. It is hard to understand why the New Zealand Naval Board warnings on 26 and 29 May of Japanese submarines operating off Sydney were ignored, unless MacArthur feared that by alerting Australian defences he would also alert the Japanese that their signals were being decyphered. There are also enough clues in the historical record that point to Churchill's pre-knowledge of the attack on Pearl Harbor and Madagascar. His most secret wartime intelligence briefs are closed for 75 years, until November 2016.

The history of war is as much a catalogue of gallant disasters as it is of successful engagements and the Japanese midget submarine raid on Sydney Harbour must fall in the former category. Like the Dieppe raid in 1942, and Gallipoli in 1915, its military objectives were not achieved; but out of failure there arose a legend of human courage and sacrifice that was eventually much more powerful than immediate military objectives. ●

Appendices

APPENDICES

APPENDIX A

OFFICIAL REPORT OF REAR-ADMIRAL-IN-CHARGE OF SYDNEY HARBOUR DEFENCES

No. B.S. 1749/201/37

From…The Rear-Admiral in Charge, H.M.A. Naval Establishments, Sydney.
To…The Secretary, Naval Board, Melbourne.
Date…16 July 1942

Subject…*Midget Submarine attack on Sydney Harbour 31 May - 1 June 1942.*

1. Submitted for the information of the Naval Board is the following report on the Midget Submarine Attack on Sydney Harbour, 31 May – 1 June 1942:
2. Appendices supporting the narrative are attached:
Appendix I – Chronological sequence of events.
Appendix II – Sources of information.
Appendix III – Submarine and Torpedo particulars [not included here].
Appendix IV – Loop indications and signatures.
Appendix V – Lessons learnt [not included here].
Appendix VI – Recommendations for recognition of personnel.
3. It is considered that four midget submarines participated in the raid. Of these, two are known by their actual Japanese numbers (No. 14 and No. 21). They are thus referred to in the following narrative. The other two unknown midgets are referred to as "MIDGET A" and "MIDGET B" respectively.
4. It is considered that the force, which attacked Sydney, consisted of five "I" class submarines, four midget submarines, and one, possibly two, float planes. These were:
"I" 21 (Float plane)
"I" 24
"I" 22
"I" 27
"I" 29 (Possibly float plane)
Midget No. 14

Midget No. 21
"Midget A"
"Midget B"

5. The attack was possibly preceded by aerial reconnaissance, which may have been carried out on 19, 30 and 31 May.

RECONNAISSANCE

6. A reconnaissance of Sydney Harbour, especially the Naval Anchorage area, was carried out by one biplane single float plane at approximately 0420K/30 May.
7. Allied warships in Sydney Harbour at that time included the following:
No. 1 Buoy – HMAS "CANBERRA"
No. 2 Buoy – USS "CHICAGO"
No. 4 Buoy – USS "PERKINS"
No. 5 Buoy – USS "DOBBIN"
No. 6 Buoy – HMAS "BUNGAREE"
Birt's Buoy – HMS "KANIMBLA"
Off Robertson Point – HMAS "AUSTRALIA" [sic - "HMAS WESTRALIA"]
8. The plane, which was burning navigational lights, approached the harbour from a northerly direction, flew over the Naval Anchorage; circled the USS "CHICAGO" twice, and departed in a due east direction.

TACTICS

9. The contents of Midget No. 21 (ample food supplies, first aid kit, charts, lists of call signs etc.) suggest that this was by no means regarded as a "suicide" venture.
10. The establishment of "picking up dispositions", rendezvous at which midgets were to rejoin their parents, had been made. Five of such rendezvous were spaced at fairly regular intervals (an average of eighteen miles apart) two to the northward and three to the southward of Sydney.
11. The waiting parent submarines were in each case spread two miles apart on a line of bearing at right angles to the coast line.

RECONSTRUCTION OF EVENTS OF 31 MAY – 1 JUNE

12. Weather conditions were reported outside the Heads at 1900K as – sea rough, moderate swell, wind S. by W. force 4, dark and overcast. The moon was full and rose at 1813K. Dawn on Monday, 1 June, was at 0545K; high tide 2125K, height 6 feet.
13. Four midget submarines (Midget 14, Midget 21, "Midget A" and "Midget B") were released (from "I" Submarines 22, 24, 27, and 29) off Sydney Heads, a short distance to seawards, but outside the loop area, during the afternoon of Sunday, 31 May.

MIDGET NO. 14 [I-27]

14. The first attempt at entry was made by Midget No. 14. and was unsuccessful. She crossed the loop 2001 and, by 2015, was caught in the nets (centre portion, close to Western Gate). She was unable to free herself, and blew herself up at 2235. Her propellers were thickly covered with grease when the wreck was recovered. No food had been touched, neither had sanitary utensils been used.

"MIDGET A" [I-24]

15. The second entry was made by "Midget A". She crossed the loop at 2148, and entered the harbour unobserved.
16. "Midget A" was not sighted until 2252. She was then sighted by "CHICAGO" and a ferry in the proximity of Garden Island. She was also sighted by Dockyard Motor Boat "NESTOR" and an officer on Ferry Wharf, Garden Island, at the same time. She was then close to Garden Island (200 yards off) and proceeding towards the Harbour Bridge.
17. "Midget A" was fired on by "CHICAGO" and apparently turned towards North Shore instead of proceeding further up the harbour. She was next sighted at 2310 from the Oil Wharf at Garden Island (by the A.M.S. Vessels "WHYALLA" and "GEELONG"), in the direction of Bradley's Head. They fired at her and kept the area under observation with searchlights for half an hour.
18. "Midget A" fired two torpedoes from the direction of Bradley's Head at 0030. One of these failed to explode, after running ashore on Garden Island. The other passed under the Dutch submarine K-9, which was lying alongside "KUTTABUL" at Garden Island, hit the sea bottom and exploded, sinking "KUTTABUL".
19. It is presumed that these torpedoes were fired at "CHICAGO" at No. 2 Buoy, who was about to slip and proceed. The dock floodlights, which would have silhouetted "CHICAGO" were extinguished just before the torpedo was fired. "Midget A" than escaped, passing over the loop on her exit from the harbour at 0158.

"MIDGET B" [I-22]

20. "Midget B" made an unsuccessful attempt to enter the harbour but failed to reach the effective loop (No. 12) or, consequently, the boom. She was sighted by "YANDRA" (the duty A/S Vessel on patrol within the Loop Area) and later by "LAURIANA" who illuminated her until intercepted between the Heads, at 2254, by "YANDRA".
21. Two separate attacks were carried out by "YANDRA" on "Midget B" during a period of nine minutes, starting from the time she attempted to ram the submarine at 2258 until her second attack – a full pattern of six depth charges – at 2307.
22. It is considered that "Midget B" was destroyed by this second attack, in position $023°$ 3.6 cables from Hornby Light.

MIDGET No. 21 [I-22]

23. Midget No. 21 entered the harbour at 0301, at which time she crossed No. 12 Loop. She proceeded up the harbour unobserved until she reached the Bradley's Head vicinity. Here she was sighted by "KANIMBLA" and fired on at 0350 and gave rise to the unconfirmed contact made by "DOOMBA" off Robertson Point at 0450.

24. She was detected in Taylor Bay and attacked with depth charges, first by "SEA MIST" at 0500, then by "YARROMA" and "STEADY HOUR" intermittently until 0827. The effect of these attacks was clearly shown in the great amount of damage done to Midget No. 21, which was evident in the wreck when it was recovered. It is probable that the first attack caused the submarine to run into the bottom, because the lower bow cap was damaged and both caps were jammed, although set to release. The torpedo tubes had both been fired, although the bow caps had jammed on release. The lower tube had been fired with the external adjustment fittings engaged, and these had sheared off when the torpedo moved in the tube. This suggests that an attempt to fire was made in a hurry, and was prompted by, or interrupted by, the depth charge attacks. The tubes can be fired only from the Control Room; the release of the bow caps can be carried out only from Forward; other operations on the tubes may be carried out from the Control Room or the forward compartment.

25. Both members of the crew were shot through the head; the demolition charges had been fired but the fuses (sic) were drowned. It is possible that the junior member of the crew had attempted to escape, as he was found with his boots off. The Captain was wearing boots. This suggests that an early depth charge attack damaged the midget, and later ones progressively wrecked her.

SUMMARY

26. It is, then, considered that four midget submarines attempted to enter the harbour, of which only two –
    "Midget A"
    "Midget 21"
succeeded in passing the boom, and of which one – "Midget A" – got away again.

27. The other three midget submarines were destroyed:

    Midget 14 in the net at 2235/31.
    "Midget B" between Heads at 2307/31.
    Midget 21 in Taylor Bay between 0500 and 0827/ June.

Signed G. C. Muirhead-Gould
A/REAR-ADMIRAL

APPENDIX I – CHRONOLOGICAL SEQUENCE OF EVENTS.

TIME (K)	EVENTS
2000	Recorded crossing on No 12 Loop.
2015 (approx.)	Watchman sighted suspicious object in the nets near Sheerlegs – Western Channel. Watchman and mate proceeded in skiff to investigate.
2130 (approx.)	Watchman proceeded to "YARROMA" and reported suspicious object. ("YARROMA" was duty Channel Patrol Boat at West Gate.) "YARROMA" would not approach owing to fear that object was a magnetic mine.
2148	Recorded crossing on No 12 Loop.
2152	"YARROMA" reported "Suspicious object in net" and was told to close and give full description.
2210	"YARROMA" reported object was metal with serrated edge on top, moving with the swell. "YARROMA" was ordered to give fuller description.
2220 (approx.)	Stoker from "YARROMA" sent in Maritime Services Board skiff to investigate and reported object as a submarine. "LOLITA" closed "YARROMA" Captain Bode, "CHICAGO", left TRESCO with suggestions that he should go to sea with "PERKINS".
2227	N.O.C.S. to All ships, Sydney – "Take A/S precautions." Port closed to outward shipping.
2230	Watchmen sent back to work. "YARROMA" reported – "Object is submarine. Request permission to open fire." "GOONAMBEE" ordered to proceed forthwith to investigate object at West Gate. Second Duty Staff Officer proceeded to CPBs not duty. ("GOONAMBEE" was duty M/S Vessel in Watsons Bay.)
2235	"YARROMA" reported submarine had blown up.
2236	N.O.C.S. TO GENERAL - "Presence of enemy submarine at boom gate is suspected. Ships are to take action against attack."
2252	"LAURIANA" noticed flurry on water ahead to port, investigated with searchlight, which showed conning tower of submarine, distance 60 feet to 80 feet. Signalled Port War Signal Station, Channel Patrol Boat and Minesweeper entering harbour and Channel Patrol Boat at boom. ("LAURIANA" was one of four duty Naval Auxiliary Patrol Boats.) No Response. "CHICAGO" to N.O.C.S. – "Submarine periscope sighted about 500 yards off our starboard bow, heading up the channel."
2250 to 2253 (approx.)	USS "CHICAGO" at No. 2 buoy switched on searchlight and opened fire towards Fort Denison – red tracers (pom-pom).

	Dockyard Motor Boat "NESTOR" halfway between ferry wharf and No. 2 Buoy noticed disturbance in water 40 yards ahead. "CHICAGO'S" searchlight then illuminated periscope of submarine, coming towards "NESTOR". Submarine was steering towards harbour bridge 200 yards off Garden Island. Officer on Ferry Wharf saw periscope in "CHICAGO'S" searchlight. Shots falling all around it.
2254	"YANDRA" sighted conning tower 400 yards away 028°-3 cables from Hornby Light. ("YANDRA" was duty A/S Vessel on patrol within Loop Area.)
2255	"YANDRA" approached to attack.
2258	"YANDRA" attempted to ram submarine, which reappeared 100 yards astern, damaged, and slowing turning to starboard. Position 283° 2.5 cables from Hornby.
2259	"YANDRA" carried out A/S Sweep. Negative results.
2300 Channel.	"GOONAMBEE" proceeded to Watsons Bay to Gate in West Patrolled Bradley's Head to Gate. "YANDRA" at West Gate.
2303	"YANDRA" sighted conning tower 600 yards away.
2304	A/S contact obtained. "YANDRA" prepared to attack.
2307	"YANDRA" fired pattern 6 depth charge set to 100 feet. Position 023°3.6 cables from Hornby Light. Submarine was not seen after explosions.
2310	"GEELONG" fired at suspicious object in line to left of Bradley's Head and, with "WHYALLA", swept with searching lights for half an hour. ("GEELONG" was A.M.S. refitting alongside oil wharf.) ("WHYALLA" A/S vessel self refitting alongside "GEELONG")
2314	N.O.C.S. signal – "All ships to be darkened"
2315	"BINGERA" ordered to immediate notice. ("BINGERA" was Stand Off A/S vessel at No. 7 Buoy.) U.S.S. "PERKINS" slipped and was ordered back to buoy by "CHICAGO" securing again at 2340 to No. 4 Buoy. ("PERKINS" at four hours' notice at No. 4 Buoy.)
2330	"BINGERA" to N.O.C.S. – "Ready to proceed"
2334	"BINGERA" ordered to "slip and carry out A/S search in harbour. Submarine reported passing – proceeding towards harbour bridge."
2336	"BINGERA" reported – "Ready to proceed." Rear-Admiral and Chief Staff Officer proceeded down harbour.
2340	"PERKINS" secured again No. 4 Buoy. "BINGERA" slipped and proceeded up the harbour.
0000	Rear-Admiral and Chief Staff Officer boarded "LOLITA".
0025	Flood lights new dock extinguished by orders N.O.C.S.
0030	"KUTTABUL" hit by torpedo. All lights on the Island were extinguished by the explosion and the telephones went out of order.

0034	Lights and telephone switchboard, Garden Island, came into service.
0045	"BOMBAY, "WHYALLA" ordered to raise steam. ("BOMBAY" was A.M.S. at four hours' notice at No. 9 Buoy.)
0045	"PERKINS" slipped.
0103	"BINGERA" ordered to sweep between Bradley's Head and Garden Island.
0110	N.O.C.S. – General – "Enemy Submarine is present in the harbour and 'KUTTABUL' has been torpedoed."
0120	Submarine K-9 slipped and proceeded up harbour in tow. (K-9 was alongside "KUTTABUL".)
0121	"ADELE" ready. Told to remain at Buoy. ("ADELE" was Stand Off Examination Vessel at Watsons Bay.)
0125	"SAMUEL BENBOW" reported – "Crew at action stations raising steam." ("SAMUEL BENBOW" was Stand Off M/S Vessel at Watsons Bay.)
0158	Crossing reported on No. 12 Loop.
0214	"CHICAGO" to N.O.C.S. – "Proceeding to sea."
0230	"WHYALLA" to N.O.C.S. – "Slipped and proceeding to sea."
0230 to 0245	Staff Officer, Channel Patrol Boats, received orders to proceed and patrol when ready vicinity Bradley's Head. "TOOMAREE" – East Boom Gate. "MARLEAN" – West Boom Gate. Stand off Channel Patrol "SEA MIST" – West Boom Gate. Boats at Farm Cove. "STEADY HOUR" to contact Duty CPBs at boom – "LOLITA" and "YARROMA".
0243	"PERKINS" to sea" reported by P.W.S.S.
0245 (approx.)	"STEADY HOUR" ordered "SEA MIST" to patrol Bradley's Head – Boom.
0256	"CHICAGO" to sea" reported by P.W.S.S.
0300	"CHICAGO" reported – "Submarine entering harbour."
0301	Crossing reported on No. 12 Loop.
0305	"WHYALLA" to sea" reported by P.W.S.S.
0307	N.O.C.S. ordered "BINGERA" – "Carry out A/S patrol in vicinity of 'CANBERRA'."
0320	"BOMBAY" reported – "Ready to proceed."
0335	CPBs proceeded on patrol. Lieutenant Adams embarked in H.M.I.S. "BOMBAY" and proceeded to sea on A/S Search as per N.O.C.S. 1735z/31.
0340	LFB 92 reported sighting submarine five miles off Port Hacking at 0105k/1 June.
0350	"KANIMBLA" switched on to searchlight and opened fire. "BINGERA" searched area. ("KANIMBLA" was 12 hours' notice at Burts (sic) Buoy.)
0450 (approx.)	"DOOMBA" signalled "BINGERA" about submarine contact off

	Robertson Point. This was investigated without result. "CANBERRA" signalled unconfirmed sighting torpedo track from Bradley's Head at 0440. ("CANBERRA" at four hours' notice at No. 1 Buoy.) (At immediate notice from 0115 (pencilled addition to report).)
0500	"YARROMA" and "SEA MIST" and "STEADY HOUR" all patrolling. Red Verey's Light seen in Taylor Bay by "YARROMA" and depth charge explosion heard. "YARROMA" proceeded to scene at full speed and en route saw three more Verey Lights and heard further detonations.
0500 (approx.)	"STEADY HOUR" sighted suspicious object. Whilst proceeding up West Channel "SEA MIST" attacked and fired Verey light (red). "SEA MIST" reported three submarines.
0500 (approx.)	"SEA MIST", at request of "GOONAMBEE", investigated suspicious object in Taylor Bay. Fired two depth charges on each occasion firing a red Verey light before so doing. Aldis lamp was used to illuminate target.
0511	N.O.C.S. stopped all sailings from Newcastle and Port Kembla.
0532	"BOMBAY" to sea.
0540	P.W.S.S. reported two red flares, apparently from ship anchored on bank. Rear-Admiral-in-Charge and Chief Staff Officer proceeded down harbour.
0545	"BOMBAY", "WHYALLA", "YANDRA" on patrol outside Heads.
0640	"STEADY HOUR" dropped depth charge ("STEADY HOUR", "SEA MIST" on patrol Chowder Bay – Bradley's Head.)
	"STEADY HOUR" dropped second charge and marked buoy in same place.
0658	"YARROMA" picked up A/S contact of submarine – confirmed dropped one charge.
0718 to 0721	"YARROMA" – second attack – one charge. Brown oily tinge in disturbance – oily smear arose.
0725	"STEADY HOUR" reported attacking definite ASDIC contact – oil and air bubbles.
0730	"WHYALLA" and "BOMBAY" joined company and conducted search. C.S.O. proceeded down harbour.
	On "WINBAH'S" arrival at Taylor Bay:
	Reported by Commanding Officer, "STEADY HOUR", that his anchor had caught up in submarine and light oil film and large bubbles clearly visible.
0755	"YARROMA'S" third attack – same attack as 0718-0721. (Then stationary.)
0827	"YARROMA" – fourth and last attack – Oil and air bubbles continued to rise.

APPENDIX II – SOURCES OF INFORMATION.

(a) <u>Documents recovered from Midget 21</u> (Translated at Navy Office, Melbourne).
These disclosed the existence of an "Advanced Detachment" comprising:
Four Surface Vessels.
Eleven "I" Class submarines: I-10, I-16, I-18, I-20, I-21, I-22, I-24, I-27, I-28, I-29, I-30.
Eight "Midgets": 9, 21, 22, 23, 25, 26, 27, 28.
Call signs for aircraft attached to I-10, I-21, I-29, I-30.
It is interesting to note that Midget No. 14 is not mentioned.

(b) <u>Charts recovered from Midget 21</u>
Picking up "Dispositions" apparently placed five "I" class submarines at various rendezvous North and South of Sydney. Therse were: I-21, I-22, I-24, I-27, I-29. Two of these, I-21 and I-29, were allotted aircraft call signs.
The courses from Sydney to the rendezvous off Broken Bay (shown on photostat of chart attached) led to four "I" class submarines (I-22, I-24, I-27 and I-29), leaving I-21 apparently free to act as leader and possibly with her aircraft in lieu of, and not in addition to, a midget.
A working chart showed fixes due east of Sydney heads, the seaward one being marked "1625". These fixes (marked on attached photostat of portion of charts were:
    Outer South Head Light 260° 7.2 miles.
    Outer South Head Light 253° 4.1 miles.
    Outer South Head Light 247° 3.6 miles.
    Outer South Head Light 260° 1.7 miles.
Courses were marked on a Sydney Harbour chart recovered from Midget No. 21.

APPENDIX IV – LOOP INDICATIONS AND SIGNATURES.

Although two loops were in operation (No 11, laid in 14/15 fathoms, and No. 12, laid in 6/7 fathoms) signatures were registered on No 12. only.

Four signatures were observed on this loop, at 2001, 2148, 0158 and 0301. At first these were all believed to indicate inward crossings. Subsequently, however, it was decided that the 0158 signature could have recorded a crossing in the opposite direction from the other three. It has accordingly been taken as an outward crossing. Prints of signature are attached.

APPENDIX VI – RECOMMENDATIONS FOR RECOGNITION OF PERSONNEL.

RECOMMENDATIONS FOR RECOGNITION OF PERSONNEL

The following are recommended to the notice of the Naval Board for their display of zeal and determination throughout the operation:

Mr James Cargill, for his vigilance and initiative and for his personnel efforts to report a suspicious circumstance to the proper authorities; and

To a lesser degree Mr W. Nangle who helped him.

Lieutenant A. G. Townley RANVR and the crew of HMAS "STEADY HOUR".

Sub-Lieutenant J. A. Doyle, RANR(S) and crew of HMAS "SEA MIST". [Lieutenant R. T. Andrew was in command of *Sea Mist* at the time.]

Lieutenant J. A. Taplin, RANR(S) and the crew of HMAS "YANDRA".

Engineer Captain A. B. Doyle, CBE, R.A.N.

Commander (E) C. C. Clark, R.A.N. These officers arrived at the scene minutes after the explosion and commendable fortitude in searching the vessel for any men who might have been trapped. In doing so, they had to wade in deep water and in hazardous conditions in darkness, as it was not known at the time which portions of the decks had been rendered dangerous by the explosion. They rendered assistance to a number of men who had been shocked by the suddenness and force of the action.

Bandsman M. N. Cumming, Official Number, 20501. This rating, who was on board "KUTTABUL" at the time of the explosion, showed determination in diving into the water from the vessel, swimming a few yards and assisting a rating on to "KUTTABUL'S" deck. He also again dived into the water into "KUTTABUL'S" wreckage in order to see whether anyone needed assistance. Although no great courage or endurance was necessary, he displayed commendable initiative.

Mr F. J. Lingard (Torpedo Fitter). For the removal of pistols and primers from torpedoes, and demolition charges from submarines, this work being carried out entirely voluntarily.

The Skipper and crew of Naval Auxiliary Patrol Boat, "LAURIANA". For prompt action in illuminating submarine.

The Captain and crew of HMAS "YARROMA". For their part in the sinking of Midget 21. It is considered that this action redeemed, to some extent, their earlier failure.

All personnel of the Dockyard First Aid Party. For their efficient handling of casualties.

APPENDIX B - PRELIMINARY REPORT

No B.S. 1518/201/37
Date 22 June 1942

SUBJECT JAPANESE MIDGET SUBMARINE ATTACK ON SYDNEY HARBOUR

Be pleased to lay before the Naval Board the attached chronological narrative relating to the entry of Japanese midget Submarines into Port Jackson on the 31 May/1 June, 1942, and operations in connection therewith. All times mentioned in this report are K (Zone-10).

2. There was a regrettable failure on the part of the watchkeepers to identify the unusual crossings at 2001 and 2148. Crossings at these times were noticed by the watchkeeper but disregarded as being tugs. It is however possible that the submarines took advantage of the approach to the Harbour of a tug to follow close in her wake and thus, inadvertently no doubt, to share her signature on the loop. Subsequent crossings, or at least the crossings at 0159, were reported as "unidentified" but the "battle" was in full swing and nothing could be done about it. The crossing at 0301 was that of submarine sighted by "CHICAGO".
3. I consider that the loop system fully justified itself, though, naturally I must deplore the fact that the human element failed.
4. The loop operators having failed, it is apparent that a Midget submarine was in the harbour for about two hours. It was seen by Mr James Cargill of the Maritime Services Board Staff who took some time to collect a friend and to communicate this vital information to the Channel Patrol Boat on patrol. "YARROMA" did not open fire because he thought it might be a mine. This is deplorable and inexplicable.
5. Great difficulty has been experienced in making out any sort of chronological plot. A great many ships and boats and, therefore, people were concerned in these operations, and all were so busy that they had not thought for recording actual time of incidents.
6. From a preliminary examination of the evidence, I reported that I considered that "STEADY HOUR" was responsible for the sinking of No. 4 submarine in Taylor Bay. Further investigations show that "YARROMA" and "SEA MIST" were equally concerned in this attack, and "YARROMA" thus to some extent made up for her previous indecision.
7. Although "SEA MIST's" report, at 0500, that she had seen three submarines in Chowder Bay sounded at that time fantastic, it is now considered that this was actually possible. Examination of the captured charts shows what may have been the position of the submarine in this area. "SEA MIST's" subsequent reports give great promise of a successful attack in Chowder Bay. Members of her crew drew a most convincing sketch of the stern cage of the submarine, which they claim to have seen. At this time, no one was aware that these submarines had tail cages. It is unfortunate that all efforts to locate this submarine have failed.

8. I realise that I have still failed to account for all four crossings. One was sunk in the net, one was sunk in Taylor Bay, one was probably sunk in Chowder Bay. But there were four crossings. All inward and none outward, so "YANDRA's" victim is a fifth. It may be that a third submarine was sunk in Chowder or Taylor Bay's by the "SEA MIST", "STEADY HOUR", "YARROMA" combination, or that the reports of "NEREUS" ["SILVER CLOUD" pencilled in over this word] that she had sunk a submarine in Vaucluse Bay the following night were genuine.
9. There are several lessons to be learnt from these events and steps have already been taken to correct mistakes.

There was a great congestion in signal traffic through the Port War Signal Station. It is evident that Port War Signal Station is not capable of, and was never intended to cope with, such a situation. It was impossible for the Operational Room at Garden Island to communicate with these boats direct, and the only alternative method was by boat. In order to ascertain exactly what was happening I had myself go down to the boom and interview Officers on the spot and return with the information to Garden Island. Channel Patrol Boats and Naval Auxiliary patrol boats have no signalmen and this complicates V/S communications. It is evident that R/T communication between Boats on patrol and Garden Island Operations Room is essential and proposals are being examined for obtaining them. The R/T set at Port War Signal Station was out of action at the time of the incident.

Some comment has been made that ferries were allowed to continue to run. This was done by my direct order as I felt that once there was a submarine, or more than one submarine in the Harbour, the more boats that were moving about at high speed the better chances of keeping the submarines down until daylight.

A far bigger question arises – that of the effect of ferries and Maritime Service Board tugs and barges crossing the loops during the dark hours. It is certain that the complete cessation of all traffic across the loops at night would greatly facilitate the task of the loop operators, but it is impossible to assess the inconvenience, which would be caused to the inhabitants of Manly and elsewhere. I have informed the Premier and the Ferry Company that I had felt obliged to consider stopping the ferries altogether from sunset to sunrise, but that, realising the inconvenience which this would have caused. I would for the present only request them to make arrangements for the ferries to stop immediately, or to remain at their Wharves, or return to their departure wharves, on a request being made by an authorised Naval Officer. At the same time I have asked the Maritime Services Board to restrict their nightly operations of tugs and barges as much as possible, and I have asked them and the ferry services to provide me with a table of the times at which their craft will normally pass the Boom Gates. By this means I hope in future to be able to check all Loop Crossings.

The following action has been taken:
Naval Auxiliary Patrol vessels have been armed with depth charges.
A modified Mark IV depth charge pistol with similar characteristics to the Mark VIII

pistol, viz, able to fire in less than 42 feet of water, has been developed as being supplied to Channel Patrol Boats and Naval Auxiliary Patrol Boats.

An R/T set for Garden Island Operations Room is being provided.

Signed G. C. Muirhead-Gould
A/REAR-ADMIRAL

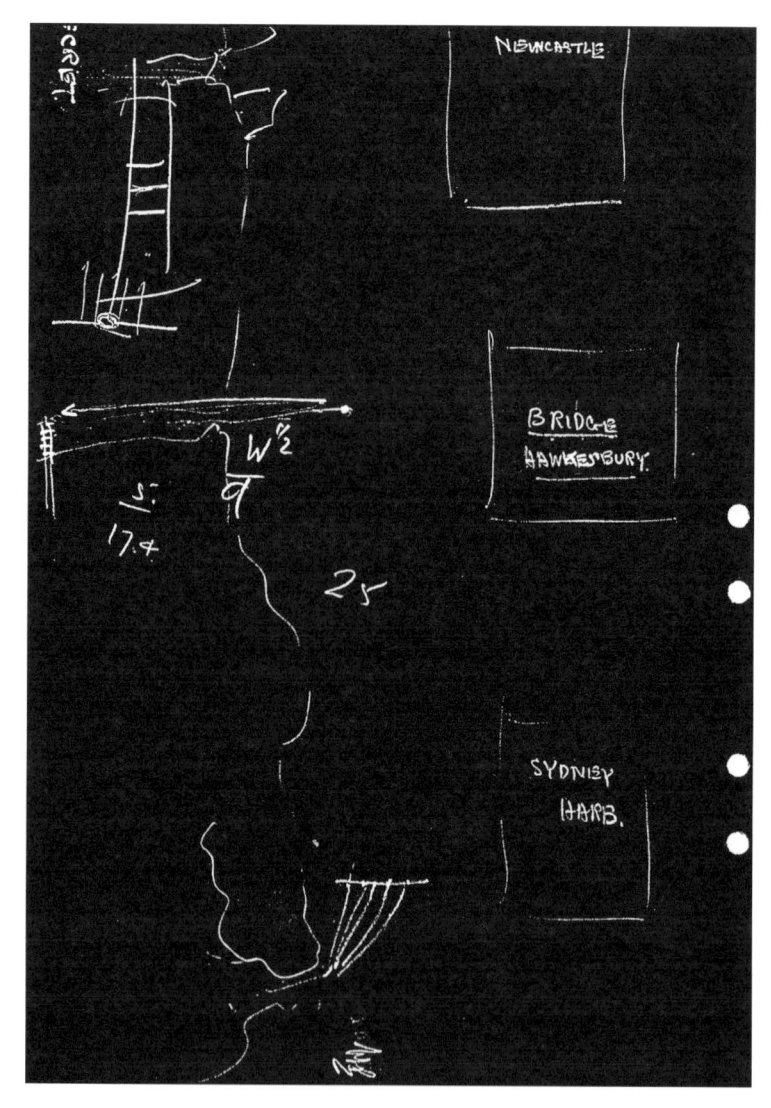

APPENDIX C

Reproduction of hand-drawn chart recovered from midget submarine I-22 (Midget 21). The Hawkesbury Bridge is clearly shown.

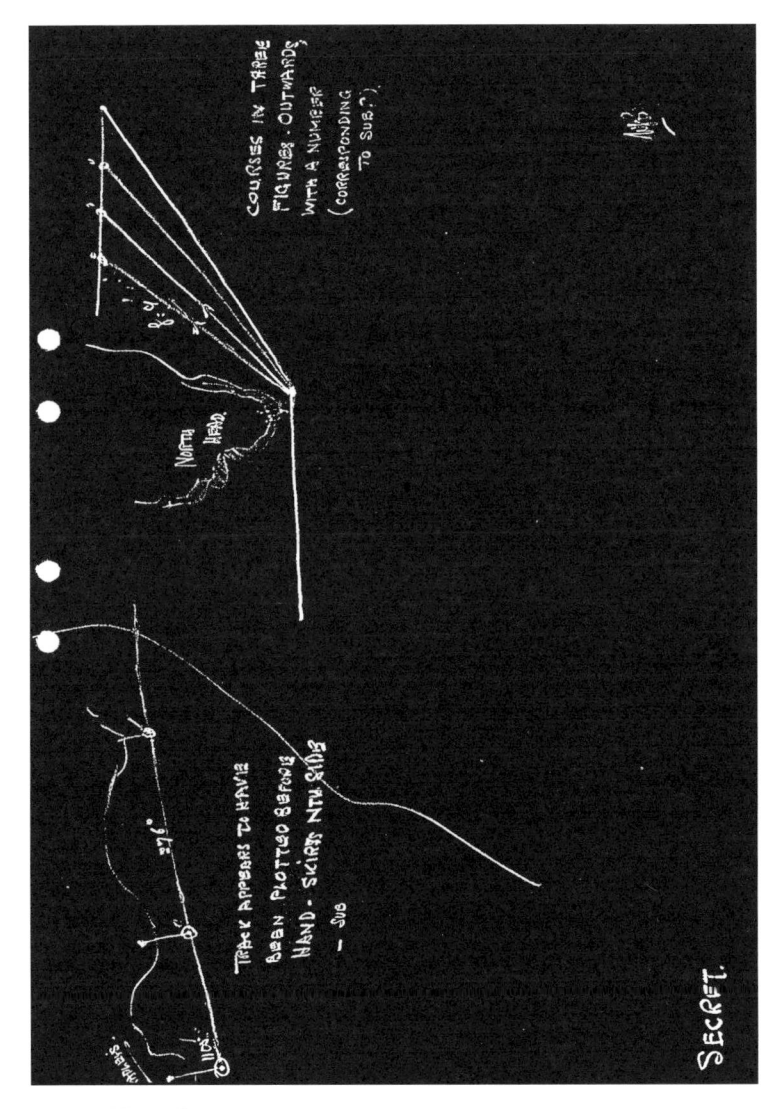

APPENDIX D
The track from Bradley's Head follows the western channel and appears to be an inward course by Lieutenant Matsuo in I-22 (Midget 21).

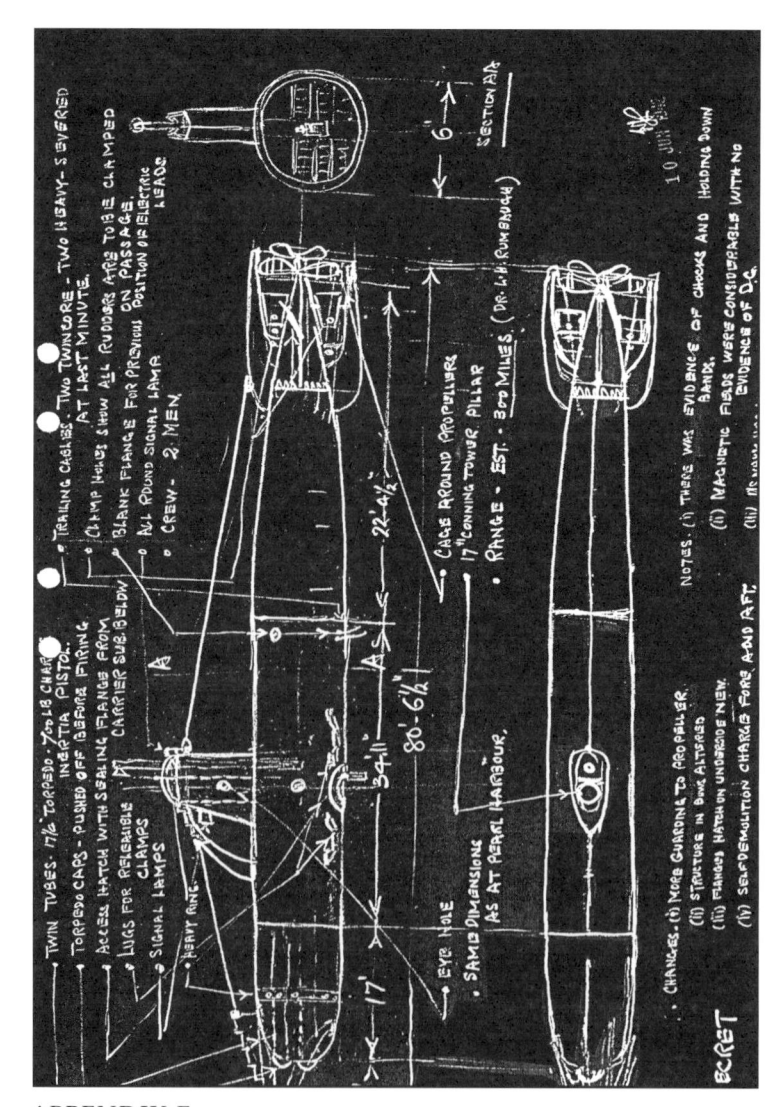

APPENDIX E

Hand-drawn reconstruction of the midget submarine, 10 June 1942.

BIBLIOGRAPHY

BIBLIOGRAPHY

MONOGRAPHS
Auchmuty, J. J., *The Voyage of Governor Phillip to Botany Bay*, Angus and Robertson, Sydney, 1970.
Carruthers, S. L., *Australia Under Siege: Japanese Submarine Raiders 1942*. Solus Books, Sydney 1982.
Clarke, H. and Yamashita, T., *To Sydney by Stealth*, Horwitz, Sydney 1966.
Clarke, H., *Fire One*, Angus & Robertson, Sydney, 1978.
Connell, B., *Return of the Tiger,* Evans, London, 1960.
Costello, J., *The Pacific War,* Rawson, Wade, New York, 1981.
Cusack, D. and James, F., *Come in Spinner,* Angus & Robertson, Sydney, 1951.
Feldt, E., *The Coastwatchers,* Ballantine Books, New York, 1959.
Garret, R., *Submarines,* Little, Brown, Boston, 1977.
Gill, G. H., *Royal Australian Navy 1942-1945,* Australian War Memorial, Canberra.
Hall, T., *Darwin 1942,* Methuen, Sydney, 1981.
Hashimoto, M., *Sunk,* Cassel, London, 1954.
Hasluck, P., *The Government and the People 1939-1945,* Australian War Memorial, Canberra.
Hoehling, A. A., *The Day the Admirals Slept Late,* Zebra Books, New York, 1978.
Ind, A. W., *Spy Ring Pacific,* Weidenfeld & Nicolson, London, 1958.
Ind, A. W., *A History of Modern Espionage,* Hodder & Stoughton, London, 1965.
Jenkins, D., *Battle Surface: Japan's Submarine War Against Australia 1942-44,* Random House Australia, Sydney, 1992.
Kanrogi, O., *Hirohito,* Gateway, Los Angeles, 1975.
King, J., *Waltzing Materialism,* Harper & Row, Sydney, 1978.
Loney, J., *The Price of Admiralty,* Marine History Pub., Geelong.
Loney, J., *Wrecks on the Queensland Coast*, Volume 2, Maritime History Publication, 1987.
MacArthur, D., *Reminiscences,* McGraw-Hill, New York, 1964.
Macken, J. J., *Pittwater's War*, Anchor Publications, Sydney, 2005.
Masanori, I., *The End of the Imperial Japanese Navy,* Weidenfeld & Nicolson, London, 1962.
McKie, R., *The Heroes,* Angus & Robertson, Sydney, 1978.
Meo, L. D., *Japan's Radio War on Australia 1941-1945,* Melbourne U.P., 1968.
Moore, J. H., *Over-Sexed, Over-Paid and Over Here,* University of Queensland Press, St Lucia, 1981.
Morison, S. E., *History of U.S. Naval Operations in World War II,* Little, Brown, Boston, 1947.
O'Neill, R., *Suicide Squads,* Lansdowne Press, Sydney, 1981.
Pearl, C., *Australia's Yesterdays,* Reader's Digest, Sydney, 1974.
Prange, G. W., *At Dawn We Slept,* Michael Joseph Ltd, London, 1981.
Rhys, L., *My Ship is So Small,* Georgian House, Melbourne, 1946.
Rush, C, W., Chambliss, W. C. & Gimpel. H. J., *The Complete Book of Submarines,* World Publishing, Cleveland, 1958.
Stevenson, W., *A Man Called Intrepid,* Sphere Books, London, 1977.
Warner, P., and Seno, S., *The Coffin Boats: Japanese midget submarine operations in the Second World War*, Lee Cooper, London, 1986.
Watts, A. J. and Gorden, B. J., *The Imperial Japanese Navy,* Doubleday, New York, 1971.
Williamson, K., *The Last Bastion*, Lansdowne, Sydney, 1984.
Winterbotham, F. W., *The Ultra Secret,* Futura, London, 1975.
Wisniewski, R. A., *Pearl Harbor and the USS Arizona Memorial: A pictorial History,* Pacific Basin Enterprises, Honolulu, 1977.

AUSTRALIAN PERIODICALS AND NEWSPAPERS
Argus – 2, 3, 4, 5, 6, 8, 9, 10 & 16 June; 16 July 1942; 3, 10, 19, 20, 21, 24, 28 & 30 Nov 1942; 1 & 16 December 1942.
Australia's Heritage, Part 43, Paul Hamlyn, Sydney, 1970.
Daily Telegraph, 29 May 1950.
Fort Scratchley, Perfection Printing, Newcastle, 1979.
Geelong Advocate, 5 June 1982.

Port City Pictorial, Port Macquarie RSL Club Ltd, Vol 1, No. 9, October 1982.
Ports of N.S.W., Volume 2, No.1., June 1978.
Shipmate, May 1976 (US Naval Academy Alumni Association & Foundation).
Shipmate, March 1981.
Smith's Weekly, 8 and 13 June 1942.
Sun News-Pictorial, 1 June 1982.
Sydney Morning Herald, 2, 3, 4, 5, 6, 8 and 9 June 1942 and 31 July 1945.
The Age, 2 & 3 June 1942.
The Bulletin, 22 and 25 May 1982, 29 June 1982 and 10 August 1982.
The Sun, 1, 5, 6, 7, June 1942.
The Sunday Mail, 14 November 1982.
The Sunday Sun and Guardian, 8 March 1942.
White Ensign, Vol 1 No 2, December 1945.

JAPANESE PERIODICALS AND NEWSPAPERS
Asahi Shimbun, No. 20186, 6 June 1942.
Showa, No. 20479, 28 March 1943.
Mainichi, Japan, 1942.
Japan (Nippon) Times, 7 June 1942, 28 March 1943.
Yomiusi Shimbun, March 1942.

PERSONAL CORRESPONDENCE
Ernest James Higgins, 4 June 1986, 15 June 1986 (*HMAS Kuttabul*).
Fletcher, G. L., Rear-Admiral, USN, 1 January 1982 (*USS Perkins*).
George W. Chipley, USN, 12 Jan 1982; 3, 10, 11, 14 May 1982, (*USS Chicago*).
Hirokazu Sano, 26 September 1981 (Japan Midget Submarine Association).
Hermon J. Mecklenburg, Captain, USN, 13 January 1982 (*USS Chicago*).
Itsuo Ashibe, 12 April 1978.
James Cargill, October 1992 (Maritime Services Board Watchman).
Jikyo Ishino, 1 September 1988 (Japan Midget Submarine Association).
Kazou Uyeda, 26 January 1989.
Koichi Ban, 13 April 1978.
Laurie E. C. Hinchliffe, Lt-Commander, RAN, 3 March 1982 (NOIC Staff Officer).
Professor Iwashiwa Hisao, Chief War History Department, Japan, 1978.
Reginald T. Andrew, Lieutenant, RAN, 23 May, 23 June, 25 September, 10 November 1978; 26 February, 28 May, 5 October 1979; 27 January, 8 & 26 May, 23 June, 16 July, 17 Aug 1980; 16 January, 11 February, 6 Apr, 14 May, 7, 24 & 25 June, 24 December 1981; 7 May, 4 & 23 July 1982 (*HMAS Sea Mist*).
Richard Sargent, 30 June 1986 (*HMAS Yarroma*).
Robert A. Allen, Ensign, USN, 16 January 1982 (*USS Perkins*).
Roland J. Obey, Captain, USN, 28 January 1982 (*USS Perkins*).
Saeki Matsuo, 18 October 1988.
Walter C. Ford, Rear-Admiral, USN, 28 January 1982 (*USS Perkins*).
William O. Floyd, Rear-Admiral, USN, 9 February 1982 (*USS Chicago*).
William W. South, Commander, USN (*USS Chicago*).
Yasuaki Imaizumi, Defence Attache, Embassy of Japan, London, June 1979.

INTERVIEWS
Charles "Charlie" Brown, Able-Seaman, RAN, 1988 (*HMAS Kuttabul*).
George W. Chipley, USN, 1982 (*USS Chicago*).
George W. Kittredge, Rear-Admiral, USN, 1982 (*USS Chicago*).

Harold F. Anderson, 1980.
James Nelson, Able-Seaman, 1981 (*HMAS Lolita*).
Laurie E. C. Hinchliffe, Lt-Commander, NOIC Staff Officer, RAN, 3 March 1981.
Reginald T Andrew, 1978-1982 (*HMAS Sea Mist*).
Robert Nelson, First Class Petty Officer, USN, 1982 (*USS Chicago*).
William O. Floyd, Rear-Admiral, USN, 1982 (*USS Chicago*).
William W. South, Commander, USN, 1982 (*USS Chicago*).
Tieji Yamaki, Sub-Lieutenant, Japanese Navy, 1982.

AUSTRALIAN WAR MEMORIAL

AWM52   AIF and Militia Unit War Diaries, 1939-1945.
4/19/4 Sydney Coastal Artillery, December 1940 – October 1942.

AWM54   MP 2026/21/22: Report from Rear-Admiral-in-Charge, HMA Naval Establishments, Sydney. "Midget Submarine Attack on Sydney Harbour 31 May-1 June, 1942".

MP1587/1: Midget Submarine Attack on Sydney Harbour - Signals. Series accession number B6121/3.

Intelligence - Reports, enemy plans and preparation and situation reports: Fraser Island Intelligence Report. Subject: (1) Gulf incident; (2) Intercept Japanese radio; (3) Reported submarine Glendower Point; (4) Fraser Island intelligence report by "B" Group Volunteer Defence Corps - Queensland. Subject 4 (1) Intelligence report; (2) Covering letter to First Australian Army; (3) Covering letter to Naval Staff Office 505/6/7 Plans and photos of submarines.

Plans and diagrams, photographs of midget (Japanese) submarine and components, involved in Sydney Harbour attack, 1942.

Appreciations - Japanese submarine movements in Australian waters, May 1943.

General Staff Intelligence, New Guinea Force, Collation Cards - Chronological sequence of events, SWPA (Patrols - Coast Watching Activities, Shipping sighting, Shipping losses - Enemy air raids), 1943. [Intelligence - Reports, enemy plans and preparation and situation reports:].

Intelligence - Reports, enemy plans and preparation and situation reports: Japanese preparations for war and plans for Australia Contents 1 - Historical Background; 2 - Preparations and planning, 1942.

Directorate of Military Intelligence: chronological sequence of events SWPA with brief summaries of fighting, strengths and dispositions, 1942-1945.

Translations of Japanese answers to questionnaire submitted by Historical Staff, Australian War Memorial - Battle plan of Japanese Fleets in 1942, including Sydney Harbour attack, and effectiveness of Australian coast-watching organisations, 1942-1948.

War establishments and amendments - [Intelligence:] [Air Liaison Group New Guinea Int Corps; Army Air Photo Interpretation Group or Unit, Combined Operations Intelligence Centre; Interpreter Unit; Corps Section Intelligence Corps; Intelligence Corps; Combined Services Detailed Interrogation Centre, BCOF; LHQ Section Intelligence Corps; Advanced LHQ Section Intelligence Corps; Allied Translater and Interpreter Signal Section; Central Bureau Intelligence Corps; Special Intelligence Ppersonnel Group; Army Intelligence Section; Corps Section], 1942-1952.

Naval (inc. Enemy) - Submarines and anti-sub devices: Submarine tactics, air intelligence, southern area collated information bulletins, 1942.

Documents recovered from crashed Japanese Bomber at Gaile (near Port Moresby) 10 July 1942. Report No 14 - A Forms for reporting enemy dispositions; B Forms for meteorological reports, Report No 15 - Set of maps together with a bag labelled in Japanese "Reconnaissance Satchel", Report No 18 - Among documents found there was a reference chart of directions for navigation in South Sea Base Area, a photograph of this chart is reproduced in Appendix "A" of this file and translated in Appendix "B", Report No 12 - Naval comment on the table of Japanese Fleet Organisation - Speed by eye - indicator, 1942.

AWM61	Report on Coastal Defence, Sydney, Newcastle and Port Kembla, 1940-1942.
AWM69	Official History, 1939-45 War: Records of G Hermon Gill: Manuscript and typescript notes for Naval War History, 1940-1941. [Mainly events of June 1942] (1941-1943).
AWM102	Transcript of Rear-Admiral Muirhead-Gould's radio speech on 2FC in July 1942.
AWM123	Headquarters Allied Air Forces SWPA. Directorate of Intelligence. Consolidated index. Intelligence summaries 1-53 (inclusive), Dec 1942.
	Naval operations, Midway Island and Aleutian Islands, Jun 1942. File No 1 - Intelligence summaries, Advisory War Council minutes, press cuttings, May 1942 - Sep 1945.
	Japanese naval strength - Intelligence summaries, War Cabinet and Advisory War Council minutes, press cuttings, Jun 1942 - Jan 1943
AWM124	"Artic" messages from New Zealand Naval Board. 1941-1942.
	Messages to Australian Minister [R G Casey] and Australian Naval Attache in Washington, and Prime Minister Curtin, 1942.
	Report of investigation into a Japanese torpedo, fired from a midget submarine during the attack on Sydney Harbour, 7-8 June 1942.
	Report of investigation into a Japanese torpedo, fired from a midget submarine during the attack on Sydney Harbour, 7-8 June 1942.
AWM188	Japanese Submarine Activity in the South West Pacific, 1942-1947.
AWM246	Port Jackson Fixed Defence Indicator Loops. Tracing showing alterations and repairs to Indicator Loops, 4 Jun 1942 to 28 Dec 1942.
AWM315	Relics - Official: Australian Navy. Japanese submarine sunk in Sydney Harbour, 31 May 1942 and incidental relics.

AUSTRALIAN NATIONAL ARCHIVES

A981	Political Warfare Intelligence Summary of Monitored Far Eastern Broadcasts.
A1608	War Records Exhibition of Japanese Submarine for Patriotic Purposes, 1942-1944
A3300	British Embassy - Intelligence, 1942.
A5954	Headquarters Allied Air Forces. South West Pacific Area. Directorate of Intelligence. Intelligence Summary. Serial Nos. 74, 160.
	Strategical Situation in Southwest Pacific Area. Relation to Global Strategy, Request for concentration of Naval Forces and Question of Return of 9th Division. 25/8/42 - 8/1/43. File No 1.
	Circulation of cablegrams to Commander-in-Chief, Southwest Pacific Area, and Commanders, Allied Naval and Air Forces, 1942.
	Operations in South West Pacific Area. Japanese submarine activity off coast of Australia, 1942. [Press cuttings]
	Naval Operations in Pacific. Enemy Submarine Activity off Coast of Australia, 1942-1945.
A12728	Folder of inwards cables master sheets - Most Secret and Top Secret - WINCH prefix - 27 December 1941 (WINCH 12) to 8 April 1945 (WINCH 8) - Prime Minister of The United Kingdom (Great Britain) (Winston Churchill) to Prime Minister of Australia (John Curtin), 27 Dec 1941 - 8 Apr 1945.

	Folder of outwards cables master sheets - Most Secret and Top Secret - JOHCU and ARDEN prefixes - 4 October 1941 (ARDEN 1) to 30 January 1945 (JOHCU 88) - Prime Minister of Australia (Arthur Fadden, John Curtin) to Prime Minister of The United Kingdom (Great Britain) (Winston Churchill), 4 Oct 1941 - 30 Jan 1945.
B5555	FRUMEL records (incomplete) of communications intelligence relating to the Midway Battle, 1942.
	FRUMEL records (incomplete) of communications intelligence relating to the Coral Sea Battle, 1942.
B5436	Central Bureau Technical Records Part E- Naval Short Weather Synoptic weather reports - JN36, circa 1942 - circa 1945.
B6121	Guadalcanal battle of November 1942 - Solomons Campaign Naval Operations.
	Signals - Macarthur to Various Addressees Concerning Expected Japanese Attack Against Port Moresby and NE Australia, 1942.
	Signals - Midget Submarine Attack on Sydney Harbour; *SS Allara* - Damage by Japanese Submarine; *SS Mamutu* - Sinking of by Japanese Submarine; *SS Orestes* - Damage by Japanese Submarine I24 and I21; *SS Guatemala* - Sinking of by Japanese Submarine; *SS Iron Crown* - sinking of by Japanese submarine; *SS Age* - abortive attack on by Japanese submarine; *SS Barwon* - Abortive Attack on by Japanese Submarine; and *SS Chloe* - Sinking by Japanese submarine, 1942.
A6923	Australian Military Forces - [Director of Military Intelligence - Central Bureau - Special Intelligence, ULTRA, related to the interception of enemy wireless traffic including Y signals and X (Typex) cypher machines- technical and other Allied administrative arrangements for collection of Y Intelligence; Special Intelligence, ULTRA; Cryptographic Intelligence, PEARL and Traffic Analysis, THUMB]. 1942-1946.
	Australian Military Forces - Central Bureau - administration of [Special Intelligence related to the interception of enemy wireless traffic including Y signals and X (Typex) cypher machines
A9519	Attacks - Naval - Submarines, 1942-1944.
A10913	Secret Admiralty Weekly Intelligence Report, number 116, 29 May 1942.
BP132/2	Naval auxiliary patrol boats - Provision of anti-submarine equipment.
BP262/2	Demolition - Works General [includes secret correspondence from Prime Minister to Qld Premier outlining steps to implement denials of resources to the enemy and "scorched earth" policy; preparation for demolition of army, naval and air force facilities in Qld.
C320	NSW Security Service file - Japanese fifth column activities: 1 Jan 1942 - 15 Dec 1945 - CA 946, Security Service, New South Wales. Short wave radio messages [allegedly between Japanese].
	NSW Security Service file - Japanese naval personnel in Australia before war.
MP1049/5	Indications of Submarine activity off Darwin, 1942.
MP138/1	Dr Clynes enemy alien examination of Japanese Submarine, 1942
MP150/1	Boom Defence equipment [report from District Contract Board]; Naval Auxiliary Patrol enrolment and special submissions.
MP151/1	Appointment of NOIC [Naval Officer in Charge], 1942.
	Awards in connection with Japanese midget submarine attack on Sydney Harbour, 1942.
	List of personnel killed as a result of enemy action by Japanese submarine in Sydney Harbour, 1942.
MP401/1	Darwin Air Raid Inquiry - exhibits - including Duty Officers Log, ARP Nominal Rolls, Naval message, 1942.
MP1049/5	Attack by midget submarines on Sydney - appreciation from study of Japanese charts and magnetic surveys.
	Report on demolition charge from Japanese submarine recovered at Sydney.

MP1185/8	Ashes of Japanese naval men whose bodies were recovered from Sydney Harbour [10 folios, contains 4 photographs of the bodies of Japanese naval men recorered from Sydney Harbour, these images may casue distress].
PP227/2	Grading of Intelligence - Admiralty System, 1939-1942.
SP109/3	Censorship Naval and Shipping. Information re Sinkings of Ships, 1942-1945.
SP112/1	Questions relating to the reception of radio broadcasts from Japanese-controlled Stations, and broadcasting of messages by Australian and Allied prisoners-of-war: 1 Jan 1939 - 31 Dec 1946 - CA 34, Department of Information, Central Office - Press Division.
SP300/3	'Eyewitness Accounts' [Radio talk presented by ABC war correspondent on Japanese Submarine sinking in Sydney Harbour], 1942.
SP338/1	Japanese Midget Submarine Attack on Sydney Harbour, 31 May-1 June 1942.

UNITED STATES SOURCES

Department of the Navy, The Historical Centre, Japanese Naval Ships, Type A, B & C Midget Submarines (http://www.history.navy.mil/photos/sh-fornv/japan/japtp-ss/mdg-a-2.htm).

Hawaiin University, Hawaii Undersea Research Laboratory (HURL), Analysis of Hole in Conning Tower of Midget Sub, 20 December 2003 (http://www.soest.hawaii.edu/HURL/midget.html

National Museum of the Pacific War (http://www.nimitz-museum.org/).

The Honolulu Star-Bulletin, 1st, 2nd and 3rd Extra, 7 December; 8, 9, 10 and 11 December 1941; 2 May 2002.

The Pacific Digest, The Sakamaki Midget Submarine, by Heber A. Holbrook, 3 January 2001.

US Naval Institute, Pearl Harbor - Attack from Below, by Commander John Rodgaard, USNR (Rtd) (http://www.usni.org/navalhistory/Articles99/Nhrodgaard.htm).

USS Arizona Memorial, Submerged Cultural Resources Study, The Japanese Midget Submarines at Pearl Harbor, 27 April 2001.

OTHER SOURCES

Bullard, W. L., Leading Seaman Diver, RAN Report of diving operations 1-8 June, 1942.
Chief War History Department, Japan - Attack on Sydney Harbour (translated JETS, Embassy of Japan, Canberra).
Commonwealth Department of Veterans' Affairs, Publications, *The Sinking of the Centaur* (http://www.dva.gov.au/media/publicat/2003/centaur/index.htm).
HMAS Lauriana's running log - from 1210K/31 May to 0740K/1 June 1942: L. H. Winkworth Flotilla Skipper "P" "*Lauriana*" No. 6 Patrol, 31 May 1942, to: The Squadron Skipper, Naval Auxiliary Patrol.
Japanese report by K. Nakamura – Representing the Imperial Japanese Second Demobilisation Minister.
Maritime Services Board of NSW – Report, James Cargill, 3 June 1942.
Maritime Services Board of NSW – Memorandum, A. B. Shaw, Acting Secretary, Maritime Services Board of NSW, 3 June 1942.
Maritime Services Board of NSW – Memorandum, E. A. Lucas, Secretary to Rear Admiral-in-Charge, Sydney, Department of the Navy, 6 October 1942.
Naval Message – *HMAS Silver Cloud*, Lt-Cdr, Senior Officer, Channel Patrol Flotilla, 10 October 1942 (R. T. Andrew Estate).
HMAS Lolita, handwritten report, Warrant Officer H. S. Anderson, June 1942 (H. F. Anderson).
Naval Message – Naval Officer in Charge, Sydney, to *HMAS Lolita*, 3 June 1942. ●

INDEX

Adelaide (Australian Cruiser) - 39, 103, 104, 155
Adele (Australian examination vessel) - 39, 239
Admiralty House - 41
Age (Aust. merchant steamer) - 190, 191, 198
Ageta, Kiyoi, Cdr - 46, 48, 49, 51, 85, 115, 215, 216, 219
AIB see Allied Intelligence Bureau - 77, 78
Akeida, Lt Saburo - 93
Aleutian Islands - 206, 216
Alice Springs - 68
Allara (Australian steamer) - 198
Allied Air Command - 179
Allied Intelligence Bureau (AIB) - 77, 78
Allura, (NAP) - 39, 41, 123, 155
Anderson, H. S., Warrant Officer - 11, 37, 121, 122, 123, 125, 136, 180, 255
Andrew, Reginald T., Lt - 11, 37, 110, 111, 112, 120, 157, 159, 162, 163, 164, 179, 242, 253, 255
Antares (American auxiliary vessel) - 53
Arizona (American battleship) - 57
Arnott, Harold - 107, 129
Arunta (Australian corvette) - 87
ASDIC (underwater detection equipment) - 133, 159, 164, 240
Ashibe, Mamoru - 17, 85, 129, 155, 183, 184, 217
Astoria (American heavy cruiser) - 181
ATIS (Allied Translator Interpreter Section) - 76
Auckland - 59, 60, 85, 88, 89, 173, 174, 175
Auchmuty, J. J. - 103, 251
Australia (Australian heavy cruiser) - 229, 234
Australian Declaration of War - 62, 64, 66
Australian Governor-General - 40, 41, 64
Australian Hudson aircraft - 64, 193, 195
Australian *National Security Act* - 67
Australian Naval Board - 17, 88, 108, 109, 176, 193, 254
Australian Naval Intelligence - 65, 179, 187, 254
Australian Parliament - 63, 64, 67, 181, 189
Australian War Cabinet - 64, 65, 67, 79, 169
Australian War Memorial - 184, 187, 211, 222, 223, 224, 251, 253
Australian Wirraway aircraft - 30
Axis powers, defeat of - 73
Ban Katsuhisa, Sub-Lt - 17, 18, 46, 85, 129, 133, 136, 138, 139, 155, 183, 184, 217
see also I-24 (midget submarine)
Bang, A. G., Capt - 199
Barnes, Brig-Gen - 67
Barwon (Australian merchant steamer) - 191, 198
Battle of Midway see Midway Islands
Battle of Rennell Island - 181, 182

Battle of the Coral Sea see Coral Sea Battle
"Beat Hitler first" policy - 69, 75, 206, 224
BELCONNEN (Central Bureau) - 205, 206
Bellevue Hill - 197
Bingera (Australian anti-submarine vessel) - 39, 155, 159, 161, 179, 191, 238, 239
Birubi (Australian pilot steamer) - 196, 197
Blamey, General Sir Thomas - 77
Bland, Leslie, Able-Seaman - 29, 145, 152
Bletchley Park (London) - 74, 75, 76, 205
Blue Mountains 195
Bode, H. D., Capt - 41, 123, 129, 137, 175, 181, 237
Bombay (Indian corvette) - 39, 159, 239, 240
Boom net (anti-submarine) - 23, 37, 38, 58, 89, 105, 109, 116, 117, 119, 121, 123, 124, 131, 155, 157, 160, 176, 177, 178, 181, 212, 213, 235, 236, 237, 239, 244, 254
Botany Bay - 103, 116, 173, 189, 251
Bougainville - 74
Brady, Second Officer - 191
Breydon, E., Lt-Cdr - 37, 179
Brisbane - 76, 83, 85, 168, 174, 189, 200, 201
British Admiralty - 23, 64, 91, 94, 109, 176, 254
British Government - 67, 68
British Loyalty (British tanker) - 23, 90, 93
British Navy - 64
British Prime Minister see Churchill, Winston
British Secret Service - 73, 74, 75
British Security Co-ordination (BSC) - 74, 75, 77
Broken Bay - 87, 116, 184, 241
Brown, Charlie, Able-Seaman - 11, 145, 146, 147, 225
Brown, Tulla - 11, 167, 168, 169
BSC see British Security Co-ordination
Buhl, C. F., US Navy Diver - 221
Bungaree (Australian minelayer) - 39, 104, 234
Burlingame, Burl - 55
Burma - 68
Caiger, George 78
Calana (Aust. steamer) - 198
California (American battleship) - 57
Canberra - 68, 167, 224, 251, 255
Canberra (Australian heavy cruiser) - 39, 103, 39, 155, 159, 181, 234, 239, 240
Cape Ambon (Madagascar) - 90, 93
Cape Banks - 187, 188
Cargill, James - 11, 109, 117, 119, 121, 176, 177, 178, 180, 242, 243, 252, 255
Caroline Islands - 85, see also Truk Islands
Censorship, government - 19, 25, 67, 167-169, 224

JAPANESE SUBMARINE RAIDERS 1942 *A Maritime Mystery* .259

Centaur (Australian hospital ship) - 200, 201 Central Bureau *see* BELCONNEN
Channel patrol boat flotilla - 37
Charrette (American destroyer) - 216
Chicago (American heavy cruiser) - 19, 30, 31, 36, 39, 78, 83, 89, 91, 123, 129, 133, 135, 136, 137, 139, 145, 155, 157, 158, 160, 174, 175, 176, 181, 182, 234, 235, 237, 238, 239, 243, 252, 253
Chiyoda (Japanese carrier) - 47, 60, 83, 174
Chloe (Greek merchant steamer) - 85, 174
Chuma, Lt Kenshi - 18, 46, 47, 86, 117, 119, 123, 129, 177, 212, 213, 217, 219 *see also* I-27 (midget submarine)
Churchill, Winston - 67, 68, 69, 73, 74, 75, 77, 79, 206, 224, 230, 254, 259
Circular Quay - 35, 135, 167
Clark, Cdr C. C. - 149, 242
Clarke Island - 145, 212, 214
Coast Farmer (American steamer) - 198
Cobargo (Australian merchant steamer) - 37
Cockatoo Island - 30, 37, 59, 89
Collins, John, Commodore - 229
Combat Intelligence Unit (HYPO) - 205, 206, 207
Combers, L. T., Ordinary-Seaman - 147
Combined Defence Headquarters - 41
Cook, Capt James 116
Coolana (Australian steamer) - 198
Coral Sea - 23, 35, 37, 77, 78, 79, 80, 85, 97, 169, 174, 206
Coral Sea Battle - 77, 79, 97, 206
Costello, John - 205, 251
Coventry, and Ultra - 75, 79
Crace, Rear-Admiral - 78, 83
Crowe, James, Able-Seaman - 121, 123, 136
"Crusader" *see* Safford, Laurence F.
Cumming, M. N., Bandsman - 147, 242
Curie, Colin, Gunner -197
Curtin Government *see* Australian Government Curtin, John - 25, 63, 64, 65, 66, 67, 68, 69, 73, 75, 77, 78, 79, 168, 169, 179, 206, 224, 254
Curtiss (American seaplane tender) - 55
Cutler, Roden, VC - 37
Daigo, Vice-Admiral - 83, 85, 91, 117, 174, 187, 189
Daily Telegraph - 31, 167, 168, 175, 252
Darwin - 18, 19, 23, 24, 25, 65, 67, 68, 169, 173, 251
Davao (Philippines) - 219
Davey, Jack - 107
Davies, A. F. - 227
Davies, E., Able-Seaman - 145
Dechaineux, Emile, Capt - 229

Deloraine (Australian corvette) - 65
Department of Information - 64, 189
Diego Suarez Bay, *see also* Madagascar - 23, 48, 90, 91, 92, 93, 94, 175, 217, 219
Dieppe - 230
Dobbin (American destroyer tender) - 39, 104, 155, 234
Donovan, William "Wild Bill" - 75, 77
Doomba (Australian minesweeper) - 39, 159, 164, 199, 236, 239
Doyle, A. B., Capt - 121, 149, 242
Dureenbee (Australian trawler) - 198
East Indies - 63, 68, 78, 151
Eastern Suburbs - 31, 195, 197, 194, 212
Echunga (Australian steamer) - 198
Eighth Submarine Squadron - 55, 60, 91, 92, 94
Elizabeth Bay - 41, 123
"Enigma" machine *see* Ultra
Erinna (British merchant steamer) - 37
Esmerelda (CPB) - 39
Eta Jima (Japan) - 221
Evatt. Minister of External Affairs, Dr - 66, 69
Eyres, H. C., Sub-Lt - 37, 121, 123
Fair (American destroyer) - 216
Far East - 64, 68, 77
Farm Cove - 37, 38, 107, 110, 157, 159, 160, 161, 162, 177, 179, 239
Fiji - 59, 65, 79, 83, 85, 189, 207
First Submarine Squadron - 49, 51
Fletcher, F. J. Rear-Admiral - 78
Fletcher, G. L., Rear-Admiral - 252
Flinders Naval Base - 110
Forde, Deputy Prime-Minister - 189
Fort Scratchley - 196, 197, 199, 252
Fukutome, Vice-Admiral Shigeru - 83
Furuno, Shigemi - 46, 51, 218
Gabo Island - 191, 198
Gallipoli - 230
Garden Island - 13, 23, 24, 29, 30, 35, 38, 41, 59, 103, 107, 124, 136, 137, 139, 143, 157, 160, 168, 173, 175, 177, 225, 226, 235, 238, 239
Garden Island Operations Room - 31, 89, 110, 119, 121, 174, 176, 187, 244, 245
Geelong (Australian corvette) - 39, 136, 145, 155, 235, 238
Germany - 69, 181, 187, 195
Gill, G. Hermon - 30, 88, 115, 139, 175, 177
Goonambee (Australian minesweeper) - 39, 155, 159, 162, 237, 238, 240, 261
Gowrie, A. H., Lord - 40, 41, 64
"Grand Strategy" document - 69, 224

G.S. Livanos (Greek steamer) - 198
Guadalcanal - 83, 181, 207, 216, 217, 220
Guatemala (Panamanian merchant steamer) - 191, 198, 201
Hanafusa, Hiroshi, Cdr - 46, 85
Harvey, W. J., Capt - 197
Hashimoto, Mochitsura - 51, 199, 251
Hasluck, Sir Paul 67, 100, 168, 169, 251
Hawaii 49, 51, 52, 53, 59, 65, 78, 205, 221, 254
Hawaii Undersea Research Laboratory (HURL) - 221
Helena (American light cruiser) - 57
Helm (American destroyer) - 53
Hinchliffe, L. E. C., Lt-Cdr - 11, 137, 192, 253
Hirohito, Emperor - 251
Hiroo, Akira - 45, 46, 51, 218, 221
Hitchcock, G. J., Flight-Lt - 11, 193, 195
Hobart - 32, 59
Hobart (Australian light cruiser) - 145, 146, 147
Hoehling, A. A. - 155, 251
"Hollywood Fleet" - 107
Houston (American light cruiser) - 65
Hunter Valley - 195
HYPO (US Pacific Fleet Combat Intelligence Unit) - 205, 206, 207
I-class submarines (Japanese submarine) - 29, 32, 49
I-1 (Japanese submarine) - 200
I-2 (Japanese submarine) - 200
I-3 (Japanese submarine) - 200
I-10 (Japanese submarine) - 91, 94, 241
I-11 (Japanese submarine) - 200, 201
I-16 (Japanese submarine) - 46, 48, 49, 51, 57, 91, 93, 216, 241
I-16 (midget submarine) - 57, 93
I-18 (Japanese submarine) - 49, 46, 91, 241
I-18 (midget submarine) - 51, 93
I-20 (Japanese submarine) - 46, 49, 51, 91, 93, 216, 241
I-20 (midget submarine) - 20, 93
I-21 (Japanese submarine) - 60, 83, 85, 87, 89, 116, 173, 174, 175, 187, 188, 189, 190, 191, 197, 199, 200, 201, 216, 241
I-22 (Japanese submarine) - 46, 49, 51, 57, 60, 48, 83, 85, 86, 88, 89, 115, 174, 188, 189, 200, 216, 241,
I-22 (midget submarine) - 84, 85, 88, 132, 134, 155, 158, 160, 213, 214, 221, 235, 236, 246, 247
I-24 (Japanese submarine) - 17, 46, 49, 51, 53, 60, 83, 85, 89, 116, 174, 188, 190, 191, 195, 197, 199, 200, 201, 216, 241
I-24 (midget submarine) - 17, 51, 53, 60, 88, 104, 160, 129, 130, 138, 156, 183, 184, 189, 219, 235
I-25 (Japanese submarine) - 32, 59, 85, 173

I-26 (Japanese submarine) - 200, 201
I-27 (Japanese submarine) - 60, 83, 85, 86, 89, 116, 174, 189, 191, 193, 200, 216, 241
I-27 (midget submarine) - 85, 116, 118, 160, 188, 213, 214, 235, 241
I-28 (Japanese submarine) - 60, 83, 85, 174
I-29 (Japanese submarine) - 60, 83, 85, 87, 88, 89, 116, 188, 173, 174, 187, 189, 200, 216, 241
I-30 (Japanese submarine) - 91, 241
I-124 (Japanese submarine) - 65, 200
I-174 (Japanese submarine) - 200, 201
I-175 (Japanese submarine) - 200, 201
I-177 (Japanese submarine) - 200
I-178 (Japanese submarine) - 200
I-180 (Japanese submarine) - 200
Inagaki, Kiyoshi - 46, 51, 53, 55, 218
Ind, Allison W. - 77, 78
Indian Ocean - 59, 83, 91, 201
Indicator loops - 38, 39, 109, 110, 124, 129, 155, 157, 160, 176, 183, 184, 233, 234 , 235, 236, 237, 238, 239, 242, 244, 260, 261
Indicator Loop signature - 104, 118, 130, 156, 158
Indicator Loop Station - 38, 110, 129, 155, 157, 160, 176, 177
Institute for Counter Terrorism - 230
Inter-Allied Services Department (IASD) - 77
Iron Chieftain (Australian merchant steamer) - 190, 191, 198
Iron Crown (Australian steamer) - 193, 198
Ishizaki, Rear-Admiral Noburo - 59, 91, 93, 94
Ito, Susumo, Flying Warrant Officer - 29, 30, 32, 91, 103, 107, 175, 181
Iura, Capt Shojiro - 49
Iwasa, Lt Naoji - 46, 47, 49, 51, 218, 221
Iwase, Sub-Lt Katsusuke 93, 217
Japanese codes - 73, 74, 79, 174, 205
Japanese Combined Fleet - 32, 45, 50, 59, 207
Japanese decoy periscopes - 192, 193
Japanese Government - 64 .
Japanese Imperial Forces - 63
Japanese Imperial Army Air Force - 229
Japanese Imperial Navy - 13, 207, 215
Japanese High Command - 73
Japan Midget Submarine Association - 11, 84, 226, 227
Japanese Planning Board - 91
Japanese sympathisers - 91
John Adams (American steamer) - 83, 85
Jomard Passage - 83
K-9 (Dutch submarine) - 23, 39, 121, 136, 143, 143, 151, 235, 239

JAPANESE SUBMARINE RAIDERS 1942 *A Maritime Mystery* .261

Kaiten - 25, 227, 229, 230

Kamakura Maru (Japanese freighter) - 215

Kamikazi attacks - 25, 224, 229, 230

Kanimbla (British armed merchant cruiser) - 39, 164

Katayama, Yoshio - 51, 46, 218, 221

Katoomba (Australian corvette) - 65

Kawai, Tatsuo 212

Kikuchi Clan - 227

Kimmel, Husband E., Admiral - 53, 221

King, E. J., Admiral - 206

King of England - 64

Kings Cross - 98

Kirby, F., Able-Seaman - 149, 152

Kirribilli - 38, 41, 160

Kuramia (Australian gate vessel) - 109

Kure Naval Base - 49

Kure Naval College - 45, 219

Kuroshima, Kameto, Capt - 59

Kuttabul (Australian depot ship) - 19, 41, 39, 103, 136, 137, 139, 143-155, 160, 177, 179, 201, 225, 226, 235, 238, 239, 242, 252, 253

Lauriana (NAP) - 37, 39, 41, 107, 123, 129, 131, 133, 134, 155, 235, 237, 242, 255

Lebanese Civil War - 230

Leilani (CPB) - 37, 39, 157,

Lexington (American aircraft carrier) - 78, 79, 83, 174

Leyte Island - 229

Lithgow (Australian corvette) - 65

Littleby, J., Petty Officer - 149

Lolita (CPB) - 37, 39, 119, 120, 121, 122, 123, 125, 136, 155, 162, 179, 180, 237, 238, 239, 253, 254, 255

London - 64, 69, 75, 76, 77, 94, 109, 195

Long, R. B. M., Cdr - 65, 68

Louisville (American heavy cruiser) - 182

Lucas, E. A - 179, 255

Lunga Anchorage - 216, 219

Luzon Island - 216

MacArthur, Gen. Douglas - 25, 68, 69, 73, 76, 77, 78, 79, 103, 169, 174, 179, 187, 189, 205, 206, 207, 230, 251, 254

Madagascar - 23, 90, 91, 92, 93, 94, 176, 205, 230

"Magic" *see* Ultra

Makin, N.J.O. (Minister of the Navy) - 66, 181, 189

Malaya - 59, 64, 91, 149

Malay Barrier - 67

Maldive Islands - 216

Man-of-War Anchorage - 29, 30, 37, 38, 41, 129, 133, 136, 137, 155, 157, 175

Manila - 64, 205

Manly ferry - 35, 117, 133, 135

Maritime Services Board - 244

Marlean (CPB) - 37, 39, 157, 189, 239

Marshall Islands - 57, 59, 216

Martinez, Dan - 55

Maryland (American battleship) - 57

Mascot aerodrome - 30

Mashbir, Col. Sydney F. - 78

Matsuo, Lt Keiu - 18, 32, 45, 46, 47, 84, 85, 86, 115, 116, 129, 131, 133, 155, 157, 164, 177, 179, 211, 212, 215, 217, 227, 229, 225, 247

Matsuo, Matsue, 211, 227

Mecklenberg, H. J., Lt-Cdr - 11, 133, 137

Mediterranean - 110, 136

Melbourne - 32, 41, 59, 64, 65, 68, 76, 77, 78, 99, 149, 168, 179, 187, 189, 199, 205, 224, 222, 223, 241, 254

Australian Naval Intelligence Centre ("Airlie") - 77

Midway Islands - 59, 73, 205, 206

MI (Midway) Operation - 73, 79, 169, 205, 206, 207

Middle East - 37, 59, 230

Mills, C. F., Lt-Cdr - 30, 41

Mindanao (Philippines) - 219

Miramar (CPB) - 39, 148

MO (Port Moresby) Operation - 83, 173, 206, 207

Monaghan (American destroyer) - 55

Moore, John Hammond - 98, 103

Morison, Samuel, Rear-Admiral - 129, 251

Mortlake Bank (Aust. Merchant steamer) - 37

Morton, A. T., Flight-Sgt - 139

Mott, G. S., Col - 77, 78

Mozambique Channel - 94

Muirhead-Gould, Gerald C., Rear-Admiral - 30, 31, 40, 41, 87, 93, 107, 106, 108,110, 117, 119, 121, 123, 124, 129, 136, 137, 139, 143, 150, 151, 155, 157, 164, 168, 174, 175, 176, 177, 178, 179, 181, 191, 193, 212, 215, 224, 229, 236, 245

Murada (Australian steamer) - 198

Nagumo, Chuichi, Vice-Admiral - 65

Nakamura, K. - 216, 254

Nangle, William - 109, 117, 177, 242

NAP *see* Naval auxiliary patrol boat flotilla

"Nappies" ("Nap-Naps") *see* Naval Auxiliary Patrol Boat Flotilla

National Emergency Service - 31, 97, 109

Nauru Island - 78, 79, 206

Naval Auxiliary Patrol Boat Flotilla (NAP) - 107

NEGAT (Washington Naval Headquarters) - 206, 207

Nelson, James, Able-Seaman - 11, 121, 122, 123, 136, 253
Neosho (American oil tanker) - 57
Nestor (Australian dockyard motorboat) - 135
Netherlands East Indies - 63
Nevada (American battleship) - 57
New Caledonia - 59, 65, 79, 83, 207
Newcastle - 24, 31, 65, 87, 143, 174, 190, 191, 193, 196, 197, 198, 199, 240, 254
Newcastle Harbour - 87, 191, 196, 197
Newcombe, Harvey M., Capt - 11, 110, 129, 155, 176, 177
New Guinea - 65, 75, 77, 78, 80, 83, 169, 179, 206, 216
New Hebrides - 65
Newton, S., Bombardier - 199,
New York - 24, 74, 75, 77, 230
New Zealand - 31, 59, 60, 65, 85, 88, 89, 145, 147, 174, 189, 206
New Zealand Naval Board - 31, 88, 89, 230
New Zealand naval authorities - 31, 88, 89, 174
Nimitz, Chester W., Admiral - 77, 78, 205, 206, 207
Nimitz Museum - 221, 254
Nisshin (Japanese carrier) - 47, 59, 91
Noumea (New Caledonia) - 60, 78, 83, 85, 173, 174
Oahu Island (Hawaiian Islands) - 51, 54, 224
Ocean Islands - 78, 79, 206
Office of Strategic Service (OSS) - 75, 77
Ohmori, Takeshi - 117, 212
Oklahoma (American battleship) - 55, 57, 224
Orange - 195
Oranje (Dutch/Australian hospital ship) - 137
Orestes (British merchant steamer) - 199
Oshigaha, A.G. - 215
Ota, N., Capt - 216
Outerbridge, William, Capt - 53
Pacific Ocean - 32, 60
Pacific War - 69, 73, 173, 205, 206, 207, 212, 221, 229, 254
Pago Pago - 59
Paladin (British destroyer) - 216
Parnell Place (Newcastle) - 196, 197, 199
PC487 (American patrol boat) - 216
Pearl Harbor - 18, 23, 24, 31, 32, 35, 45, 46, 47, 48, 49, 50, 51, 52, 53, 54, 55, 57, 58, 59, 63, 64, 65, 68, 69, 78, 85, 103, 105, 109, 115, 119, 176, 205, 206, 207, 216, 218, 219, 220, 221, 224, 229, 252, 254
Penang (Malaya) - 59, 91
Perkins (American destroyer) - 19, 31, 36, 37, 39, 78, 83, 87, 123, 137, 155, 174, 199, 234, 237, 238, 239, 252, 253
Petard (British destroyer) - 216
Philippines - 64, 68, 88, 205, 216, 219, 224
Port Hacking - 88, 89, 116, 183, 184, 187, 188, 189, 239

Port Kembla - 240
Port Moresby - 23, 25, 60, 77, 78, 79, 80, 83, 173, 206
Port War Signal Station - 38, 110, 121, 123, 124, 131, 136, 160, 176, 237, 244, 254
Prange, Gordon W. - 57, 251
Queen Carola Harbour - 60, 83, 85, 174
Queen Elizabeth I (British transport ship) - 37
Queen Mary I (British transport ship) - 37, 40
Quincy (American heavy cruiser) - 181
Rabaul (New Britain) - 63, 65, 79, 83, 201, 206
Radio direction finding (RDF) - 89, 91
Ramilles (British battleship) - 23, 90, 91, 92, 93, 94, 175
Repulse (British battleship) - 149
Richmond Airbase - 30
RO 33 (Japanese submarine) - 200
Roberts, W. Owen C., Lt-Cdr - 11
Roberts, N., Able-Seaman - 11, 146, 147
Robertson Point - 159, 164, 234, 236, 240
Robson, N., Marine-Engineer - 149, 152
Rodgaard, Jogn, Capt - 55, 254
Roosevelt, F. D. - 68, 69, 73, 74, 75, 79, 187, 224
Rose Bay - 38, 160, 195
Darwin - 18, 19, 23, 24, 25, 63, 65, 67, 68, 169, 173
Rumbaugh, L. A., Professor - 155
Rushcutters Bay - 37, 38, 110, 160
Safford, Laurence F., Cdr ("Crusader") - 76
Saipan Island - 206
Sakamaki, Kazuo, Sub-Lt - 46, 51, 53, 55, 218, 219, 221, 254
Samarai - 229, 230
Samoa (American) - 59, 65, 79
Samuel Benbow (Australian minesweeper) - 39, 239
San Michele (Australian trawler) - 187
Sandford, Alastair W., Col - 76
Sano, Hirokazu - 11, 46, 50, 218
Sasaki, Hankyu, Capt. - 32, 49, 50, 51, 57, 60, 78, 80, 85, 87, 88, 89, 91, 116, 117, 174, 175, 187, 189, 191, 193, 195, 197, 215, 216
Sasaki, Naokichi, Petty Officer - 46, 49, 51, 218, 221
Sawfish (American submarine) - 216
Scrivener, P. E. - 108
Sea Mist (CPB) - 37, 39, 107, 110, 11, 112, 157, 159, 162, 163, 164, 179, 183, 236, 239, 240, 242, 243, 244, 253
Senninbari - 212
Seto Inland Sea - 47, 49
Sheraton, Cyril, Naval Gunner - 191
Shaw, Archibald - 99, 255
Shoho (Japanese aircraft carrier) - 79
Silver Cloud (CPB) - 37, 39, 244, 255

Singapore - 68, 75, 77, 97, 107
Smith's Weekly - 175, 252
Solomon Islands - 58, 78, 83, 145, 172, 206, 216, 220
Solomon Sea - 78, 83, 174
Special Liaison Units (SLUs) - 76
Special Operations Executive (SOE) - 77
Steady Hour (CPB) - 37, 39, 157, 161, 162, 164, 179, 180, 236, 239, 240, 242, 243, 244
Stephenson, Sir William - 73, 74, 75, 76, 77
Stevenson, William - 74, 251
Suva (Fiji) - 59, 74, 85
Sydney Harbour Bridge - 38, 143, 160, 173
Sydney Morning Herald - 66, 119, 144, 148, 150, 191, 206, 214, 252
Taiyo Maru (Japanese ocean liner) - 49
Takada, Takazo, Petty Officer - 93
Takada, Koozoo, Petty Officer - 217
Takemoto, Masami, Petty Officer - 93, 217
Takeo Yoshikawa - 49
Tamil Tigers - 229, 230
Tasmania - 189, 191
Tautog (American submarine) - 85
Taylor Bay - 38, 159, 160, 162, 164, 177, 178, 179, 183, 213, 227, 236, 240, 243, 244
Tennessee (American battleship) - 57
Thailand - 65
Third Submarine Company - 32, 37, 41, 60, 78, 80, 83, 85, 87, 88, 89, 115, 187, 189, 193, 201, 206, 216
Tippecanoe (American fleet oiler) - 78
Titanic - 221
Tojo, Hideki, Gen - 224
Tokyo - 64, 78, 215, 254
Tokyo Naval College - 49
Toomaree (CPB) - 39, 157
Townley, Athol G., Lt - 24, 37, 157, 180, 242
Townsville - 79, 207
"Tresco" - 41, 181, 237
Trimcomalee - 108, 230
Trist, Boy D. - 149, 152
Tromp (Dutch cruiser) - 31, 87
Truk Islands - 74, 85, 201
Truk Lagoon - 85, 216, 229
Tsuzuku, Masas - 85, 87, 115, 116, 129, 155, 212, 217, 229
Tulagi (Solomon Islands) - 78, 83, 206
Uyeda, Sadaji, Sub-Lt - 46, 51, 57, 218, 224
Ultra - 25, 73, 74, 75, 76, 77, 79, 88, 252
United Kingdom - 63, 68
US Army's Signal Intelligence Service - 74

US Pacific Fleet - 23, 53, 57, 59, 73, 78, 205, 206, 221
US Western Pacific Fleet - 57
Vestal (American collier) - 57
Victoria - 110, 145, 222
Vietnam War - 24
Vincennes (American heavy cruiser) - 181
Walsh Bay - 37, 38, 160
Ward (American destroyer) - 53, 221, 224
Warren, I. J. Launchmaster - 135
Washington (USA) - 64, 74, 76, 77, 176, 205, 206
Washington Naval Headquarters (NEGAT) - 76, 205, 206,
Watson's Bay - 38, 155, 160, 167, 178, 237, 238, 239,
Watson, Walter, Capt - 197
Wellen (Russian steamer) - 31, 87, 198
Wellington (New Zealand) - 59
Westralia (Australian armed merchant cruiser) - 39, 107, 155, 234
West Virginia (American battleship) - 57
Whitfield, Colin R., Able-Seaman - 147
Whyalla (Australian corvette) - 39, 133, 136, 155, 158, 179, 189, 191, 196, 197, 199, 235, 238, 239, 240
Wilkinson, J. B., Lt-Cdr - 173
William Dawes (American liberty ship) - 198
Williams, Seaman William - 145
Willoughby, C., Col - 77, 78
Wilson, P. F., Lt - 30, 41, 139, 157, 175, 177
Winkworth, L. H. - 37, 41, 123, 129, 131, 133, 134, 255
Winterbotham, Fred W. - 74, 76, 252
Wichita (American heavy cruiser) - 182
Woods, C.J.W., Lt-Cdr - 110
Yamaki, Teiji, Sub-Lt - 11, 46, 47, 85, 229, 217, 253
Yamamoto, Isoroku, Admiral - 32, 45, 50, 51, 58, 59, 74, 78, 79, 205, 206, 207, 216
Yamashita, Takeo - 215, 216, 219, 251
Yamazuki Maru (Japanese transport ship) - 220
Yandra (Australian anti-submarine vessel) - 39, 41, 123, 131, 132, 133, 155, 179, 235, 238, 242, 244
Yarrawonga (NAP) - 39, 41, 123, 155
Yarroma (CPB) - 37, 39, 41, 119, 120, 121, 123, 125, 155, 162, 164, 179, 236, 240, 243, 242, 237, 253
"Yellow Peril" - 63, 195
Yokoyama, Kunhan, Petty Officer - 46, 51
Yokoyama, Masaharu, Sub-Lt - 46, 51, 57, 218, 224
Yokoyama, Shigenori, Sub-Lt - 218
Yorktown (US aircraft carrier) - 78, 79, 83, 174
Yoshimura, Iwao, Cdr - 85 ●